C-4936   CAREER EXAMINATION SERIES

This is your
PASSBOOK for...

Head Driver Improvement Examiner

Test Preparation Study Guide
Questions & Answers

COPYRIGHT NOTICE

This book is SOLELY intended for, is sold ONLY to, and its use is RESTRICTED to individual, bona fide applicants or candidates who qualify by virtue of having seriously filed applications for appropriate license, certificate, professional and/or promotional advancement, higher school matriculation, scholarship, or other legitimate requirements of education and/or governmental authorities.

This book is NOT intended for use, class instruction, tutoring, training, duplication, copying, reprinting, excerption, or adaptation, etc., by:

1) Other publishers
2) Proprietors and/or Instructors of "Coaching" and/or Preparatory Courses
3) Personnel and/or Training Divisions of commercial, industrial, and governmental organizations
4) Schools, colleges, or universities and/or their departments and staffs, including teachers and other personnel
5) Testing Agencies or Bureaus
6) Study groups which seek by the purchase of a single volume to copy and/or duplicate and/or adapt this material for use by the group as a whole without having purchased individual volumes for each of the members of the group
7) Et al.

Such persons would be in violation of appropriate Federal and State statutes.

PROVISION OF LICENSING AGREEMENTS – Recognized educational, commercial, industrial, and governmental institutions and organizations, and others legitimately engaged in educational pursuits, including training, testing, and measurement activities, may address request for a licensing agreement to the copyright owners, who will determine whether, and under what conditions, including fees and charges, the materials in this book may be used them. In other words, a licensing facility exists for the legitimate use of the material in this book on other than an individual basis. However, it is asseverated and affirmed here that the material in this book CANNOT be used without the receipt of the express permission of such a licensing agreement from the Publishers. Inquiries re licensing should be addressed to the company, attention rights and permissions department.

All rights reserved, including the right of reproduction in whole or in part, in any form or by any means, electronic or mechanical, including photocopying, recording, or by any information storage and retrieval system, without permission in writing from the Publisher.

Copyright © 2024 by
National Learning Corporation

212 Michael Drive, Syosset, NY 11791
(516) 921-8888 • www.passbooks.com
E-mail: info@passbooks.com

PASSBOOK® SERIES

THE *PASSBOOK® SERIES* has been created to prepare applicants and candidates for the ultimate academic battlefield – the examination room.

At some time in our lives, each and every one of us may be required to take an examination – for validation, matriculation, admission, qualification, registration, certification, or licensure.

Based on the assumption that every applicant or candidate has met the basic formal educational standards, has taken the required number of courses, and read the necessary texts, the *PASSBOOK® SERIES* furnishes the one special preparation which may assure passing with confidence, instead of failing with insecurity. Examination questions – together with answers – are furnished as the basic vehicle for study so that the mysteries of the examination and its compounding difficulties may be eliminated or diminished by a sure method.

This book is meant to help you pass your examination provided that you qualify and are serious in your objective.

The entire field is reviewed through the huge store of content information which is succinctly presented through a provocative and challenging approach – the question-and-answer method.

A climate of success is established by furnishing the correct answers at the end of each test.

You soon learn to recognize types of questions, forms of questions, and patterns of questioning. You may even begin to anticipate expected outcomes.

You perceive that many questions are repeated or adapted so that you can gain acute insights, which may enable you to score many sure points.

You learn how to confront new questions, or types of questions, and to attack them confidently and work out the correct answers.

You note objectives and emphases, and recognize pitfalls and dangers, so that you may make positive educational adjustments.

Moreover, you are kept fully informed in relation to new concepts, methods, practices, and directions in the field.

You discover that you are actually taking the examination all the time: you are preparing for the examination by "taking" an examination, not by reading extraneous and/or supererogatory textbooks.

In short, this PASSBOOK®, used directedly, should be an important factor in helping you to pass your test.

HEAD DRIVER IMPROVEMENT EXAMINER

DUTIES
As a Head Driver Improvement Examiner, you would supervise a section containing several units. You would review all training programs, handle cases that go beyond the expertise of the Supervising Driver Improvement Examiner, set production standards, review production reports, and recommend and initiate corrective action where needed.

SCOPE OF THE EXAMINATION
The written test will cover knowledge, skills and/or abilities in such areas as:

1. **Preparing written material** - These questions test for the ability to present information clearly and accurately, and to organize paragraphs logically and comprehensibly. For some questions, you will be given information in two or three sentences followed by four restatements of the information. You must then choose the best version. For other questions, you will be given paragraphs with their sentences out of order. You must then choose, from four suggestions, the best order for the sentences.
2. **Understanding and interpreting written material based on the Vehicle and Traffic law, rules and regulations** - These questions test for the ability to read, understand and interpret various provisions of the above named law, rules or regulations. This part of the test will contain several reading selections based on or extracted from a passage of legal text. The candidate must read each selection and then answer one or more questions based upon it. All factual information needed to answer these questions is contained in the reading selections. No prior knowledge of that information is necessary to answer the questions correctly.
3. **Evaluating conclusions in light of known facts** - These questions will consist of a set of facts and a conclusion. You must decide if the conclusion is proved by the facts, disproved by the facts or if the facts are not sufficient to prove or disprove the conclusion. The questions will not be specific to a particular field.
4. **Administrative supervision** - These questions test for knowledge of the principles and practices involved in directing the activities of a large subordinate staff, including subordinate supervisors. Questions relate to the personal interactions between an upper level supervisor and his/her subordinate supervisors in the accomplishment of objectives. These questions cover such areas as assigning work to and coordinating the activities of several units, establishing and guiding staff development programs, evaluating the performance of subordinate supervisors, and maintaining relationships with other organizational sections.

HOW TO TAKE A TEST

I. YOU MUST PASS AN EXAMINATION

A. WHAT EVERY CANDIDATE SHOULD KNOW

Examination applicants often ask us for help in preparing for the written test. What can I study in advance? What kinds of questions will be asked? How will the test be given? How will the papers be graded?

As an applicant for a civil service examination, you may be wondering about some of these things. Our purpose here is to suggest effective methods of advance study and to describe civil service examinations.

Your chances for success on this examination can be increased if you know how to prepare. Those "pre-examination jitters" can be reduced if you know what to expect. You can even experience an adventure in good citizenship if you know why civil service exams are given.

B. WHY ARE CIVIL SERVICE EXAMINATIONS GIVEN?

Civil service examinations are important to you in two ways. As a citizen, you want public jobs filled by employees who know how to do their work. As a job seeker, you want a fair chance to compete for that job on an equal footing with other candidates. The best-known means of accomplishing this two-fold goal is the competitive examination.

Exams are widely publicized throughout the nation. They may be administered for jobs in federal, state, city, municipal, town or village governments or agencies.

Any citizen may apply, with some limitations, such as the age or residence of applicants. Your experience and education may be reviewed to see whether you meet the requirements for the particular examination. When these requirements exist, they are reasonable and applied consistently to all applicants. Thus, a competitive examination may cause you some uneasiness now, but it is your privilege and safeguard.

C. HOW ARE CIVIL SERVICE EXAMS DEVELOPED?

Examinations are carefully written by trained technicians who are specialists in the field known as "psychological measurement," in consultation with recognized authorities in the field of work that the test will cover. These experts recommend the subject matter areas or skills to be tested; only those knowledges or skills important to your success on the job are included. The most reliable books and source materials available are used as references. Together, the experts and technicians judge the difficulty level of the questions.

Test technicians know how to phrase questions so that the problem is clearly stated. Their ethics do not permit "trick" or "catch" questions. Questions may have been tried out on sample groups, or subjected to statistical analysis, to determine their usefulness.

Written tests are often used in combination with performance tests, ratings of training and experience, and oral interviews. All of these measures combine to form the best-known means of finding the right person for the right job.

II. HOW TO PASS THE WRITTEN TEST

A. NATURE OF THE EXAMINATION

To prepare intelligently for civil service examinations, you should know how they differ from school examinations you have taken. In school you were assigned certain definite pages to read or subjects to cover. The examination questions were quite detailed and usually emphasized memory. Civil service exams, on the other hand, try to discover your present ability to perform the duties of a position, plus your potentiality to learn these duties. In other words, a civil service exam attempts to predict how successful you will be. Questions cover such a broad area that they cannot be as minute and detailed as school exam questions.

In the public service similar kinds of work, or positions, are grouped together in one "class." This process is known as *position-classification*. All the positions in a class are paid according to the salary range for that class. One class title covers all of these positions, and they are all tested by the same examination.

B. FOUR BASIC STEPS

1) Study the announcement

How, then, can you know what subjects to study? Our best answer is: "Learn as much as possible about the class of positions for which you've applied." The exam will test the knowledge, skills and abilities needed to do the work.

Your most valuable source of information about the position you want is the official exam announcement. This announcement lists the training and experience qualifications. Check these standards and apply only if you come reasonably close to meeting them.

The brief description of the position in the examination announcement offers some clues to the subjects which will be tested. Think about the job itself. Review the duties in your mind. Can you perform them, or are there some in which you are rusty? Fill in the blank spots in your preparation.

Many jurisdictions preview the written test in the exam announcement by including a section called "Knowledge and Abilities Required," "Scope of the Examination," or some similar heading. Here you will find out specifically what fields will be tested.

2) Review your own background

Once you learn in general what the position is all about, and what you need to know to do the work, ask yourself which subjects you already know fairly well and which need improvement. You may wonder whether to concentrate on improving your strong areas or on building some background in your fields of weakness. When the announcement has specified "some knowledge" or "considerable knowledge," or has used adjectives like "beginning principles of..." or "advanced ... methods," you can get a clue as to the number and difficulty of questions to be asked in any given field. More questions, and hence broader coverage, would be included for those subjects which are more important in the work. Now weigh your strengths and weaknesses against the job requirements and prepare accordingly.

3) Determine the level of the position

Another way to tell how intensively you should prepare is to understand the level of the job for which you are applying. Is it the entering level? In other words, is this the position in which beginners in a field of work are hired? Or is it an intermediate or advanced level? Sometimes this is indicated by such words as "Junior" or "Senior" in the class title. Other jurisdictions use Roman numerals to designate the level – Clerk I, Clerk II, for example. The word "Supervisor" sometimes appears in the title. If the level is not indicated by the title, check the description of duties. Will you be working under very close supervision, or will you have responsibility for independent decisions in this work?

4) Choose appropriate study materials

Now that you know the subjects to be examined and the relative amount of each subject to be covered, you can choose suitable study materials. For beginning level jobs, or even advanced ones, if you have a pronounced weakness in some aspect of your training, read a modern, standard textbook in that field. Be sure it is up to date and has general coverage. Such books are normally available at your library, and the librarian will be glad to help you locate one. For entry-level positions, questions of appropriate difficulty are chosen – neither highly advanced questions, nor those too simple. Such questions require careful thought but not advanced training.

If the position for which you are applying is technical or advanced, you will read more advanced, specialized material. If you are already familiar with the basic principles of your field, elementary textbooks would waste your time. Concentrate on advanced textbooks and technical periodicals. Think through the concepts and review difficult problems in your field.

These are all general sources. You can get more ideas on your own initiative, following these leads. For example, training manuals and publications of the government agency which employs workers in your field can be useful, particularly for technical and professional positions. A letter or visit to the government department involved may result in more specific study suggestions, and certainly will provide you with a more definite idea of the exact nature of the position you are seeking.

III. KINDS OF TESTS

Tests are used for purposes other than measuring knowledge and ability to perform specified duties. For some positions, it is equally important to test ability to make adjustments to new situations or to profit from training. In others, basic mental abilities not dependent on information are essential. Questions which test these things may not appear as pertinent to the duties of the position as those which test for knowledge and information. Yet they are often highly important parts of a fair examination. For very general questions, it is almost impossible to help you direct your study efforts. What we can do is to point out some of the more common of these general abilities needed in public service positions and describe some typical questions.

1) General information

Broad, general information has been found useful for predicting job success in some kinds of work. This is tested in a variety of ways, from vocabulary lists to questions about current events. Basic background in some field of work, such as sociology or economics, may be sampled in a group of questions. Often these are principles which have become familiar to most persons through exposure rather than through formal training. It is difficult to advise you how to study for these questions; being alert to the world around you is our best suggestion.

2) Verbal ability

An example of an ability needed in many positions is verbal or language ability. Verbal ability is, in brief, the ability to use and understand words. Vocabulary and grammar tests are typical measures of this ability. Reading comprehension or paragraph interpretation questions are common in many kinds of civil service tests. You are given a paragraph of written material and asked to find its central meaning.

3) Numerical ability

Number skills can be tested by the familiar arithmetic problem, by checking paired lists of numbers to see which are alike and which are different, or by interpreting charts and graphs. In the latter test, a graph may be printed in the test booklet which you are asked to use as the basis for answering questions.

4) Observation

A popular test for law-enforcement positions is the observation test. A picture is shown to you for several minutes, then taken away. Questions about the picture test your ability to observe both details and larger elements.

5) Following directions

In many positions in the public service, the employee must be able to carry out written instructions dependably and accurately. You may be given a chart with several columns, each column listing a variety of information. The questions require you to carry out directions involving the information given in the chart.

6) Skills and aptitudes

Performance tests effectively measure some manual skills and aptitudes. When the skill is one in which you are trained, such as typing or shorthand, you can practice. These tests are often very much like those given in business school or high school courses. For many of the other skills and aptitudes, however, no short-time preparation can be made. Skills and abilities natural to you or that you have developed throughout your lifetime are being tested.

Many of the general questions just described provide all the data needed to answer the questions and ask you to use your reasoning ability to find the answers. Your best preparation for these tests, as well as for tests of facts and ideas, is to be at your physical and mental best. You, no doubt, have your own methods of getting into an exam-taking mood and keeping "in shape." The next section lists some ideas on this subject.

IV. KINDS OF QUESTIONS

Only rarely is the "essay" question, which you answer in narrative form, used in civil service tests. Civil service tests are usually of the short-answer type. Full instructions for answering these questions will be given to you at the examination. But in case this is your first experience with short-answer questions and separate answer sheets, here is what you need to know:

1) **Multiple-choice Questions**

Most popular of the short-answer questions is the "multiple choice" or "best answer" question. It can be used, for example, to test for factual knowledge, ability to solve problems or judgment in meeting situations found at work.

A multiple-choice question is normally one of three types—
- It can begin with an incomplete statement followed by several possible endings. You are to find the one ending which *best* completes the statement, although some of the others may not be entirely wrong.
- It can also be a complete statement in the form of a question which is answered by choosing one of the statements listed.

- It can be in the form of a problem – again you select the best answer.

Here is an example of a multiple-choice question with a discussion which should give you some clues as to the method for choosing the right answer:

When an employee has a complaint about his assignment, the action which will *best* help him overcome his difficulty is to
    A. discuss his difficulty with his coworkers
    B. take the problem to the head of the organization
    C. take the problem to the person who gave him the assignment
    D. say nothing to anyone about his complaint

In answering this question, you should study each of the choices to find which is best. Consider choice "A" – Certainly an employee may discuss his complaint with fellow employees, but no change or improvement can result, and the complaint remains unresolved. Choice "B" is a poor choice since the head of the organization probably does not know what assignment you have been given, and taking your problem to him is known as "going over the head" of the supervisor. The supervisor, or person who made the assignment, is the person who can clarify it or correct any injustice. Choice "C" is, therefore, correct. To say nothing, as in choice "D," is unwise. Supervisors have and interest in knowing the problems employees are facing, and the employee is seeking a solution to his problem.

2) True/False Questions

The "true/false" or "right/wrong" form of question is sometimes used. Here a complete statement is given. Your job is to decide whether the statement is right or wrong.

SAMPLE: A roaming cell-phone call to a nearby city costs less than a non-roaming call to a distant city.

This statement is wrong, or false, since roaming calls are more expensive.

This is not a complete list of all possible question forms, although most of the others are variations of these common types. You will always get complete directions for answering questions. Be sure you understand *how* to mark your answers – ask questions until you do.

V. RECORDING YOUR ANSWERS

Computer terminals are used more and more today for many different kinds of exams.
For an examination with very few applicants, you may be told to record your answers in the test booklet itself. Separate answer sheets are much more common. If this separate answer sheet is to be scored by machine – and this is often the case – it is highly important that you mark your answers correctly in order to get credit.
An electronic scoring machine is often used in civil service offices because of the speed with which papers can be scored. Machine-scored answer sheets must be marked with a pencil, which will be given to you. This pencil has a high graphite content which responds to the electronic scoring machine. As a matter of fact, stray dots may register as answers, so do not let your pencil rest on the answer sheet while you are pondering the correct answer. Also, if your pencil lead breaks or is otherwise defective, ask for another.

Since the answer sheet will be dropped in a slot in the scoring machine, be careful not to bend the corners or get the paper crumpled.

The answer sheet normally has five vertical columns of numbers, with 30 numbers to a column. These numbers correspond to the question numbers in your test booklet. After each number, going across the page are four or five pairs of dotted lines. These short dotted lines have small letters or numbers above them. The first two pairs may also have a "T" or "F" above the letters. This indicates that the first two pairs only are to be used if the questions are of the true-false type. If the questions are multiple choice, disregard the "T" and "F" and pay attention only to the small letters or numbers.

Answer your questions in the manner of the sample that follows:

32. The largest city in the United States is
    A. Washington, D.C.
    B. New York City
    C. Chicago
    D. Detroit
    E. San Francisco

1) Choose the answer you think is best. (New York City is the largest, so "B" is correct.)
2) Find the row of dotted lines numbered the same as the question you are answering. (Find row number 32)
3) Find the pair of dotted lines corresponding to the answer. (Find the pair of lines under the mark "B.")
4) Make a solid black mark between the dotted lines.

VI. BEFORE THE TEST

Common sense will help you find procedures to follow to get ready for an examination. Too many of us, however, overlook these sensible measures. Indeed, nervousness and fatigue have been found to be the most serious reasons why applicants fail to do their best on civil service tests. Here is a list of reminders:

- Begin your preparation early – Don't wait until the last minute to go scurrying around for books and materials or to find out what the position is all about.
- Prepare continuously – An hour a night for a week is better than an all-night cram session. This has been definitely established. What is more, a night a week for a month will return better dividends than crowding your study into a shorter period of time.
- Locate the place of the exam – You have been sent a notice telling you when and where to report for the examination. If the location is in a different town or otherwise unfamiliar to you, it would be well to inquire the best route and learn something about the building.
- Relax the night before the test – Allow your mind to rest. Do not study at all that night. Plan some mild recreation or diversion; then go to bed early and get a good night's sleep.
- Get up early enough to make a leisurely trip to the place for the test – This way unforeseen events, traffic snarls, unfamiliar buildings, etc. will not upset you.
- Dress comfortably – A written test is not a fashion show. You will be known by number and not by name, so wear something comfortable.

- Leave excess paraphernalia at home – Shopping bags and odd bundles will get in your way. You need bring only the items mentioned in the official notice you received; usually everything you need is provided. Do not bring reference books to the exam. They will only confuse those last minutes and be taken away from you when in the test room.
- Arrive somewhat ahead of time – If because of transportation schedules you must get there very early, bring a newspaper or magazine to take your mind off yourself while waiting.
- Locate the examination room – When you have found the proper room, you will be directed to the seat or part of the room where you will sit. Sometimes you are given a sheet of instructions to read while you are waiting. Do not fill out any forms until you are told to do so; just read them and be prepared.
- Relax and prepare to listen to the instructions
- If you have any physical problem that may keep you from doing your best, be sure to tell the test administrator. If you are sick or in poor health, you really cannot do your best on the exam. You can come back and take the test some other time.

VII. AT THE TEST

The day of the test is here and you have the test booklet in your hand. The temptation to get going is very strong. Caution! There is more to success than knowing the right answers. You must know how to identify your papers and understand variations in the type of short-answer question used in this particular examination. Follow these suggestions for maximum results from your efforts:

1) Cooperate with the monitor

The test administrator has a duty to create a situation in which you can be as much at ease as possible. He will give instructions, tell you when to begin, check to see that you are marking your answer sheet correctly, and so on. He is not there to guard you, although he will see that your competitors do not take unfair advantage. He wants to help you do your best.

2) Listen to all instructions

Don't jump the gun! Wait until you understand all directions. In most civil service tests you get more time than you need to answer the questions. So don't be in a hurry. Read each word of instructions until you clearly understand the meaning. Study the examples, listen to all announcements and follow directions. Ask questions if you do not understand what to do.

3) Identify your papers

Civil service exams are usually identified by number only. You will be assigned a number; you must not put your name on your test papers. Be sure to copy your number correctly. Since more than one exam may be given, copy your exact examination title.

4) Plan your time

Unless you are told that a test is a "speed" or "rate of work" test, speed itself is usually not important. Time enough to answer all the questions will be provided, but this does not mean that you have all day. An overall time limit has been set. Divide the total time (in minutes) by the number of questions to determine the approximate time you have for each question.

5) Do not linger over difficult questions

If you come across a difficult question, mark it with a paper clip (useful to have along) and come back to it when you have been through the booklet. One caution if you do this – be sure to skip a number on your answer sheet as well. Check often to be sure that you have not lost your place and that you are marking in the row numbered the same as the question you are answering.

6) Read the questions

Be sure you know what the question asks! Many capable people are unsuccessful because they failed to *read* the questions correctly.

7) Answer all questions

Unless you have been instructed that a penalty will be deducted for incorrect answers, it is better to guess than to omit a question.

8) Speed tests

It is often better NOT to guess on speed tests. It has been found that on timed tests people are tempted to spend the last few seconds before time is called in marking answers at random – without even reading them – in the hope of picking up a few extra points. To discourage this practice, the instructions may warn you that your score will be "corrected" for guessing. That is, a penalty will be applied. The incorrect answers will be deducted from the correct ones, or some other penalty formula will be used.

9) Review your answers

If you finish before time is called, go back to the questions you guessed or omitted to give them further thought. Review other answers if you have time.

10) Return your test materials

If you are ready to leave before others have finished or time is called, take ALL your materials to the monitor and leave quietly. Never take any test material with you. The monitor can discover whose papers are not complete, and taking a test booklet may be grounds for disqualification.

VIII. EXAMINATION TECHNIQUES

1) Read the general instructions carefully. These are usually printed on the first page of the exam booklet. As a rule, these instructions refer to the timing of the examination; the fact that you should not start work until the signal and must stop work at a signal, etc. If there are any *special* instructions, such as a choice of questions to be answered, make sure that you note this instruction carefully.

2) When you are ready to start work on the examination, that is as soon as the signal has been given, read the instructions to each question booklet, underline any key words or phrases, such as *least, best, outline, describe* and the like. In this way you will tend to answer as requested rather than discover on reviewing your paper that you *listed without describing*, that you selected the *worst* choice rather than the *best* choice, etc.

3) If the examination is of the objective or multiple-choice type – that is, each question will also give a series of possible answers: A, B, C or D, and you are called upon to select the best answer and write the letter next to that answer on your answer paper – it is advisable to start answering each question in turn. There may be anywhere from 50 to 100 such questions in the three or four hours allotted and you can see how much time would be taken if you read through all the questions before beginning to answer any. Furthermore, if you come across a question or group of questions which you know would be difficult to answer, it would undoubtedly affect your handling of all the other questions.

4) If the examination is of the essay type and contains but a few questions, it is a moot point as to whether you should read all the questions before starting to answer any one. Of course, if you are given a choice – say five out of seven and the like – then it is essential to read all the questions so you can eliminate the two that are most difficult. If, however, you are asked to answer all the questions, there may be danger in trying to answer the easiest one first because you may find that you will spend too much time on it. The best technique is to answer the first question, then proceed to the second, etc.

5) Time your answers. Before the exam begins, write down the time it started, then add the time allowed for the examination and write down the time it must be completed, then divide the time available somewhat as follows:
    - If 3-1/2 hours are allowed, that would be 210 minutes. If you have 80 objective-type questions, that would be an average of 2-1/2 minutes per question. Allow yourself no more than 2 minutes per question, or a total of 160 minutes, which will permit about 50 minutes to review.
    - If for the time allotment of 210 minutes there are 7 essay questions to answer, that would average about 30 minutes a question. Give yourself only 25 minutes per question so that you have about 35 minutes to review.

6) The most important instruction is to *read each question* and make sure you know what is wanted. The second most important instruction is to *time yourself properly* so that you answer every question. The third most important instruction is to *answer every question*. Guess if you have to but include something for each question. Remember that you will receive no credit for a blank and will probably receive some credit if you write something in answer to an essay question. If you guess a letter – say "B" for a multiple-choice question – you may have guessed right. If you leave a blank as an answer to a multiple-choice question, the examiners may respect your feelings but it will not add a point to your score. Some exams may penalize you for wrong answers, so in such cases *only*, you may not want to guess unless you have some basis for your answer.

7) Suggestions
    a. Objective-type questions
        1. Examine the question booklet for proper sequence of pages and questions
        2. Read all instructions carefully
        3. Skip any question which seems too difficult; return to it after all other questions have been answered
        4. Apportion your time properly; do not spend too much time on any single question or group of questions

5. Note and underline key words – *all, most, fewest, least, best, worst, same, opposite,* etc.
6. Pay particular attention to negatives
7. Note unusual option, e.g., unduly long, short, complex, different or similar in content to the body of the question
8. Observe the use of "hedging" words – *probably, may, most likely,* etc.
9. Make sure that your answer is put next to the same number as the question
10. Do not second-guess unless you have good reason to believe the second answer is definitely more correct
11. Cross out original answer if you decide another answer is more accurate; do not erase until you are ready to hand your paper in
12. Answer all questions; guess unless instructed otherwise
13. Leave time for review

   b. Essay questions
     1. Read each question carefully
     2. Determine exactly what is wanted. Underline key words or phrases.
     3. Decide on outline or paragraph answer
     4. Include many different points and elements unless asked to develop any one or two points or elements
     5. Show impartiality by giving pros and cons unless directed to select one side only
     6. Make and write down any assumptions you find necessary to answer the questions
     7. Watch your English, grammar, punctuation and choice of words
     8. Time your answers; don't crowd material

8) Answering the essay question

Most essay questions can be answered by framing the specific response around several key words or ideas. Here are a few such key words or ideas:

M's: manpower, materials, methods, money, management
P's: purpose, program, policy, plan, procedure, practice, problems, pitfalls, personnel, public relations

   a. Six basic steps in handling problems:
     1. Preliminary plan and background development
     2. Collect information, data and facts
     3. Analyze and interpret information, data and facts
     4. Analyze and develop solutions as well as make recommendations
     5. Prepare report and sell recommendations
     6. Install recommendations and follow up effectiveness

   b. Pitfalls to avoid
     1. *Taking things for granted* – A statement of the situation does not necessarily imply that each of the elements is necessarily true; for example, a complaint may be invalid and biased so that all that can be taken for granted is that a complaint has been registered

2. *Considering only one side of a situation* – Wherever possible, indicate several alternatives and then point out the reasons you selected the best one
3. *Failing to indicate follow up* – Whenever your answer indicates action on your part, make certain that you will take proper follow-up action to see how successful your recommendations, procedures or actions turn out to be
4. *Taking too long in answering any single question* – Remember to time your answers properly

IX. AFTER THE TEST

Scoring procedures differ in detail among civil service jurisdictions although the general principles are the same. Whether the papers are hand-scored or graded by machine we have described, they are nearly always graded by number. That is, the person who marks the paper knows only the number – never the name – of the applicant. Not until all the papers have been graded will they be matched with names. If other tests, such as training and experience or oral interview ratings have been given, scores will be combined. Different parts of the examination usually have different weights. For example, the written test might count 60 percent of the final grade, and a rating of training and experience 40 percent. In many jurisdictions, veterans will have a certain number of points added to their grades.

After the final grade has been determined, the names are placed in grade order and an eligible list is established. There are various methods for resolving ties between those who get the same final grade – probably the most common is to place first the name of the person whose application was received first. Job offers are made from the eligible list in the order the names appear on it. You will be notified of your grade and your rank as soon as all these computations have been made. This will be done as rapidly as possible.

People who are found to meet the requirements in the announcement are called "eligibles." Their names are put on a list of eligible candidates. An eligible's chances of getting a job depend on how high he stands on this list and how fast agencies are filling jobs from the list.

When a job is to be filled from a list of eligibles, the agency asks for the names of people on the list of eligibles for that job. When the civil service commission receives this request, it sends to the agency the names of the three people highest on this list. Or, if the job to be filled has specialized requirements, the office sends the agency the names of the top three persons who meet these requirements from the general list.

The appointing officer makes a choice from among the three people whose names were sent to him. If the selected person accepts the appointment, the names of the others are put back on the list to be considered for future openings.

That is the rule in hiring from all kinds of eligible lists, whether they are for typist, carpenter, chemist, or something else. For every vacancy, the appointing officer has his choice of any one of the top three eligibles on the list. This explains why the person whose name is on top of the list sometimes does not get an appointment when some of the persons lower on the list do. If the appointing officer chooses the second or third eligible, the No. 1 eligible does not get a job at once, but stays on the list until he is appointed or the list is terminated.

X. HOW TO PASS THE INTERVIEW TEST

The examination for which you applied requires an oral interview test. You have already taken the written test and you are now being called for the interview test – the final part of the formal examination.

You may think that it is not possible to prepare for an interview test and that there are no procedures to follow during an interview. Our purpose is to point out some things you can do in advance that will help you and some good rules to follow and pitfalls to avoid while you are being interviewed.

What is an interview supposed to test?

The written examination is designed to test the technical knowledge and competence of the candidate; the oral is designed to evaluate intangible qualities, not readily measured otherwise, and to establish a list showing the relative fitness of each candidate – as measured against his competitors – for the position sought. Scoring is not on the basis of "right" and "wrong," but on a sliding scale of values ranging from "not passable" to "outstanding." As a matter of fact, it is possible to achieve a relatively low score without a single "incorrect" answer because of evident weakness in the qualities being measured.

Occasionally, an examination may consist entirely of an oral test – either an individual or a group oral. In such cases, information is sought concerning the technical knowledges and abilities of the candidate, since there has been no written examination for this purpose. More commonly, however, an oral test is used to supplement a written examination.

Who conducts interviews?

The composition of oral boards varies among different jurisdictions. In nearly all, a representative of the personnel department serves as chairman. One of the members of the board may be a representative of the department in which the candidate would work. In some cases, "outside experts" are used, and, frequently, a businessman or some other representative of the general public is asked to serve. Labor and management or other special groups may be represented. The aim is to secure the services of experts in the appropriate field.

However the board is composed, it is a good idea (and not at all improper or unethical) to ascertain in advance of the interview who the members are and what groups they represent. When you are introduced to them, you will have some idea of their backgrounds and interests, and at least you will not stutter and stammer over their names.

What should be done before the interview?

While knowledge about the board members is useful and takes some of the surprise element out of the interview, there is other preparation which is more substantive. It *is* possible to prepare for an oral interview – in several ways:

1) Keep a copy of your application and review it carefully before the interview

This may be the only document before the oral board, and the starting point of the interview. Know what education and experience you have listed there, and the sequence and dates of all of it. Sometimes the board will ask you to review the highlights of your experience for them; you should not have to hem and haw doing it.

2) Study the class specification and the examination announcement

Usually, the oral board has one or both of these to guide them. The qualities, characteristics or knowledges required by the position sought are stated in these documents. They offer valuable clues as to the nature of the oral interview. For example, if the job involves supervisory responsibilities, the announcement will usually indicate that knowledge of modern supervisory methods and the qualifications of the candidate as a supervisor will be tested. If so, you can expect such questions, frequently in the form of a hypothetical situation which you are expected to solve. NEVER go into an oral without knowledge of the duties and responsibilities of the job you seek.

3) Think through each qualification required

Try to visualize the kind of questions you would ask if you were a board member. How well could you answer them? Try especially to appraise your own knowledge and background in each area, *measured against the job sought*, and identify any areas in which you are weak. Be critical and realistic – do not flatter yourself.

4) Do some general reading in areas in which you feel you may be weak

For example, if the job involves supervision and your past experience has NOT, some general reading in supervisory methods and practices, particularly in the field of human relations, might be useful. Do NOT study agency procedures or detailed manuals. The oral board will be testing your understanding and capacity, not your memory.

5) Get a good night's sleep and watch your general health and mental attitude

You will want a clear head at the interview. Take care of a cold or any other minor ailment, and of course, no hangovers.

What should be done on the day of the interview?

Now comes the day of the interview itself. Give yourself plenty of time to get there. Plan to arrive somewhat ahead of the scheduled time, particularly if your appointment is in the fore part of the day. If a previous candidate fails to appear, the board might be ready for you a bit early. By early afternoon an oral board is almost invariably behind schedule if there are many candidates, and you may have to wait. Take along a book or magazine to read, or your application to review, but leave any extraneous material in the waiting room when you go in for your interview. In any event, relax and compose yourself.

The matter of dress is important. The board is forming impressions about you – from your experience, your manners, your attitude, and your appearance. Give your personal appearance careful attention. Dress your best, but not your flashiest. Choose conservative, appropriate clothing, and be sure it is immaculate. This is a business interview, and your appearance should indicate that you regard it as such. Besides, being well groomed and properly dressed will help boost your confidence.

Sooner or later, someone will call your name and escort you into the interview room. *This is it.* From here on you are on your own. It is too late for any more preparation. But remember, you asked for this opportunity to prove your fitness, and you are here because your request was granted.

What happens when you go in?

The usual sequence of events will be as follows: The clerk (who is often the board stenographer) will introduce you to the chairman of the oral board, who will introduce you to the other members of the board. Acknowledge the introductions before you sit down. Do not be surprised if you find a microphone facing you or a stenotypist sitting by. Oral interviews are usually recorded in the event of an appeal or other review.

Usually the chairman of the board will open the interview by reviewing the highlights of your education and work experience from your application – primarily for the benefit of the other members of the board, as well as to get the material into the record. Do not interrupt or comment unless there is an error or significant misinterpretation; if that is the case, do not hesitate. But do not quibble about insignificant matters. Also, he will usually ask you some question about your education, experience or your present job – partly to get you to start talking and to establish the interviewing "rapport." He may start the actual questioning, or turn it over to one of the other members. Frequently, each member undertakes the questioning on a particular area, one in which he is perhaps most competent, so you can expect each member to participate in the examination. Because time is limited, you may also expect some rather abrupt switches in the direction the questioning takes, so do not be upset by it. Normally, a board member will not pursue a single line of questioning unless he discovers a particular strength or weakness.

After each member has participated, the chairman will usually ask whether any member has any further questions, then will ask you if you have anything you wish to add. Unless you are expecting this question, it may floor you. Worse, it may start you off on an extended, extemporaneous speech. The board is not usually seeking more information. The question is principally to offer you a last opportunity to present further qualifications or to indicate that you have nothing to add. So, if you feel that a significant qualification or characteristic has been overlooked, it is proper to point it out in a sentence or so. Do not compliment the board on the thoroughness of their examination – they have been sketchy, and you know it. If you wish, merely say, "No thank you, I have nothing further to add." This is a point where you can "talk yourself out" of a good impression or fail to present an important bit of information. Remember, *you close the interview yourself*.

The chairman will then say, "That is all, Mr. _____, thank you." Do not be startled; the interview is over, and quicker than you think. Thank him, gather your belongings and take your leave. Save your sigh of relief for the other side of the door.

How to put your best foot forward

Throughout this entire process, you may feel that the board individually and collectively is trying to pierce your defenses, seek out your hidden weaknesses and embarrass and confuse you. Actually, this is not true. They are obliged to make an appraisal of your qualifications for the job you are seeking, and they want to see you in your best light. Remember, they must interview all candidates and a non-cooperative candidate may become a failure in spite of their best efforts to bring out his qualifications. Here are 15 suggestions that will help you:

1) Be natural – Keep your attitude confident, not cocky

If you are not confident that you can do the job, do not expect the board to be. Do not apologize for your weaknesses, try to bring out your strong points. The board is interested in a positive, not negative, presentation. Cockiness will antagonize any board member and make him wonder if you are covering up a weakness by a false show of strength.

2) Get comfortable, but don't lounge or sprawl

Sit erectly but not stiffly. A careless posture may lead the board to conclude that you are careless in other things, or at least that you are not impressed by the importance of the occasion. Either conclusion is natural, even if incorrect. Do not fuss with your clothing, a pencil or an ashtray. Your hands may occasionally be useful to emphasize a point; do not let them become a point of distraction.

3) Do not wisecrack or make small talk

This is a serious situation, and your attitude should show that you consider it as such. Further, the time of the board is limited – they do not want to waste it, and neither should you.

4) Do not exaggerate your experience or abilities

In the first place, from information in the application or other interviews and sources, the board may know more about you than you think. Secondly, you probably will not get away with it. An experienced board is rather adept at spotting such a situation, so do not take the chance.

5) If you know a board member, do not make a point of it, yet do not hide it

Certainly you are not fooling him, and probably not the other members of the board. Do not try to take advantage of your acquaintanceship – it will probably do you little good.

6) Do not dominate the interview

Let the board do that. They will give you the clues – do not assume that you have to do all the talking. Realize that the board has a number of questions to ask you, and do not try to take up all the interview time by showing off your extensive knowledge of the answer to the first one.

7) Be attentive

You only have 20 minutes or so, and you should keep your attention at its sharpest throughout. When a member is addressing a problem or question to you, give him your undivided attention. Address your reply principally to him, but do not exclude the other board members.

8) Do not interrupt

A board member may be stating a problem for you to analyze. He will ask you a question when the time comes. Let him state the problem, and wait for the question.

9) Make sure you understand the question

Do not try to answer until you are sure what the question is. If it is not clear, restate it in your own words or ask the board member to clarify it for you. However, do not haggle about minor elements.

10) Reply promptly but not hastily

A common entry on oral board rating sheets is "candidate responded readily," or "candidate hesitated in replies." Respond as promptly and quickly as you can, but do not jump to a hasty, ill-considered answer.

11) Do not be peremptory in your answers

A brief answer is proper – but do not fire your answer back. That is a losing game from your point of view. The board member can probably ask questions much faster than you can answer them.

12) Do not try to create the answer you think the board member wants

He is interested in what kind of mind you have and how it works – not in playing games. Furthermore, he can usually spot this practice and will actually grade you down on it.

13) Do not switch sides in your reply merely to agree with a board member

Frequently, a member will take a contrary position merely to draw you out and to see if you are willing and able to defend your point of view. Do not start a debate, yet do not surrender a good position. If a position is worth taking, it is worth defending.

14) Do not be afraid to admit an error in judgment if you are shown to be wrong

The board knows that you are forced to reply without any opportunity for careful consideration. Your answer may be demonstrably wrong. If so, admit it and get on with the interview.

15) Do not dwell at length on your present job

The opening question may relate to your present assignment. Answer the question but do not go into an extended discussion. You are being examined for a *new* job, not your present one. As a matter of fact, try to phrase ALL your answers in terms of the job for which you are being examined.

Basis of Rating

Probably you will forget most of these "do's" and "don'ts" when you walk into the oral interview room. Even remembering them all will not ensure you a passing grade. Perhaps you did not have the qualifications in the first place. But remembering them will help you to put your best foot forward, without treading on the toes of the board members.

Rumor and popular opinion to the contrary notwithstanding, an oral board wants you to make the best appearance possible. They know you are under pressure – but they also want to see how you respond to it as a guide to what your reaction would be under the pressures of the job you seek. They will be influenced by the degree of poise you display, the personal traits you show and the manner in which you respond.

ABOUT THIS BOOK

This book contains tests divided into Examination Sections. Go through each test, answering every question in the margin. We have also attached a sample answer sheet at the back of the book that can be removed and used. At the end of each test look at the answer key and check your answers. On the ones you got wrong, look at the right answer choice and learn. Do not fill in the answers first. Do not memorize the questions and answers, but understand the answer and principles involved. On your test, the questions will likely be different from the samples. Questions are changed and new ones added. If you understand these past questions you should have success with any changes that arise. Tests may consist of several types of questions. We have additional books on each subject should more study be advisable or necessary for you. Finally, the more you study, the better prepared you will be. This book is intended to be the last thing you study before you walk into the examination room. Prior study of relevant texts is also recommended. NLC publishes some of these in our Fundamental Series. Knowledge and good sense are important factors in passing your exam. Good luck also helps. So now study this Passbook, absorb the material contained within and take that knowledge into the examination. Then do your best to pass that exam.

EXAMINATION SECTION

EXAMINATION SECTION
TEST 1

DIRECTIONS: Each question or incomplete statement is followed by several suggested answers or completions. Select the one that BEST answers the question or completes the statement. *PRINT THE LETTER OF THE CORRECT ANSWER IN THE SPACE AT THE RIGHT.*

1. The administrator who allows his staff to suggest ways to do their work will usually find that

    A. this practice contributes to high productivity
    B. the administrator's ideas produce greater output
    C. clerical employees suggest inefficient work methods
    D. subordinate employees resent performing a management function

2. In considering how to distribute among employees the various tasks which must be accomplished, an administrator should bear in mind that MOST people

    A. are working mainly for money, so the particular task they do is usually unimportant
    B. would rather work with a congenial group, but since this lowers output, it is better to have people work alone
    C. want recognition as outstanding workers, but since only one can be best, it is better policy to stress equality
    D. are concerned with being part of a group and also hope to be outstanding, and the administrator must consider both

3. A coordinator may be the supervisor of several employees. As such, he is their leader. The style of leadership which is MOST effective is a style in which

    A. the coordinator's behavior is tailored to the situation
    B. the coordinator lets his subordinates solve their own problems
    C. the coordinator consults with his subordinates about any work being done
    D. subordinates are told firmly what to do, how and when

4. As a coordinator you may be required to set up a records retention program. To set up such a program, the FIRST step you should take is to

    A. find out how long the records will be needed
    B. determine what types of records are maintained
    C. investigate storage facilities
    D. revise the filing system

5. You are responsible for supervising the work of several subordinates who deal directly with people seeking specific help from your department. One of your subordinates is faced with an angry citizen who has brought his troubles to the wrong department, but who refuses to believe this and is loudly demanding to *see the manager*. The subordinate asks you to step in and take over. Which of the following is probably the MOST effective way of handling this situation?

   A. Tell your subordinate that since this is obviously not a matter for your department, his request that you take over is inappropriate.
   B. Remind your subordinate firmly that it is his job to deal with the public, and that he must learn to handle people who are confused and angry.
   C. Do not stop what you are doing, but call out to the angry citizen that whatever your subordinate told him is correct.
   D. Step in and direct the angry citizen to a department which can help him.

6. A supervisor is one who is responsible for the actions of others working for him and at the same time is responsible to others above him in the organization chart.
   The foregoing statement IMPLIES, in effect, that the supervisor

   A. has full authority for his actions
   B. can delegate his responsibilities to his assistants
   C. accepts direction from his own supervisor
   D. has higher status than a coordinator

7. In issuing requested supplies to employees of the office, there is a great deal of merit in limiting the quantity issued at any one time to about a two-week supply.
   In MOST cases, this policy is

   A. *bad*, because employees should be allowed as large a quantity of supplies as they feel they need
   B. *bad*, because, if larger quantities were issued, employees would have to ask for supplies less often
   C. *good*, because the smaller the quantity issued, the more efficiently the office can be managed
   D. *good*, because a larger amount would encourage waste and a smaller amount would necessitate more trips to the stockroom

8. As a coordinator, assume that there is a rule in your office that all correspondence to other agencies must be signed personally by the hearing officer.
   If the hearing officer is unexpectedly absent on a day when an important letter which has not yet been signed is scheduled to be mailed out, the MOST appropriate action for you to take is to

   A. seek advice from the superior of the hearing officer
   B. sign the letter with the name of the hearing officer and your own initials
   C. telephone the hearing officer at home
   D. wait until the next day

9. Unless otherwise directed, a car should be parked parallel to and within 12 inches of a curb or edge of a roadway, facing in the same direction as traffic on the car's side of the road.
Of the following, the MOST likely reason for this regulation is to

   A. allow the car's passengers adequate room to open its doors
   B. make sure that the road can be washed effectively by Sanitation Department equipment
   C. prevent the car from blocking the smooth flow of traffic
   D. allow another vehicle enough room to double-park

10. Parking meters are generally installed in shopping and commercial districts.
Of the following, the MOST likely reason for this practice is to

    A. promote an equitable rotation of short-term parking opportunities
    B. prevent trucks from stopping to unload and receive deliveries
    C. discourage overnight parking of vehicles by local residents
    D. maximize the revenue gained from these meters to offset the cost of purchasing and maintaining them

11. In the city, the large numbers of criminal cases have made it difficult for the court system to assure a defendant a speedy trial.
The MAIN result of this situation has been that

    A. judges are imposing longer sentences to reduce the number of cases
    B. defense attorneys and prosecutors often engage in plea bargaining
    C. judges are being selected more rapidly by special *blue-ribbon* panels
    D. juries are now given a limit of 48 hours within which they must deliver a verdict

12. The transit fare in the city may have to be raised to meet higher transit authority costs.
The one of the following which is MOST likely to be the PRINCIPAL cause of such higher costs is

    A. equipment repair
    B. equipment replacement
    C. salary increases
    D. conversion to air conditioning

Questions 13–16.

DIRECTIONS: Questions 13 through 16 are to be answered on the basis of the following table.

AVERAGE HOURLY CARRYING CAPACITIES OF
SINGLE-LANE TRANSPORT FACILITIES

MODE OF TRANSPORT	NO. OF PASSENGERS
Autos on surface streets	1,575
Autos on elevated highways	2,025
Buses on surface streets	9,000
Streetcars on surface streets	13,500
Streetcars in subways	20,000
Local subway trains	40,000
Express subway trains	60,000

13. For a group of elevated highways to approximately equal the carrying capacity of a two-lane local subway train facility, the TOTAL number of lanes required would be MOST NEARLY

    A. 80 B. 60 C. 40 D. 20

14. Buses on surface streets using a single lane can carry approximately what percentage of the passengers that express subway trains in one lane can carry?

    A. 20% B. 15% C. 10% D. 5%

15. The average number of passengers that can be carried by autos on surface streets in one day is MOST NEARLY

    A. 1,575 B. 2,025 C. 37,800 D. 48,600

16. If one lane of a surface street were used for buses and another lane were used for streetcars, the number of passengers that could be carried by both lanes together in one hour would probably be MOST NEARLY

    A. 9,000 B. 11,250 C. 13,500 D. 22,500

17. The one of the following which is MOST likely to result from a change from a centralized plan for records management to a decentralized plan is

    A. a loss of time for personnel who use the records
    B. greater specialization of record keeping personnel
    C. authority and responsibility for the records management program being vested in one person within the organization
    D. easier access to the records for personnel most concerned with such records

18. The *grapevine* is an informal means of communication in an organization.
    The attitude of a supervisor with respect to the grapevine should be to

    A. ignore it since it deals mainly with rumors and sensational information
    B. regard it as a serious danger which should be eliminated
    C. accept it as a real line of communications which should be listened to
    D. utilize it for most purposes instead of the official line of communication

19. The supervisor of an office that must deal with the public should realize that planning in this type of work situation

    A. is useless because he does not know how many people will request service or what service they will request
    B. must be done at a higher level but that he should be ready to implement the results of such planning
    C. is useful primarily for those activities that are not concerned with public contact
    D. is useful for all the activities of the office, including those that relate to public contact

20. Which of the following factors is MOST important in planning the location of work stations and other aspects of office layout? 20.____

    A. Preferences of the office employees
    B. Nature and flow of work in the office
    C. Volume of work in the office
    D. Seniority of employees in the office

KEY (CORRECT ANSWERS)

1.	A	11.	B
2.	D	12.	C
3.	A	13.	C
4.	B	14.	B
5.	D	15.	C
6.	C	16.	D
7.	D	17.	D
8.	A	18.	C
9.	C	19.	D
10.	A	20.	B

TEST 2

DIRECTIONS: Each question or incomplete statement is followed by several suggested answers or completions. Select the one that BEST answers the question or completes the statement. *PRINT THE LETTER OF THE CORRECT ANSWER IN THE SPACE AT THE RIGHT.*

1. It is usually MOST desirable for a work supervisor for a large group of clerical workers to have a work station which

    A. provides a view of the entire room
    B. is in another room away from all the clerical workers
    C. is isolated from all workers except for a secretary or assistant
    D. is located so that he can receive all visitors

1.____

Questions 2-5.

DIRECTIONS: Questions 2 through 5 must be answered on the basis of the following passage.

Analysis of current data reveals that motor vehicle transportation actually requires less space than was used for other types of transportation in the pre-automobile era, even including the substantial area taken by freeways. The reason is that when the fast moving through traffic is put on built-for-the-purpose arterial roads, then the amount of ordinary space needed for strictly local movement and for access to property drops sharply. Even the amount of land taken for urban expressways turns out to be surprisingly small in terms either of total urban acreage or of the volume of traffic they carry. No existing or contemplated urban expressway system requires as much as 3 percent of the land in the areas it serves, and this would be exceptionally high. The Los Angeles freeway system occupies only 2 percent of the available land; the same is true of the District of Columbia, where only 0.75 percent is pavement, with the remaining 1.25 percent as open space. California studies estimate that, in a typical California urban community, 1.6 to 2 percent of the area should be devoted to freeways, which will handle 50 to 60 percent of all traffic needs, and about ten times as much land to the ordinary roads and streets that carry the rest of the traffic. By comparison, when John A. Sutter laid out Sacramento in 1850, he provided 38 percent of the area for streets and sidewalks. The French architect, Pierre L' Enfant, proposed 59 percent of the area of the District of Columbia for roads and streets; urban renewal in Southwest Washington, incorporating a modern street network, reduced the acreage of space for pedestrian and vehicular traffic in the renewal area from 48.2 to 41.5 percent of the total. If we are to have a reasoned consideration of the impact of highway transportation on contemporary urban development, it would be well to understand these relationships.

2. The passage states that

    A. modern transportation uses less space than was used for transportation before the auto age
    B. expressways require more space than streets in terms of urban acreage
    C. typical urban communities were poorly designed in terms of relationship between space used for traffic and that used for other purposes
    D. the need for local and access roads would increase if the number of expressways were increased

2.____

3. According to the above passage, it was originally planned that the percent of the area to be used for roads and streets in the District of Columbia should be MOST NEARLY

    A. 40% B. 45% C. 50% D. 60%

3.____

4. The above passage states that the amount of space needed for local traffic

   A. *increases* when arterial highways are constructed
   B. *decreases* when arterial highways are constructed
   C. *decreases* when there is more land available
   D. *increases* when there is more land available

5. According to the above passage, studies estimate that, in a typical California urban community, the amount of land devoted to ordinary roads and streets as compared with that devoted to freeways should be MOST NEARLY _____ as much.

   A. one-half
   B. one-tenth
   C. twice
   D. ten times

Questions 6–8.

DIRECTIONS: Questions 6 through 8 must be answered on the basis of the following passage.

A glaring exception to the usual practice of the judicial trial as a means of conflict resolution is the utilization of administrative hearings. The growing tendency to create administrative bodies with rule-making and quasi-judicial powers has shattered many standard concepts. A comprehensive examination of the legal process cannot neglect these newer patterns.

In the administrative process, the legislative, executive, and judicial functions are mixed together, and many functions, such as investigating, advocating, negotiating, testifying, rule-making, and adjudicating, are carried out by the same agency. The reason for the breakdown of the separation-of-powers formula is not hard to find. It was felt by Congress, and state and municipal legislatures, that certain regulatory tasks could not be performed efficiently, rapidly, expertly, and with due concern for the public interest by the traditional branches of government. Accordingly, regulatory agencies were delegated powers to consider disputes from the earliest stage of investigation to the final stages of adjudication entirely within each agency itself, subject only to limited review in the regular courts.

6. The above passage states that the usual means for conflict resolution is through the use of

   A. judicial trial
   B. administrative hearing
   C. legislation
   D. regulatory agencies

7. The above passage *implies* that the use of administrative hearing in resolving conflict is a(n) _____ approach.

   A. traditional
   B. new
   C. dangerous
   D. experimental

8. The above passage states that the reason for the breakdown of the separation-of-powers formula in the administrative process is that

   A. Congress believed that certain regulatory tasks could be better performed by separate agencies
   B. legislative and executive functions are incompatible in the same agency
   C. investigative and regulatory functions are not normally reviewed by the courts
   D. state and municipal legislatures are more concerned with efficiency than with legality

9. An employee examining the summonses of individuals appearing for hearings noticed that the address on one summons was the same as that of an individual who had appeared earlier that day. He asked the second respondent if he knew the first respondent.
The MOST appropriate evaluation of the employee's behavior is that he should

   A. not have mentioned any other respondent to the second respondent
   B. not waste time inspecting summonses in such detail
   C. be commended for inspecting summonses so carefully
   D. be commended for his investigation of the respondents

10. An employee is assigned to maintain all types of frequently used reference material such as booklets and technical papers. He keeps these in a pile on a shelf in order of arrival. When new material arrives, he puts it on top of the pile.
Which of the following BEST evaluates the employee's handling of this reference material?
His system is most likely to result in_____ filing and _____ retrieval.

   A. fast; slow
   B. slow; slow
   C. fast; fast
   D. slow; fast

11. An employee computes statistics relating to proceedings. The method he devised consists of organizing his source and summary documents in such a manner that at any time another employee can assume the work. This method takes a little more time than other possible methods.
Which of the following statements BEST evaluates the judgment of the employee in devising such a method?
The employee has used

   A. *good* judgment because it is important to provide for continuity
   B. *poor* judgment because he is not using the fastest method
   C. *good* judgment because if a job is done as fast as possible, it becomes tiring
   D. *poor* judgment because it is not an employee's responsibility to prepare for a replacement

12. Assume that it is your job to receive incoming telephone calls. Those calls which you cannot handle yourself have to be transferred to the appropriate office.
If you receive an outside call for an extension line which is busy, the one of the following which you should do FIRST is to

   A. interrupt the person speaking on the extension and tell him a call is waiting
   B. tell the caller the line is busy and let him know every thirty seconds whether or not it is free
   C. leave the caller on *hold* until the extension is free
   D. tell the caller the line is busy and ask him if he wishes to wait

13. On one occasion in a certain office, an elderly employee collapsed, apparently the victim of a heart attack. Chaos broke out in the office as several people tried to help him, and several others tried to get assistance.
Of the following, the MOST certain way of avoiding such chaos in the future is to

    A. keep a copy of heart attack procedures on file so that it can be referred to by any member of the staff when an emergency occurs
    B. provide each member of the staff with a first aid book which is to be kept in an accessible location
    C. train all members of the staff in the proper procedure for handling such emergencies, assigning specific responsibilities
    D. post, in several places around the office, a list of specific procedures to follow in each of several different emergencies

14. Your superior has subscribed to several publications directly related to your division's work, and he has asked you to see to it that the publications are circulated among the supervisory personnel in the division. There are eight supervisors involved.
The BEST method of insuring that all eight see these publications is to

    A. place the publication in the division's general reference library as soon as it arrives
    B. inform each supervisor whenever a publication arrives and remind all of them that they are responsible for reading it
    C. prepare a standard slip that can be stapled to each publication, listing the eight supervisors and saying, *Please read, initial your name, and pass along*
    D. send a memo to the eight supervisors saying that they may wish to purchase individual subscriptions in their own names if they are interested in seeing each issue

15. Assume that you have been asked to prepare a narrative summary of the monthly reports submitted by employees in your division.
In preparing your summary of this month's reports, the FIRST step to take is to

    A. read through the reports, noting their general content and any unusual features
    B. decide how many typewritten pages your summary should contain
    C. make a written summary of each separate report, so that you will not have to go back to the original reports again
    D. ask each employee which points he would prefer to see emphasized in your summary

16. Your superior has telephoned a number of key officials in your agency to ask whether they can meet at a certain time next month. He has found that they can all make it, and he has asked you to confirm the meeting.
Which of the following is the BEST way to confirm such a meeting?

    A. Note the meeting on your superior's calendar
    B. Post a notice of the meeting on the agency bulletin board
    C. Call the officials on the day of the meeting to remind them of the meeting
    D. Write a memo to each official involved repeating the time and place of the meeting

17. Of the following, the worker who is MOST likely to create a problem in maintaining safety is one who

    A. disregards hazards
    B. feels tired
    C. resents authority
    D. gets bored

18. Assume that a new regulation requires that certain kinds of private organizations file information forms with your department. You have been asked to write the short explanatory message that will be printed on the front cover of the pamphlet containing the forms and instructions.
    Which of the following would be the MOST appropriate way of beginning this message?

    A. Get the readers' attention by emphasizing immediately that there are legal penalties for organizations that fail to file before a certain date
    B. Briefly state the nature of the enclosed forms and the types of organizations that must file
    C. Say that your department is very sorry to have to put organizations to such an inconvenience
    D. Quote the entire regulation adopted by the city, even if it is quite long and is expressed in complicated legal language

19. Suppose that you have been told to make up the vacation schedule for the 15 employees in a particular unit. In order for the unit to operate effectively, only a few employees can be on vacation at the same time.
    Which of the following is the MOST advisable approach in making up the schedule?

    A. Draw up a schedule assigning vacations in alphabetical order
    B. Find out when the supervisors want to take their vacations, and randomly assign whatever periods are left to the non-supervisory personnel
    C. Assign the most desirable times to employees of longest standing, and the least desirable times to the newest employees
    D. Have all employees state their own preference, and then work out any conflicts in consultation with the people involved

20. Assume that you have been asked to prepare job descriptions for various positions in your department.
    Which of the following are the BASIC points that should be covered in a job description?

    A. General duties and responsibilities of the position, with examples of day-to-day tasks
    B. Comments on the performances of present employees
    C. Estimates of the number of openings that may be available in each category during the coming year
    D. Instructions for carrying out the specific tasks assigned to your department

KEY (CORRECT ANSWERS)

1.	A	11.	A
2.	A	12.	D
3.	D	13.	C
4.	B	14.	C
5.	D	15.	A
6.	A	16.	D
7.	B	17.	A
8.	A	18.	B
9.	A	19.	D
10.	A	20.	A

EXAMINATION SECTION
TEST 1

DIRECTIONS: Each question or incomplete statement is followed by several suggested answers or completions. Select the one that BEST answers the question or completes the Statement. *PRINT THE LETTER OF THE CORRECT ANSWER IN THE SPACE AT THE RIGHT.*

1. Your superior has asked you to notify division employees of an important change in one of the operating procedures described in the division manual. Every employee presently has a copy of this manual.
   Which of the following is *normally* the MOST practical way to get the employees to understand such a change?

   A. Notify each employee individually of the change and answer any questions he might have
   B. Send a written notice to key personnel, directing them to inform the people under them
   C. Call a general meeting, distribute a corrected page for the manual, and discuss the change
   D. Send a memo to employees describing the change in general terms and asking them to make the necessary corrections in their copies of the manual

1.____

2. A supervisor was directed by the head of his division to report figures for overtime wages. The supervisor asked a clerk under his supervision to give him the figures, and he passed the clerk's figures along to his superior without questioning them. It was then discovered that the clerk had carelessly supplied the wrong information. Who can PROPERLY be held responsible for the mistake, the supervisor or the payroll clerk?

   A. Only the supervisor, because he should have known that the clerk would be careless
   B. Only the clerk, because it should be unnecessary for supervisors to check the work of their subordinates except for work which is unusually complex or important
   C. Neither of them, because it is perfectly understandable that such mistakes will occur from time to time
   D. Both of them, because the person to whom a task is delegated is responsible to the supervisor who delegated the task, and the supervisor is responsible to his superior

2.____

3. As a supervisor, it is necessary for you to show a new employee how to enter information on standard forms that he will have to prepare. These forms have a number of blanks to be filled in, but the job is fairly simple once a person becomes familiar with it.
   The BEST way to show the new employee how to do the job is to

   A. explain how to do it and have him fill out a few forms, helping him with any difficulties
   B. give him a completed form to use as a model, and tell him to do all the others exactly the same way
   C. put him on his own immediately, and assume that he will learn for himself through trial and error
   D. give him several dozen completed forms to read, and ask him to check back with you in a few hours when he feels ready to start work

3.____

4. An administrative position carries with it a certain amount of authority. Management theorists feel that the exercise of authority is ESSENTIAL in carrying out the goals of an organization because

   A. administrators enjoy having the power to order people around, and they would not be willing to give it up
   B. administrators must work through others to accomplish objectives, so they must have the right to direct others to act in certain ways
   C. most employees are not able to carry out tasks on their own initiative, and they need a stern supervisor to make sure that the work gets done
   D. once authority is recognized, it can be carefully limited so that no administrator makes unreasonable demands or sets himself up as a petty tyrant

5. Assume that the work in your department involves the use of many technical terms. In such a situation, when you are answering inquiries from the general public, it would *usually* be BEST to

   A. use simple language and avoid the technical terms
   B. use the technical terms whenever possible
   C. use technical terms freely, but explain each term in parentheses
   D. apologize if you are forced to use a technical term

6. You are answering a letter that was written on the letterhead of the ABC Company and signed by James H. Block, Treasurer. What is usually considered to be the CORRECT salutation to use in your reply?
   Dear

   A. ABC Company: B. Sirs:
   C. Mr. Block: D. Mr. Treasurer:

7. Assume that one of your duties is to handle routine letters of inquiry from the public. The one of the following which is *usually* considered to be MOST desirable in replying to such a letter is a

   A. detailed answer handwritten on the original letter of inquiry
   B. phone call, since you can cover details more easily over the phone than in a letter
   C. short letter giving the specific information requested
   D. long letter discussing all possible aspects of the questions raised

8. The CHIEF reason for dividing a letter into paragraphs is to

   A. make the message clear to the reader by starting a new paragraph for each new topic
   B. make a short letter occupy as much of the page as possible
   C. keep the reader's attention by providing a pause from time to time
   D. make the letter look neat and business like

9. Your superior has asked you to send a letter via fax from your agency to a government agency in another city. He has written the letter and provided you with all contact information.
Which of the following does not need to be included on the fax cover sheet to be sent along with your superior's letter?

   A. Today's date
   B. A final sentence such as, *We would appreciate hearing from your agency in reply as soon as is convenient for you*
   C. Name of the contact person or department at the other agency
   D. Name of sender

10. Suppose that a usually competent employee whom you supervise has suddenly begun having difficulty completing his assignments. You ask the employee to speak to you privately about this situation and he agrees that he would appreciate this opportunity because of a problem he is having.
Of the following, which one would be the BEST technique for you to use in speaking with him?

   A. Criticize the employee's performance as soon as he mentions his difficulty in completing his assignments
   B. Listen patiently to what the employee has to say before making any comments on your own
   C. Refuse to discuss any personal factors which the employee mentions when he tries to explain his recent work difficulty
   D. Allow the employee to argue with you but plan your attack and defense carefully

11. Suppose that you receive a telephone call from someone identifying himself as an employee in another department who asks to be given information which your own department regards as confidential.
Which of the following is the BEST way of handling such a request?

   A. Give the information requested, since your caller has official standing
   B. Grant the request, provided the caller gives you a signed receipt
   C. Refuse the request, because you have no way of knowing whether the caller is really who he claims to be
   D. Explain that the information is confidential and inform the caller of the channels he must go through to have the information released to him

12. The MAIN purpose of transferring materials from active to inactive files is to

   A. keep current reference files from growing to a size where they become inefficient and unmanageable
   B. distinguish between important business and less important matters
   C. provide a means of storing letters that need not be answered
   D. make sure that there is some way of retrieving information from previous years

13. The one of the following for which a cross-index is MOST likely to be needed is a

   A. file of reference material arranged by subject
   B. file of individual personnel records arranged alphabetically
   C. card file containing addresses and phone numbers for various organizations
   D. supervisor's tickler file

14. The CHIEF advantage of a rotary file is that

    A. it holds much more material than a standard file cabinet
    B. it provides a temporary location for material that is due to be placed in the permanent files
    C. items can be easily located and scanned without being removed from the file
    D. less time is required for placing an item on a rotary file than for placing it in a standard upright file

15. Centralization of office activities has become an important technique for achieving greater efficiency in clerical work.
    Which of the following is NOT a result that could *normally* be gained by centralization of a clerical activity?

    A. More even distribution of work loads among employees performing the same kind of clerical tasks
    B. Increased opportunities for clerical workers to learn new skills and become better qualified for promotion to administrative positions
    C. Cost savings on office equipment whose use can now be shared by several employees
    D. Establishment of uniform standards and procedures for various clerical activities

16. Assume that certain work processed in your office is then sent to another office for further processing. One of the employees in your office tells you that the supervisor in the other office has been complaining about your office's method of handling the work.
    Of the following, the MOST appropriate action for you to take is to

    A. get all the details from the employee and then speak to the other supervisor
    B. ignore the situation and continue to do the best you can
    C. remind the supervisor that it is not his function to evaluate your work
    D. refrain from reporting the matter to your superior

17. It is the practice in your department to make objective evaluations of the performance of different units. This requires looking at the results achieved by a particular unit during a specified period of time—for instance, the number of applications processed, the number of inquiries answered, the number of inspections made, and so forth.
    Of the following, the BEST method of evaluating the performance of each unit is to compare its results with the

    A. results achieved by all units of the same size that are performing other kinds of work
    B. goals that the unit was reasonably expected to meet during the specified period
    C. performance of the same unit during a similar period of time four or five years earlier
    D. amount of money spent to achieve these results

18. It is possible that you may be asked to submit a brief written evaluation of the work of several employees under your supervision. Such an evaluation should *normally* give LEAST emphasis to an employee's

    A. attendance record, including tardiness and absence
    B. ability to grasp new assignments and carry them out effectively
    C. educational background and previous employment experience
    D. ability to get along with co-workers

19. You have been asked to help draw up a plan for a new operation to be carried out by your department. The INITIAL step in planning should be

    A. finding out how much money is available in the budget for the operation
    B. determining the objective or objectives of the operation
    C. gathering information on similar operations elsewhere
    D. determining the most reasonable way of structuring the operation

20. Studies show that office employees place high importance on the social and human aspects of the organization. What office employees like best about their jobs is the kind of people with whom they work. So strive hard to group people who are most likely to get along well together.
    Based on this statement, it is MOST reasonable to assume that office workers are most pleased to work in a group which

    A. is congenial
    B. has high productivity
    C. allows individual creativity
    D. is unlike other groups

KEY (CORRECT ANSWERS)

1.	C	11.	D
2.	D	12.	A
3.	A	13.	A
4.	B	14.	C
5.	A	15.	B
6.	C	16.	A
7.	C	17.	B
8.	A	18.	C
9.	B	19.	B
10.	B	20.	A

TEST 2

DIRECTIONS: Each question or incomplete statement is followed by several suggested answers or completions. Select the one that BEST answers the question or completes the statement. *PRINT THE LETTER OF THE CORRECT ANSWER IN THE SPACE AT THE RIGHT.*

1. A certain coordinator does not compliment members of his staff when they come up with good ideas. He feels that coming up with good ideas is part of the job and does not merit special attention.
   This coordinator's practice is

   A. *poor,* because recognition for good ideas is a good motivator
   B. *poor,* because the staff will suspect that the coordinator has no good ideas of his own
   C. *good,* because it is reasonable to assume that employees will tell their supervisor of ways to improve office practice
   D. *good,* because the other members of the staff are not made to seem inferior by comparison

2. An employee under your supervision complains about a decision you have made in assigning work in the office. You consider the matter to be unimportant, but it seems to be very important to him. He is excited and very angry.
   Of the following, the MOST appropriate action for you to take FIRST is to

   A. listen to the details of his complaint
   B. refer him to your superior
   C. tell him to *cool off* before discussing the matter
   D. tell him to settle it with the other employees

3. An experienced employee complains to his unit supervisor that the latter's continual, very close supervision of his work is unnecessary and annoying. The unit supervisor has been recently appointed.
   Of the following, it would generally be BEST for the unit supervisor to

   A. agree to discontinue all supervision if the employee will agree, if he has any problems, to consult the supervisor
   B. assure the employee that close supervision is necessary but should not be taken personally
   C. consider with the employee what aspects of the supervision could be reduced
   D. explain that he is supervising closely only until he learns what the job is all about

4. A coordinator had a clerk assigned to help him review records. One day the coordinator asked the clerk to continue checking the records, and the clerk said, *No, I'm not doing any more of that today.*
   In this instance, the coordinator should IMMEDIATELY

   A. ask the clerk why he will not check the records
   B. ask another clerk to do the job
   C. tell the clerk he must do it or be transferred
   D. contact his own supervisor

5. Assume that you have been assigned to supervise other employees. You find that one of your subordinates makes many mistakes whenever he prepares a particular report. Of the following, the MOST desirable course of action for you to follow FIRST in such a situation is to

   A. retrain the subordinate in the preparation of the report
   B. transfer the subordinate to another unit
   C. tell the subordinate to improve or resign
   D. give the employee different duties

6. Some employees of a department have sent an anonymous letter containing many complaints to the department head. Of the following, what is this MOST likely to show about the department?

   A. It is probably a good place to work.
   B. Communications are probably poor.
   C. The complaints are probably unjustified.
   D. These employees are probably untrustworthy.

7. Of the following, the BEST reason for rotating employee work assignments is that such rotation

   A. challenges the ingenuity of supervisors in making assignments
   B. gives each employee a chance at both desirable and undesirable assignments
   C. creates specialists among all employees
   D. increases the competitive spirit among employees

8. A citizen was angry about a parking ticket which he had received, and he insisted on talking to a coordinator about a hearing. The coordinator spoke to him and explained the rules and procedures relating to the disposition of summonses for parking violations. The citizen remained angry and dissatisfied. The coordinator then appealed to the citizen's civic responsibility and asked him if he wished to be an obstructionist. This last action was incorrect.
How should the coordinator have handled this situation?

   A. Summoned a supervisor immediately and not talked with the angry citizen
   B. Been more sympathetic and shown some agreement with the citizen's complaint
   C. Limited himself to explaining the rules and regulations
   D. Shown some anger himself in order to reduce the citizen's anger

9. A coordinator has had several problems with a clerk who assists him. He calls the clerk in for a discussion of the matters.
Which of the following should comprise the MAJOR part of the discussion?

   A. All the things the clerk has done wrong
   B. The most recent things the clerk has done wrong
   C. The things the clerk has done well in addition to the things he has done wrong
   D. The clerk's previous experience and personal problems

Questions 10–14.

DIRECTIONS: Questions 10 through 14 are to be answered SOLELY on the basis of the following passage.

The laws with which criminal courts are concerned contain threats of punishment for infraction of specified rules. Consequently, the courts are organized primarily for implementation of the punitive societal reaction of crime. While the informal organization of most courts allows the judge to use discretion as to which guilty persons actually are to be punished, the threat of punishment for all guilty persons always is present. Also, in recent years a number of formal provisions for the use of non-punitive and treatment methods by the criminal courts have been made, but the threat of punishment remains, even for the recipients of the treatment and non-punitive measures. For example, it has become possible for courts to grant probation, which can be non-punitive, to some offenders, but the probationer is constantly under the threat of punishment, for, if he does not maintain the conditions of his probation, he may be imprisoned. As the treatment reaction to crime becomes more popular, the criminal courts may have as their sole function the determination of the guilt or innocence of the accused persons, leaving the problem of correcting criminals entirely to outsiders. Under such conditions, the organization of the court system, the duties and activities of court personnel, and the nature of the trial all would be decidedly different.

10. Which one of the following is the BEST description of the subject matter of the above passage?
The

   A. value of non-punitive measures for criminals
   B. effect of punishment on guilty individuals
   C. punitive functions of the criminal courts
   D. success of probation as a deterrent of crime

11. It may be INFERRED from the above passage that the present traditional organization of the criminal court system is a result of

   A. the nature of the laws with which these courts are concerned
   B. a shift from non-punitive to punitive measures for correctional purposes
   C. an informal arrangement between court personnel and the government
   D. a formal decision made by court personnel to increase efficiency

12. All persons guilty of breaking certain specified rules, according to the above passage, are subject to the threat of

   A. treatment
   B. punishment
   C. probation
   D. retrial

13. According to the above passage, the decision whether or not to punish a guilty person is a function USUALLY performed by

   A. the jury
   B. the criminal code
   C. the judge
   D. corrections personnel

14. According to the above passage, which one of the following is a possible effect of an increase in the *treatment reactions to crime*? 14.____

    A. A decrease in the number of court personnel
    B. An increase in the number of criminal trials
    C. Less reliance on probation as a non-punitive treatment measure
    D. A decrease in the functions of the court following determination of guilt

15. Which of the following actions would usually be MOST appropriate for a coordinator to take after receiving an instruction sheet from his supervisor explaining a new procedure which is to be followed? 15.____

    A. Put the instruction sheet aside temporarily until he determines what is wrong with the old procedure
    B. Call his supervisor and ask if the procedure is one he must implement immediately
    C. Write a memorandum to the supervisor asking for more details
    D. Try the new procedure and advise the supervisor of any problem or possible improvements

16. Assume that you are in charge of an office handling a large volume of various types of clerical work. 16.____
    The one of the following that must be done FIRST to promote even distribution and proper flow of work is to determine

    A. when additional work will come to the office
    B. the capabilities of the staff
    C. the type of tasks to be done and their priorities
    D. the time required for each task

17. In a miscellaneous correspondence folder in a file drawer, it is usually MOST helpful if letters are arranged according to 17.____

    A. date with the most recent date on the bottom
    B. date with the most recent date on the top
    C. subject with the subjects alphabetically arranged
    D. name with the names arranged geographically

18. Of the following, which one is considered the PRIMARY advantage of using a committee to resolve a problem in an organization? 18.____

    A. No one person will be held accountable for the decision since a group of people was involved
    B. People with different backgrounds give attention to the problem
    C. The decision will take considerable time so there is unlikely to be a decision that will later be regretted
    D. One person cannot dominate the decision-making process

19. Assume that as a coordinator you have been asked to redesign a form used in your office. 19.____
    Of the following, your MOST important consideration should be the

    A. sequence of items on the form
    B. number of items to be included on the form
    C. number of copies that are required
    D. purpose of the form

20. Employees in a certain office come to their supervisor with all their complaints about the office and the work. Almost every employee has had at least one minor complaint at some time.
   The situation with respect to complaints in this office may BEST be described as probably

   A. *good;* employees who complain care about their jobs and work hard
   B. *good;* grievances brought out into the open can be corrected
   C. *bad;* only serious complaints should be discussed
   D. *bad;* it indicates the staff does not have confidence in the administration

20.____

KEY (CORRECT ANSWERS)

1.	A	11.	A
2.	A	12.	B
3.	C	13.	C
4.	A	14.	D
5.	A	15.	D
6.	B	16.	C
7.	B	17.	B
8.	C	18.	B
9.	C	19.	D
10.	C	20.	B

SUPERVISION, ADMINISTRATION, MANAGEMENT AND ORGANIZATION

EXAMINATION SECTION
TEST 1

DIRECTIONS: Each question or incomplete statement is followed by several suggested answers or completions. Select the one that BEST answers the question or completes the statement. *PRINT THE LETTER OF THE CORRECT ANSWER IN THE SPACE AT THE RIGHT.*

1. One of the responsibilities of the supervisor is to provide top administration with information about clients and their problems that will help in the evaluation of existing policies and indicate the need for modifications.
   In order to fulfill this responsibility, it would be MOST essential for the supervisor to

   A. routinely forward all regularly prepared and recurrent reports from his subordinates to his immediate superior
   B. regularly review agency rules, regulations and policies to make sure that he has sufficient knowledge to make appropriate analyses
   C. note repeated instances of failure of staff to correctly administer a policy and schedule staff conferences for corrective training
   D. analyze reports on cases submitted by subordinates, in order to select relevant trend material to be forwarded to his superiors

2. You find that your division has a serious problem because of unusually long delays in filing reports and overdue approvals to private agencies under contract for services.
   The MOST appropriate step to take FIRST in this situation would be to

   A. request additional staff to work on reports and approvals
   B. order staff to work overtime until the backlog is eliminated
   C. impress staff with the importance of expeditious handling of reports and approvals
   D. analyze present procedures for handling reports and approvals

3. When a supervisor finds that he must communicate orally information that is significant enough to affect the entire staff, it would be MOST important to

   A. distribute a written summary of the information to his staff before discussing it orally
   B. tell his subordinate supervisors to discuss this information at individual conferences with their subordinates
   C. call a follow-up meeting of absentees as soon as they return
   D. restate and summarize the information in order to make sure that everyone understands its meaning and implications

4. Of the following, the BEST way for a supervisor to assist a subordinate who has unusually heavy work pressures is to

   A. point out that such pressures go with the job and must be tolerated
   B. suggest to him that the pressures probably result from poor handling of his workload
   C. help him to be selective in deciding on priorities during the period of pressure
   D. ask him to work overtime until the period of pressure is over

5. Leadership is a basic responsibility of the supervisor. The one of the following which would be the LEAST appropriate way to fulfill this role is for the supervisor to

    A. help staff to work up to their capacities in every possible way
    B. encourage independent judgment and actions by staff members
    C. allow staff to participate in decisions within policy limits
    D. take over certain tasks in which he is more competent than his subordinates

6. Assume that you have assigned a very difficult administrative task to one of your best subordinate supervisors, but he is reluctant to take it on because he fears that he will fail in it. It is your judgment, however, that he is quite capable of performing this task.
The one of the following which is the MOST desirable way for you to handle this situation is to

    A. reassure him that he has enough skill to perform the task and that he will not be penalized if he fails
    B. reassign the task to another supervisor who is more achievement-oriented and more confident of his skills
    C. minimize the importance of the task so that he will feel it is safe for him to attempt it
    D. stress the importance of the task and the dependence of the other staff members on his succeeding in it

7. Assume that a member of your professional staff deliberately misinterprets a new state directive because he fears that its enforcement will have an adverse effect on clients. Although you consider him to be a good supervisor and basically agree with him, you should direct him to comply.
Of the following, the MOST desirable way for you to handle this situation would be to

    A. avoid a confrontation with him by transferring responsibility for carrying out the directive to another member of your staff
    B. explain to him that you are in a better position than he to assess the implications of the new directive
    C. discuss with him the basic reasons for his misinterpretation and explain why he must comply with the directive
    D. allow him to interpret the directive in his own way as long as he assumes full responsibility for his actions

8. Of the following, the MAIN reason it is important for an administrator in a large organization to properly coordinate the work delegated to subordinates is that such coordination

    A. makes it unnecessary to hold frequent staff meetings and conferences with key staff members
    B. reduces the necessity for regular evaluation of procedures and programs, production and performance of personnel
    C. results in greater economy and stricter accountability for the organization's resources
    D. facilitates integration of the contributions of the numerous staff members who are responsible for specific parts of the total workload

9. The one of the following which would NOT be an appropriate reason for the formulation of an entirely NEW policy is that it would

   A. serve as a positive affirmation of the agency's function and how it is to be carried out
   B. give focus and direction to the work of the staff, particularly in decision-making
   C. inform the public of the precise conditions under which services will be rendered
   D. provide procedures which constitute uniform methods of carrying out operations

10. Of the following, it is MOST difficult to formulate policy in an organization where

    A. work assignments are narrowly specialized by units
    B. staff members have varied backgrounds and a wide range of competency
    C. units implementing the same policy are in the same geographic location
    D. staff is experienced and fully trained

11. For a supervisor to feel that he is responsible for influencing the attitudes of his staff members is GENERALLY considered

    A. *undesirable;* attitudes of adults are emotional factors which usually cannot be changed
    B. *desirable;* certain attitudes can be obstructive and should be modified in order to provide effective service to clients
    C. *undesirable;* the supervisor should be nonjudgmental and accepting of widely different attitudes and social patterns of staff members
    D. *desirable;* influencing attitudes is a teaching responsibility which the supervisor shares with the training specialist

12. The one of the following which is NOT generally a function of the higher-level supervisor is

    A. projecting the budget and obtaining financial resources
    B. providing conditions conducive to optimum employee production
    C. maintaining records and reports as a basis for accountability and evaluation
    D. evaluating program achievements and personnel effectiveness in accordance with goals and standards

13. As a supervisor in a recently decentralized services center offering multiple services, you are given responsibility for an orientation program for professional staff on the recent reorganization of the Department.
    Of the following, the MOST appropriate step to take FIRST would be to

    A. organize a series of workshops for subordinate supervisors
    B. arrange a tour of the new geographic area of service
    C. review supervisors' reports, statistical data and other relevant material
    D. develop a resource manual for staff on the reorganized center

14. Experts generally agree that the content of training sessions should be closely related to workers' practice.
    Of the following, the BEST method of achieving this aim is for the training conference leader to

    A. encourage group discussion of problems that concern staff in their practice
    B. develop closer working relationships with top administration

C. coordinate with central office to obtain feedback on problems that concern staff
D. observe workers in order to develop a pattern of problems for class discussion

15. The one of the following which is generally the MOST useful teaching tool for professional staff development is

    A. visual aids and tape recordings
    B. professional literature
    C. agency case material
    D. lectures by experts

16. The one of the following which is NOT a good reason for using group conferences as a method of supervision is to

    A. give workers a feeling of mutual support through sharing common problems
    B. save time by eliminating the need for individual conferences
    C. encourage discussion of certain problems that are not as likely to come up in individual conferences
    D. provide an opportunity for developing positive identification with the department and its programs

17. The supervisor, in his role as teacher, applies his teaching in line with his understanding of people and realizes that teaching is a highly individualized process, based on understanding of the worker as a person and as a learner. This statement implies, MOST NEARLY, that the supervisor must help the worker to

    A. overcome his biases
    B. develop his own ways of working
    C. gain confidence in his ability
    D. develop the will to work

18. Of the following, the circumstance under which it would be MOST appropriate to divide a training conference for professional staff into small workshops is when

    A. some of the trainees are not aware of the effect of their attitudes and behavior on others
    B. the trainees need to look at human relations problems from different perspectives
    C. the trainees are faced with several substantially different types of problems in their job assignments
    D. the trainees need to know how to function in many different capacities

19. Of the following, the MAIN reason why it is important to systemically evaluate a specific training program while it is in progress is to

    A. collect data that will serve as a valid basis for improving the agency's overall training program and maintaining control over its components
    B. insure that instruction by training specialists is conducted in a manner consistent with the planned design of the training program
    C. identify areas in which additional or remedial training for the training specialists can be planned and implemented
    D. provide data which are usable in effecting revisions of specific components of the training program

20. Staff development has been defined as an educational process which seeks to provide agency staff with knowledge about specific job responsibilities and to effect changes in staff attitudes and behavior patterns. Assume that you are assigned to define the educational objectives of a specific training program.
    In accordance with the above concept, the MOST helpful formulation would be a statement of the

    A. purpose and goals of each training session
    B. generalized patterns of behavior to be developed in the trainees
    C. content material to be presented in the training sessions
    D. kind of behavior to be developed in the trainees and the situations in which this behavior will be applied

21. In teaching personnel under your supervision how to gather and analyze facts before attempting to solve a problem, the one of the following training methods which would be MOST effective is

    A. case study   B. role playing
    C. programmed learning   D. planned experience'

22. The importance of analyzing functions traditionally included in the position of caseworker, with a view toward identifying and separating those activities to be performed by the most highly skilled personnel, has been widely discussed.
    Of the following, an IMPORTANT *secondary* gain which can result from such differential use of staff is that

    A. supporting job assignments can be given to persons unable to meet the demands of casework, to the satisfaction of all concerned
    B. documentation will be provided on workers who are not suited for all the duties now part of the caseworker's job
    C. caseworkers with a high level of competence in working with people can be rewarded through promotion or merit increases
    D. incompetent workers can be identified and categorized, as a basis for transfer or separation from the service

23. Of the following, a serious DISADVANTAGE of a performance evaluation system based on standardized evaluation factors is that such a system tends to

    A. exacerbate the anxieties of those supervisors who are apprehensive about determining what happens to another person
    B. subject the supervisor to psychological stress by emphasizing the incompatibility of his dual role as both judge and counselor
    C. create organizational conflict by encouraging personnel who wish to enhance their standing to become too aggressive in the performance of their duties
    D. lead many staff members to concentrate on measuring up in terms of the evaluation factors and to disregard other aspects of their work

24. Which of the following would contribute MOST to the achievement of conformity of staff activities and goals to the intent of agency policies and procedures?

    A. Effective communications and organizational discipline
    B. Changing nature of the underlying principles and desired purpose of the policies and procedures

C. Formulation of specific criteria for implementing the policies and procedures
D. Continuous monitoring of the essential effectiveness of agency operations

25. Job enlargement, a management device used by large organizations to counteract the adverse effects of specialization on employee performance, is LEAST likely to improve employee motivation if it is accomplished by

   A. lengthening the job cycle and adding a large number of similar tasks
   B. allowing the employee to use a greater variety of skills
   C. increasing the scope and complexity of the employee's job
   D. giving the employee more opportunities to make decisions

KEY (CORRECT ANSWERS)

1.	D	11.	B
2.	D	12.	A
3.	D	13.	A
4.	C	14.	A
5.	D	15.	C
6.	A	16.	B
7.	C	17.	B
8.	D	18.	C
9.	D	19.	A
10.	B	20.	D

21. A
22. A
23. D
24. A
25. A

TEST 2

DIRECTIONS: Each question or incomplete statement is followed by several suggested answers or completions. Select the one that BEST answers the question or completes the statement. *PRINT THE LETTER OF THE CORRECT ANSWER IN THE SPACE AT THE RIGHT.*

1. When a supervisor requires approval for case action on a higher level, the process used is known as

    A. administrative clearance
    B. going outside channels
    C. administrative consultation
    D. delegation of authority

2. In delegating authority to his subordinates, the one of the following to which a GOOD supervisor should give PRIMARY consideration is the

    A. results expected of them
    B. amount of power to be delegated
    C. amount of responsibility to be delegated
    D. their skill in the performance of present tasks

3. Of the following, the type of decision which could be SAFELY delegated to LOWER-LEVEL staff without undermining basic supervisory responsibility is one which

    A. involves a commitment that can be fulfilled only over a long period of time
    B. has fairly uncertain goals and premises
    C. has the possibility of modification built into it
    D. may generate considerable resistance from those affected by it

4. Of the following, the MOST valuable contribution made by the informal organization in a large public service agency is that such an organization

    A. has goals and values which are usually consistent with and reinforce those of the formal organization
    B. is more flexible than the formal organization and more adaptable to changing conditions
    C. has a communications system which often contributes to the efficiency of the formal organization
    D. represents a sound basis on which to build the formal organizational structure

5. Of the following, the condition under which it would be MOST useful for an agency to develop detailed procedures is when

    A. subordinate supervisory personnel need a structure to help them develop greater independence
    B. employees have little experience or knowledge of how to perform certain assigned tasks
    C. coordination of agency activities is largely dependent upon personal contact
    D. agency activities must continually adjust to changes in local circumstances

6. Assume that a certain administrator has the management philosophy that his agency's responsibility is to routinize existing operations, meet each day's problems as they arise, and resolve problems with a minimum of residual effect upon himself or his agency. The possibility that this official would be able to administer his agency without running into serious difficulties would be MORE likely during a period of

    A. economic change
    B. social change
    C. economic crisis
    D. social and economic stability

7. Some large organizations have adopted the practice of allowing each employee to establish his own performance goals, and then later evaluate himself in an individual conference with his immediate supervisor.
Of the following, a DRAWBACK of this approach is that the employee

   A. may set his goals too low and rate himself too highly
   B. cannot control those variables which may improve his performance
   C. has no guidelines for improving his performance
   D. usually finds it more difficult to criticize himself than to accept criticism from others

8. Decentralization of services cannot completely eliminate the requirement of central office approval for certain case actions. The MOST valid reason for complaint about this requirement is that

   A. unavoidable delay created by referral to central office may cause serious problems for the client
   B. it may lower morale of supervisors who are not given the authority to take final action on urgent cases
   C. the concept of role responsibility is minimized
   D. the objective of delegated responsibility tends to be negated

9. Which of the following would be the MOST useful administrative tool for the purpose of showing the sequence of operations and staff involved? A(n)

   A. organization chart
   B. flow chart
   C. manual of operating procedures
   D. statistical review

10. The prevailing pattern of organization in large public agencies consists of a limited span of control and organization by function or, at lower levels, process.
Of the following, the PRINCIPAL effect which this pattern of organization has on the management of work is that it

    A. reduces the management burden in significant ways
    B. creates a time lag between the perception of a problem and action on it
    C. makes it difficult to direct and observe employee performance
    D. facilitates the development of employees with managerial ability

11. The one of the following which would be the MOST appropriate way to reduce tensions between line and staff personnel in public service agencies is to

    A. provide in-service training that will increase the sensitivity of line and staff personnel to their respective roles
    B. assign to staff personnel the role of providing assistance only when requested by line personnel
    C. separate staff from line personnel and provide staff with its own independent reward structure
    D. give line and staff personnel equal status in making decisions

12. In determining the appropriate span of control for subordinate supervisors, which of the following principles should be followed? The more

    A. complex the work, the broader the effective span of control
    B. similar the jobs being supervised, the more narrow the effective span of control

C. interdependent the jobs being supervised, the more narrow the effective span of control
D. unpredictable the work, the broader the effective span of control

13. A method sometimes used in public service agencies to improve upward communication is to require subordinate supervisory staff to submit to top management monthly narrative reports of any problems which they deem important for consideration.
Of the following, a major DISADVANTAGE of this method is that it may

   A. enable subordinate supervisors to avoid thinking about their problems by simply referring such matters to their superiors
   B. obscure important issues so that they are not given appropriate attention
   C. create a need for numerous staff conferences in order to handle all of the reported problems
   D. encourage some subordinate supervisors to focus on irrelevant matters and compete with each other in the length and content of their reports

13.____

14. The use of a committee as an approach to the problem of coordinating interdepartmental activities can present difficulties if the committee functions PRIMARILY as a(n)

   A. means of achieving personal objectives and goals
   B. instrument for coordinating activities that flow across departmental lines
   C. device for involving subordinate personnel in the decision-making process
   D. means of giving representation to competing interest groups

14.____

15. A study was recently made of the attitudes and perceptions of a sample of workers who had experienced a major organizational change and redefinition of their jobs as a result of separation of certain functions.
Questionnaires administered to these workers indicated that a disproportionate number of workers in the larger agencies were dissatisfied with the reorganization and their new assignments.
Of the following, the MOST plausible reason for this dissatisfaction is that workers in larger agencies are

   A. less likely to be known to management and to be personally disciplined if they expressed dissatisfaction with their new roles
   B. less likely to have the opportunity to participate in planning a reorganization and to be given consideration for the assignments they preferred
   C. given a shorter lead period to implement the changes and therefore had insufficient time to plan the reorganization and carry it out efficiently
   D. usually made up of more older members who have had routinized their work according to habit and find it more difficult to adjust to change

15.____

16. An article which recently appeared in a professional journal presents a proposal for participatory leadership, in which the goal of supervision would be development of subordinates' self-reliance, with the premise that each staff member is held accountable for his own performance.
The one of the following which would NOT be a desirable outcome of this type of supervision is the

   A. necessity for subordinates to critically examine their performance
   B. development by some subordinates of skills not possessed by the supervisor

16.____

C. establishment of a quality control unit for sample checking and identification of errors
D. relaxation of demands made on the supervisor

17. The "management by objectives" concept is a major development in the administration of services organizations. The purpose of this approach is to establish a system for

    A. reduction of waiting time
    B. planning and controlling work output
    C. consolidation of organizational units
    D. work measurement

18. Assume that you encounter a serious administrative problem in implementing a new program. After consulting with the members of your staff individually, you come up with several alternate solutions.
Of the following, the procedure which would be MOST appropriate for evaluating the relative merits of each solution would be to

    A. try all of them on a limited experimental basis
    B. break the problem down into its component parts and analyze the effect of each solution on each component in terms of costs and benefits
    C. break the problem down into its component parts, eliminate all intangibles, and measure the effect of the tangible aspects of each solution on each component in terms of costs and benefits
    D. bring the matter before your weekly staff conference, discuss the relative merits of each alternate solution, and then choose the one favored by the majority of the conference

19. When establishing planning objectives for a service program under your supervision, the one of the following principles which should be followed is that objectives

    A. are rarely verifiable if they are qualitative
    B. should be few in number and of equal importance
    C. should cover as many of the activities of the program as possible
    D. should be set in the light of assumptions about future funding

20. Assume that you have been assigned responsibility for coordinating various aspects of a program in a community services center. Which of the following administrative concepts would NOT be applicable to this assignment?

    A. Functional job analysis   B. Peer group supervision
    C. Differential use of staff   D. Systems design

21. Good administrative practice includes the use of outside consultants as an effective technique in achieving agency objectives. However, the one of the following which would NOT be an appropriate role for the consultant is

    A. provision of technical or professional expertise not otherwise available in the agency
    B. administrative direction of a new program activity
    C. facilitating coordination and communication among agency staff
    D. objective measurement of the effectiveness of agency services

22. Of the following, the MOST common fault of research projects attempting to measure the effectiveness of social programs has been their

    A. questionable methodology
    B. inaccurate findings
    C. unrealistic expectations
    D. lack of objectivity

23. One of the most difficult tasks of supervision in a modern public agency is teaching workers to cope with the hostile reactions of clients. In order to help the disconcerted worker analyze and understand a client's hostile behavior, the supervisor should FIRST

    A. encourage the worker to identify with the client's frustrations and deprivations
    B. give the worker a chance to express and accept his feelings about the client
    C. ask the worker to review his knowledge of the client and his circumstances
    D. explain to the worker that the client's anger is not directed at the worker personally

24. Determination of the level of participation, or how much of the public should participate in a given project, is a vital step in community organization.
    In order to make this determination, the FIRST action that should be taken is to

    A. develop the participants
    B. fix the goals of the project
    C. evaluate community interest in the project
    D. enlist the cooperation of community leaders

25. The one of the following which would be the MOST critical factor for SUCCESSFUL operation of a decentralized system of programs and services is

    A. periodic review and evaluation of services delivered at the community level
    B. transfer of decision-making authority to the community level wherever feasible
    C. participation of indigenous non-professionals in service delivery
    D. formulation of quantitative plans for dealing with community problems wherever feasible

KEY (CORRECT ANSWERS)

1. A
2. A
3. C
4. C
5. B

6. D
7. A
8. A
9. B
10. B

11. A
12. C
13. D
14. A
15. B

16. D
17. B
18. C
19. D
20. B

21. B
22. C
23. B
24. B
25. B

TEST 3

DIRECTIONS: Each question or incomplete statement is followed by several suggested answers or completions. Select the one that BEST answers the question or completes the statement. *PRINT THE LETTER OF THE CORRECT ANSWER IN THE SPACE AT THE RIGHT.*

1. Douglas McGregor's theory of human motivation classifies worker behavior into two distinct categories: Theory X and Theory Y. Theory X, the traditional view, states that the average man dislikes to work and will avoid work if he can, unless coerced. Theory Y holds essentially the opposite view. The executive can apply both of these theories to worker behavior BEST if he   1.____

    A. follows an "open-door" policy only with respect to his immediate subordinates
    B. recognizes his subordinates' mental and social needs as well as agency needs
    C. recognizes that executive responsibility is primarily limited to fulfillment of agency productivity goals
    D. directs his subordinate managers to follow a policy of close supervision

2. In interpersonal communications it is of paramount importance to determine whether or not what has been said has been understood by others. One of the MOST important sources of such information is known as   2.____

    A. the halo effect
    B. evaluation
    C. feedback
    D. quantitative analysis

3. The grapevine most often provides a USEFUL service by   3.____

    A. correcting some of the deficiencies of the formal communication system
    B. rapidly conveying a true picture of events
    C. involving staff in current organizational changes
    D. interfering with the operation of the formal communication system

4. People who are in favor of a leadership style in which the subordinates help make decisions, contend that it produces favorable effects in a work unit. According to these people, which of the following is NOT likely to be an effect of such "participative management"?   4.____

    A. Reduced turnover
    B. Accelerated learning of duties
    C. Greater acceptance of change
    D. Reduced acceptance of the work unit's goals

5. Employees of a public service agency will be MOST likely to develop meaningful goals for both the agency and the employee and become committed to attaining them if supervisors   5.____

    A. allow them unilaterally to set their own goals
    B. provide them with a clear understanding of the premises underlying the agency's goals
    C. encourage them to concentrate on setting only short-range goals for themselves
    D. periodically review the agency's goals in order to suggest changes in accordance with current conditions

6. The insights of Chester Barnard have influenced the development of management thought in significant ways. He is MOST closely identified with a position that has become known as the

   A. acceptance theory of authority
   B. principle of the manager's or executive's span of control
   C. "Theory X" and "Theory Y" dichotomy
   D. unity of command principle

7. If a manager believes that man is primarily motivated by economic incentives and, above all, seeks security, he MOST usually should operate on the assumption that his subordinates

   A. need to be closely directed and have relatively little ambition
   B. are more responsive to the social forces of their peer group than to the incentives of management
   C. are capable of learning not only to accept but to seek responsibility
   D. are capable of responding favorably to many different kinds of managerial strategies

8. Of the following, the MOST important reason why it is in the interest of public service agencies to involve subordinate personnel in setting goals is that the more committed employees are to the goals of their agency the

   A. *more* likely they are to develop a desire for the agency's achievement of success
   B. *more* likely they are to prefer difficult rather than easy tasks
   C. *more* likely they are to perceive their individual performance as a reliable indicator of the agency's performance
   D. *less* likely they are to choose unreasonably difficult goals

9. As a result of gaining more recent knowledge about motivation, modern executives have had to rethink their notions about what motivates their subordinate managers. Which of the following factors is GENERALLY considered MOST important in modern motivation theory?

   A. Fringe benefits
   B. Working conditions
   C. Recognition of good work performance
   D. Education and experience required for the job

10. Of the following, the MAIN reason why cooperative interrelationships among personnel are more likely than competitive interrelationships to promote efficiency in the operation of a public service agency is that cooperation

    A. allows for a greater degree of specialization by function
    B. increases the opportunities for employees to check on each others' work
    C. provides a feeling of identification with the organization and enhances the desire for accomplishment
    D. improves the capacity of employees to acquire knowledge and learn new skills

11. Four statements are given below. Three of them describe approaches which are desirable in developing a program of employee motivation. The one which does NOT describe such an approach is:

    A. "Establish attainable goals to give employees a sense of achievement."
    B. "Largely discount the self-interest motive because it is impractical to consider it."
    C. "Allow for the participation of persons included in the plans."
    D. "Base plans on group considerations as well as individual considerations."

12. It is GENERALLY acknowledged that certain conditions should exist to insure that a subordinate will decide to accept a communication as being authoritative. Which of the following is LEAST valid as a condition which should exist?

    A. The subordinate understands the communication
    B. At the time of the subordinate's decision, he views the communication as consistent with the organization's purpose and his personal interest
    C. At the time of the subordinate's decision, he views the communication as more consistent with his personal purpose than with the organization's interests
    D. The subordinate is mentally and physically able to comply with the communication

13. In exploring the effects that employee participation has on putting changes in work methods into effect, certain relationships have been established between participation and productivity. It has MOST generally been found that HIGHEST productivity occurs in groups that are given

    A. participation in the process of change only through representatives of their group
    B. no participation in the change process
    C. full participation in the change process
    D. intermittent participation in the process of change

14. Of the following statements, the one which represents a trend LEAST likely to occur in the area of employee-management relations is that:

    A. Employees will exert more influence on decisions affecting their interests.
    B. Technological change will have a stronger impact on organizations' human resources.
    C. Labor will judge management according to company profits.
    D. Government will play a larger role in balancing the interests of the parties in labor-management affairs.

15. Members of an organization must satisfy several fundamental psychological needs in order to be happy and productive. The broadest and MOST basic needs are

    A. achievement, recognition and acceptance
    B. competition, recognition and accomplishment
    C. salary increments and recognition
    D. acceptance of competition and economic reward

16. Morale has been defined as the capacity of a group of people to pull together steadily for a common purpose. Morale thus defined is MOST generally dependent on which one of the following conditions?

    A. Job security
    B. Group and individual self-confidence
    C. Organizational efficiency
    D. Physical health of the individuals

17. Assume that consideration is being given to forming a committee for the purpose of getting a new program under way which requires the coordination of several organizational units. Which one of the following would be a MAJOR weakness of using the "committee" approach in this situation?   17._____

   A. Its inappropriateness for decision-making
   B. The necessity to include line and staff employees
   C. The difficulty of achieving proper representation
   D. Its independence from the formal organization

18. Which of the following techniques is NOT used as an approach to encourage communication between individuals at the same level?   18._____

   A. The informal organization   B. The chain of command
   C. Committee meetings   D. Distribution of written reports

19. In everyday actual operations, downward communications MOST often concern   19._____

   A. specific directives about job performance
   B. information about worker performance
   C. information about the rationale of the job
   D. information to indoctrinate the organization's staff on goals to be achieved

20. Communication has been thought of for a long time as a vital process in a formal organization system. Of the following, the MOST accurate statement that can be made concerning this process is that   20._____

   A. decision-making depends on communication and organizational structure
   B. communication does not interact but is interdependent with organizational structure and decision-making
   C. effective decision-making is dependent on organizational structure but not on communication
   D. communication is dependent on the decision-making process but not on organizational structure

21. In coaching a subordinate manager in the use of the type of management in which subordinate employees participate, an executive would be MOST accurate in emphasizing that participative management   21._____

   A. uses consultative as opposed to democratic techniques
   B. uses democratic as opposed to consultative techniques
   C. requires the involvement of subordinates while reserving for the superior the right to make decisions
   D. requires involving subordinates and giving them the right to make most decisions

22. In most work situations, employees tend to form informal groups and relationships. The BEST way for a supervisor interested in high productivity to deal with such groups and relationships is to   22._____

   A. take them into account as much as possible when making work assignments and schedules
   B. ignore them, since such relationships and groups usually have no effect on work productivity

C. attempt to destroy such groups and relationships since they are usually counterproductive
D. ignore them, even though they are usually counterproductive, since nothing can be done about them

23. Assume that in an office an entirely new method has been introduced in the handling of applications for service and related information. Employees USUALLY approach such a sudden change in their work routine with an attitude of

    A. *apprehension,* chiefly because such a change makes them uncertain of their position
    B. *indifference,* chiefly because most people don't care what they are doing, as long as they are paid
    C. *approval,* chiefly because such a change provides a welcome change of pace in their work
    D. *acceptance,* mainly because most people prefer changes to the same routines

23.____

24. In what order should the following steps be taken when revising office procedure?
    I. To develop the improved method as determined by time and motion studies and effective workplace layout
    II. To find out how the task is now performed
    III. To apply the new method
    IV. To analyze the current method

    The CORRECT order is:

    A. IV, II, I, III
    B. II, I, III, IV
    C. I, II, IV, III
    D. II, IV, I, III

24.____

25. In contrast to broad spans of control, narrow spans of control are MOST likely to

    A. provide opportunity for more personal contact between superior and subordinate
    B. encourage decentralization
    C. stress individual initiative
    D. foster group or team effort

25.____

KEY (CORRECT ANSWERS)

1. B
2. C
3. A
4. D
5. B

6. A
7. A
8. A
9. C
10. C

11. B
12. C
13. C
14. C
15. A

16. B
17. A
18. B
19. A
20. A

21. C
22. A
23. A
24. D
25. A

EXAMINATION SECTION

TEST 1

DIRECTIONS: Each question or incomplete statement is followed by several suggested answers or completions. Select the one that BEST answers the question or completes the statement. *PRINT THE LETTER OF THE CORRECT ANSWER IN THE SPACE AT THE RIGHT.*

1. An administrator in a department should be thoroughly familiar with modern methods of personnel administration.
   This statement is
   A. *true*, because this familiarity will help him in performing the normal functions of his office
   B. *false*, because personnel administration is not a departmental matter, but is centralized in the Civil Service Commission
   C. *true*, because this knowledge will insure the elimination of personnel problems in the department
   D. *false*, because departmental problems of a minor character are handled by the personnel representative, while major problems are the responsibility of the commissioner

2. The LEAST true of the following is that an administrative assistant in a department
   A. executes the policy laid down by the commissioner or his deputies
   B. in the main, carries out the policies of the commissioner but with some leeway where his own frame of reference is determinative
   C. is never required to formulate policy
   D. is responsible for the successful accomplishment of a section of the department's program

3. If a representative committee of employees in a large department is to meet with an administrative officer for the purpose of improve staff relations and of handling grievances, it is BEST that these meetings be held
   A. at regular intervals
   B. whenever requested by an aggrieved employee
   C. at the discretion of the administrative officer
   D. whenever the need arises

4. In the theory and practice of public administration, the one of the following which is LEAST generally regarded as a staff function is
   A. budgeting
   B. firefighting
   C. purchasing
   D. research and information

5. The LEAST essential factor in the successful application of a service rating system is
   A. careful training of reporting officers
   B. provision for self-rating
   C. statistical analysis to check reliability
   D. utilization of objective standards of performance

6. Of the following, the one which is NOT an aim of service rating plans is
   A. establishment of a fair method of measuring employee value to the employer
   B. application of a uniform measurement to employees of the same class and grade performing similar functions
   C. application of a uniform measurement to employees of the same class and grade however different their assignments may be
   D. establishment of a scientific duties plan

7. A rule or regulation relating to the internal management of a department becomes effective
   A. only after it is filed in the office of the clerk
   B. as soon as issued by the department head
   C. only after it has been published officially
   D. when approved by the mayor

8. Of the following, the one MOST generally regarded as an *administrative* power is the
   A. veto power
   B. message power
   C. power of pardon
   D. rule making power

9. In public administration functional allocation involves
   A. integration and the assignment of administrative power
   B. the assignment of a single power to a single administrative level
   C. the distribution of a number of subsidiary responsibilities among all levels of government
   D. decentralization of administrative responsibilities

10. In the field of public administration, the LEAST general result of coordination is the
    A. performance of a well-rounded job
    B. elimination of jurisdictional overlapping
    C. performance of functions otherwise neglected
    D. elimination of duplication of work

11. Of the following, the MOST complicated and difficult problem confronting the reorganizer in the field of public administration is
    A. ridding the government of graft
    B. ridding the government of crude incompetence
    C. ridding the government of excessive decentralization
    D. conditioning organization to modern social and economic life

12. The MOST accurate description of the process of integration in the field of public administration is
    A. transfer of administrative authority from a lower to a higher level of government
    B. transfer of administrative authority from a higher to a lower level of government
    C. concentration of administrative authority within one level of government
    D. formal cooperation between city and state governments to administer a function

13. The one of the following who was MOST closely allied with *scientific management* is
    A. Mosher   B. Probst   C. Taylor   D. White

14. Of the following wall colors, the one which will reflect the GREATEST amount of light, other things being equal, is
    A. buff   B. light gray   C. light blue   D. brown

15. Natural illumination is LEAST necessary in a(n)
    A. executive office
    B. reception room
    C. central stenographic bureau
    D. conference room

16. The MOST desirable relative humidity in an office is
    A. 30%   B. 50%   c. 70%   D. 90%

17. When several pieces of correspondence are filed in the same folder, they are USUALLY arranged
    A. according to subject
    B. numerically
    C. in the order in which they are received
    D. alphabetically

18. Eliminating slack in work assignment is
    A. speed-up
    B. time study
    C. motion study
    D. efficient management

19. *Time studies* examine and measure
    A. past performance
    B. present performance
    C. long-run effect
    D. influence of change

20. In making a position analysis for a duties classification, the one of the following factors which must be considered is the _____ the incumbent.
    A. capabilities of
    B. qualifications of
    C. efficiency attained by
    D. responsibility assigned to

21. The MAXIMUM number of subordinates who can be effectively supervised by one administrative assistant is BEST considered as
    A. determined by the law of *span of control*
    B. determined by the law of *span of attention*
    C. determined by the type of work supervised
    D. fixed at not more than six

22. Of the following devices used in personnel administration, the MOST basic is
    A. classification
    B. service rating
    C. appeals
    D. in-service training

23. Of the following, the LEAST important factor for sound organization is the
    A. individual and his position
    B. hierarchical form of organization
    C. location and delegation of authority
    D. standardization of salary schedules

24. *Stretch-out* is a term that originated with the
    A. imposition of a furlough
    B. system of semi-monthly relief payments
    C. development of labor technology
    D. irregular development of low-cost housing projects

25. The one of the following which is LEAST generally true of a personnel division in a large department is that it is
    A. concerned with having a certain point of view on personnel permeate the executive staff
    B. charged with aiding operating executives with auxiliary staff service, assistance and advice
    C. charged to administer a certain few operating duties of its own
    D. charged with the basic responsibility for the efficient operation of the entire department

KEY (CORRECT ANSWERS)

1. A
2. C
3. A
4. B
5. B

6. D
7. B
8. D
9. C
10. C

11. D
12. C
13. C
14. A
15. B

16. A
17. C
18. D
19. B
20. D

21. C
22. A
23. D
24. C
25. D

TEST 2

DIRECTIONS: Each question or incomplete statement is followed by several suggested answers or completions. Select the one that BEST answers the question or completes the statement. *PRINT THE LETTER OF THE CORRECT ANSWER IN THE SPACE AT THE RIGHT.*

Questions 1-10.

DIRECTIONS: Below are ten words numbered 1 through 10 and twenty other words divided into four groups—Group A, Group B, Group C, and Group D. For each of the ten numbered words, select the word in one of the four groups which is MOST NEARLY the same in meaning. The letter of that group is the answer for the item.

GROUP A	GROUP B	GROUP C	GROUP D
articulation	bituminous	assumption	scope
fusion	deductive	forecast	vindication
catastrophic	repudiation	terse	amortization
inductive	doleful	insolence	productive
leadership	prolonged	panorama	slanderous

1. abnegation   1.____
2. calumnious   2.____
3. purview   3.____
4. lugubrious   4.____
5. hegemony   5.____
6. arrogation   6.____
7. coalescence   7.____
8. prolix   8.____
9. syllogistic   9.____
10. contumely   10.____

11. In large cities the total cost of government is of course GREATER than in small cities but   11.____
    A. this is accompanied by a decrease in per capita cost
    B. the per capita cost is also greater
    C. the per capita cost is approximately the same
    D. the per capita cost is considerably less in approximately 50% of the cases

12. The one of the following which is LEAST characteristic of governmental reorganizations is the
    A. saving of large sums of money
    B. problem of morale and personnel
    C. task of logic and management
    D. engineering approach

13. The LEAST accurate of the following statements about graphic presentation is
    A. it is desirable to show as many coordinate lines as possible in a finished diagram
    B. the horizontal scale should read from left to right and the vertical scale from top to bottom
    C. when two or more curves are represented for comparison on the same chart, their zero lines should coincide
    D. a percentage curve should not be used when the purpose is to show the actual amounts of increase or decrease

14. Grouping of figures in a frequency distribution results in a *loss* of
    A. linearity   B. significance   C. detail   D. coherence

15. The true financial condition of a city is BEST reflected when its accounting system is placed upon a(n) _____ basis.
    A. cash   B. accrual   C. fiscal   D. warrant

16. When the discrepancy between the totals of a trial balance is $36, the LEAST probable cause of the error is
    A. omission of an item
    B. entering of an item on the wrong side of the ledger
    C. a mistake in addition or subtraction
    D. transposition of digits

17. For the MOST effective administrative management, appropriations should be
    A. itemized
    B. lump sum
    C. annual
    D. bi-annual

18. Of the following types of expenditure control in the practice of fiscal management, the one which is LEAST important is that which relates to
    A. past policy affecting expenditures
    B. future policy affecting expenditures
    C. prevention of improper use of funds
    D. prevention of overdraft

19. The sinking fund method of retiring bonds does NOT
    A. permit investment in a new issue of city bonds when the general market is unsatisfactory
    B. cause irreparable injury to the city's credit when the city is unable to make a scheduled contribution
    C. require periodic actuarial computations
    D. cost as much to administer as the serial bond method

20. Of the following, the statement that is FALSE is:
    A. Non-profit hospitalization plans are based on underlying principles similar to those which underlie mutual insurance.
    B. Federal, state, and local governments pay for more than half of the medical care received by more than half of the population of the country.
    C. In addition to non-profit hospitalization, non-profit organizations providing reimbursement for medical and nursing care are now being organized in this state.
    D. Voluntary health insurance must be depended on since a state system of health insurance is unconstitutional.

21. The MOST accurate of the following statements concerning birth and death rates is:
    A. A high birth rate is usually accompanied by a relatively high death rate.
    B. A high birth rate is usually accompanied by a relatively low death rate.
    C. The rate of increase in population for a given area may be obtained by subtracting the death rate from the birth rate.
    D. The rate of increase in population for a given area may be obtained by subtracting the birth rate from the death rate.

22. Empirical reasoning is based upon
    A. experience and observation
    B. *a priori* propositions
    C. application of an established generalization
    D. logical deduction

23. 45% of the employees of a certain department are enrolled in in-service training courses and 35% are registered in college courses.
    The percentage of employees NOT enrolled in either of these types of courses is
    A. 20%
    B. at least 20% and not more than 55%
    C. approximately 40%
    D. none of the above

24. A typist can address approximately R envelopes in a 7-hour day. A list containing S addresses is submitted with a request that all envelopes be typed within T hours.
    The number of typists needed to complete this task would b
    A. $\dfrac{7RS}{T}$
    B. $\dfrac{S}{7RT}$
    C. $\dfrac{R}{7ST}$
    D. $\dfrac{7S}{RT}$

4 (#2)

25. Bank X allows a customer to write without charge five checks per month for each $100 on deposit, but a check deposited or a cash deposit counts the same as a check written. Bank Y charges ten cents for every check written, requires no minimum balance and allows deposit of cash or of checks made out to customer free. A man receives two salary checks and, on the average, five other checks each month. He pays, on the average, twelve bills a month, five of which are for amounts between $5 and $10, five for amounts between $10 and $20, two for about $30. Assume that he pays these bills either by check or by Post Office money order (the charges for money orders are: $3.01 to $10-11¢; $10.01 to $20-13¢; $20.01 to $40-15¢) and that he has a savings account paying 2%. Assume also that if he has an account at Bank X, he keeps a balance sufficient to avoid any service charges.
Of the following statements in relation to this man, the one that is TRUE is that
   A. the monthly cost of an account at Bank Y is approximately as great as the cost of an account at Bank X and also the account is more convenient
   B. to use an account at Bank Y costs more than the use of money orders, but this disadvantage is offset by the fact that cancelled checks act as receipts for bills paid
   C. money orders are cheapest but this advantage is offset by the fact that one must go to the Post Office for each order
   D. an account at Bank X is least expensive and has the advantage that checks endorsed to the customer may be deposited in it

25.____

KEY (CORRECT ANSWERS)

1.	B		11.	B
2.	D		12.	A
3.	D		13.	A
4.	B		14.	C
5.	A		15.	B
6.	C		16.	C
7.	A		17.	B
8.	B		18.	A
9.	B		19.	B
10.	C		20.	D

21. A
22. A
23. B
24. D
25. D

EVALUATING CONCLUSIONS BASED ON FACTUAL INFORMATION

Test material will be presented in a multiple-choice question format.

Test Task: You will be given a set of statements and a conclusion based on the statements. You are to assume the statements are true. The conclusion is reached from these statements *only* not on what you may happen to know about the subject discussed. Each question has three possible answers. You must then select the correct answer in the following manner:

Select A, if the statements prove that the conclusion is true.
Select B, if the statements prove that the conclusion is false.
Select C, if the statements are inadequate to prove the conclusion either true or false.

SAMPLE QUESTION #1:

STATEMENTS: All uniforms are cleaned by the Conroy Company. Blue uniforms are cleaned on Mondays or Fridays; green or brown uniforms are cleaned on Wednesdays. Alan and Jean have blue uniforms, Gary has green uniforms, and Ryan has brown uniforms.

CONCLUSION: Jean's uniforms are cleaned on Wednesdays.
   A statements prove the conclusion TRUE
   B statements prove the conclusion FALSE
   C statements are INADEQUATE to prove the conclusion

The correct answer to this sample question is Choice B.

SOLUTION: The last sentence of the statements says that Jean has blue uniforms. The second sentence of the statements says that blue uniforms are cleaned on Monday or Friday. The conclusion says Jean's uniforms are cleaned on Wednesday. Wednesday is neither Monday nor Friday. Therefore, the conclusion must be false (choice B).

SAMPLE QUESTION #2

STATEMENTS: If Beth works overtime, the assignment will be completed. If the assignment is completed, then all unit employees will receive a bonus. Beth works overtime.

CONCLUSION: A bonus will be given to all employees in the unit.
   A. statements prove the conclusion TRUE.
   B. statements prove the conclusion FALSE.
   C. statements are INADEQUATE to prove the conclusion

The correct answer to this sample question is Choice A.

SOLUTION: The conclusion follows necessarily from the statements. Beth works overtime. The assignment is completed. Therefore, all unit employees will receive a bonus.

SAMPLE QUESTION #3

STATEMENTS: Bill is older than Wanda. Edna is older than Bill. Sarah is twice as old as Wanda.

CONCLUSION: Sarah is older than Edna.
A. statements prove the conclusion TRUE
B. statements prove the conclusion FALSE
C. statements are INADEQUATE to prove the conclusion

The correct answer to this sample question is Choice C.

SOLUTION: We know from the statements that both Sarah and Edna are older than Wanda. We do not have any other information about Sarah and Edna. Therefore, no conclusion about whether or not Sarah is older than Edna can be made.

EVALUATING CONCLUSIONS IN LIGHT OF KNOWN FACTS
EXAMINATION SECTION
TEST 1

DIRECTIONS: Each question or incomplete statement is followed by several suggested answers or completions. Select the one that BEST answers the question or completes the statement. *PRINT THE LETTER OF THE CORRECT ANSWER IN THE SPACE AT THE RIGHT.*

Questions 1-9.

DIRECTIONS: In Questions 1 through 9, you will read a set of facts and a conclusion drawn from them. The conclusion may be valid or invalid, based on the facts. It is your task to determine the validity of the conclusion.
For each question, select the letter before the statement that BEST expresses the relationship between the given facts and the conclusion that has been drawn from them. Your choices are:
 A. The facts prove the conclusion.
 B. The facts disprove the conclusion; or
 C. The facts neither prove nor disprove the conclusion.

1. FACTS: Lauren must use Highway 29 to get to work. Lauren has a meeting today at 9:00 A.M. If she misses the meeting, Lauren will probably lose a major account. Highway 29 is closed all day today for repairs.

   CONCLUSION: Lauren will not be able to get to work.

   A. The facts prove the conclusion.
   B. The facts disprove the conclusion.
   C. The facts neither prove nor disprove the conclusion.

2. FACTS: The Tumbleweed Follies, a traveling burlesque show, is looking for a new line dancer. The position requires both singing and dancing skills. If the show cannot fill the position by Friday, it will begin to look for a magician to fill the time slot currently held by the line dancers. Willa, who wants to audition for the line dancing position, can sing, but cannot dance.

   CONCLUSION: Willa is qualified to audition for the part of line dancer.

   A. The facts prove the conclusion.
   B. The facts disprove the conclusion.
   C. The facts neither prove nor disprove the conclusion.

3. FACTS: Terry owns two dogs, Spike and Stan. One of the dogs is short-haired and has blue eyes. One dog as a pink nose. The blue-eyed dog never barks. One of the dogs has white fur on its paws. Sam has long hair.

   CONCLUSION: Spike never barks.

   A. The facts prove the conclusion.
   B. The facts disprove the conclusion.
   C. The facts neither prove nor disprove the conclusion.

3.____

4. FACTS: No science teachers are members of the PTA. Some English teachers are members of the PTA. Some English teachers in the PTA also wear glasses. Every PTA member is required to sit on the dunking stool at the student carnival except for those who wear glasses, who will be exempt. Those who are exempt, however, will have to officiate the hamster races. All of the English teachers in the PTA who do not wear glasses are married.

   CONCLUSION: All the married English teachers in the PTA will set on the dunking stool at the student carnival.

   A. The facts prove the conclusion.
   B. The facts disprove the conclusion.
   C. The facts neither prove nor disprove the conclusion.

4.____

5. FACTS: If the price of fuel is increased and sales remain constant, oil company profits will increase. The price of fuel was increased, and market experts project that sales levels are likely to be maintained.

   CONCLUSION: The price of fuel will increase.

   A. The facts prove the conclusion.
   B. The facts disprove the conclusion.
   C. The facts neither prove nor disprove the conclusion.

5.____

6. FACTS: Some members of the gymnastics team are double-jointed, and some members of the gymnastics team ae also on the lacrosse team. Some double-jointed members of the gymnastics team are also coaches. All gymnastics team members perform floor exercises, except the coaches. All the double-jointed members of the gymnastics team who are not coaches are freshmen.

   CONCLUSION: Some double-jointed freshmen are coaches.

   A. The facts prove the conclusion.
   B. The facts disprove the conclusion.
   C. The facts neither prove nor disprove the conclusion.

6.____

3 (#1)

7. FACTS: Each member of the International Society speaks at least one foreign language, but no member speaks more than four foreign languages. Five members speak Spanish; three speak Mandarin; four speak French; four speak German; and five speak a foreign language other than Spanish, Mandarin, French, or German.

   CONCLUSION: The lowest possible number of members in the International Society is eight.

   A. The facts prove the conclusion.
   B. The facts disprove the conclusion.
   C. The facts neither prove nor disprove the conclusion.

   7.____

8. FACTS: Mary keeps seven cats in her apartment. Only three of the cats will eat the same kind of food. Mary wants to keep at least one extra bag of each kind of food.

   CONCLUSION: The minimum number of bags Mary will need to keep as extra is 7.

   A. The facts prove the conclusion.
   B. The facts disprove the conclusion.
   C. The facts neither prove nor disprove the conclusion.

   8.____

9. FACTS: In Ed and Marie's exercise group, everyone likes the treadmill or the stationary bicycle, or both, but Ed does not like the stationary bicycle. Marie has not expressed a preference, but spends most of her time on the stationary bicycle.

   CONCLUSION: Everyone in the group who does not like the treadmill likes the stationary bicycle.

   A. The facts prove the conclusion.
   B. The facts disprove the conclusion.
   C. The facts neither prove nor disprove the conclusion.

   9.____

Questions 10-17.

DIRECTIONS: Questions 10 through 17 are based on the following reading passage. It is not your knowledge of the particular topic that is being tested, but your ability to reason based on what you have read. The passage is likely to detail several proposed courses of action and factors affecting these proposals. The reading passage is followed by a conclusion or outcome based on the facts in the passage, or a description of a decision taken regarding the situation. The conclusion is followed by a number of statements that have a possible connection to the conclusion. For each statement, you are to determine whether:

A. The statement proves the conclusion.
B. The statement supports the conclusion but does not prove it.
C. The statement disproves the conclusion.
D. The statement weakens the conclusion but does not disprove it.
E. The statement has no relevance to the conclusion.

Remember that the conclusion after the passage is to be accepted as the outcome of what actually happened, and that you are being asked to evaluate the impact each statement would have had on the conclusion.

PASSAGE

The Owyhee Mission School District's Board of Directors is hosting a public meeting to debate the merits of the proposed abolition of all bilingual education programs within the district. The group that has made the proposal believes the programs, which teach immigrant children academic subjects in their native language until they have learned English well enough to join mainstream classes, inhibit the ability of students to acquire English quickly and succeed in school and in the larger American society. Such programs, they argue, are also a wasteful drain on the district's already scant resources.

At the meeting, several teachers and parents stand to speak out against the proposal. The purpose of an education, they say, should be to build upon, rather than dismantle, a minority child's language and culture. By teaching children in academic subjects in their native tongues, while simultaneously offering English language instruction, schools can meet the goals of learning English and progressing through academic subjects along with their peers.

Hiram Nguyen, a representative of the parents whose children are currently enrolled in bilingual education, stands at the meeting to express the parents' wishes. The parents have been polled, he says, and are overwhelmingly of the opinion that while language and culture are important to them, they are not things that will disappear from the students' lives if they are no longer taught in the classroom. The most important issue for the parents is whether their children will succeed in school and be competitive in the larger American society. If bilingual education can be demonstrated to do that, then the parents are in favor of continuing it.

At the end of the meeting, a proponent of the plan, Oscar Ramos, stands to clarify some misconceptions about the proposal. It does not call for a "sink or swim" approach, he says, but allows for an interpreter to be present in mainstream classes to explain anything a student finds too complex or confusing.

The last word of the meeting is given to Delia Cruz, a bilingual teacher at one of the district's elementary schools. A student is bound to find anything complex or confusing, she says, if it is spoken in a language he has never heard before. It is more wasteful to place children in classrooms where they don't understand anything, she says, than it is to try to teach them something useful as they are learning the English language.

CONCLUSION: After the meeting, the Owyhee Mission School District's Board of Directors votes to terminate all the district's bilingual education programs at the end of the current academic year, but to maintain the current level of funding to each of the schools that have programs cut.

10. A poll conducted by the *Los Angeles Times* at approximately the same time as the Board's meeting indicated that 75% of the people were opposed to bilingual education; among Latinos, opposition was 84%.
    A. The statement proves the conclusion.
    B. The statement supports the conclusion but does not prove it.
    C. The statement disproves the conclusion.
    D. The statement weakens the conclusion but does not disprove it.
    E. The statement has no relevance to the conclusion.

    10.____

11. Of all the studies connected on bilingual education programs, 64% indicate that students learned English grammar better in "sink or swim" classes without any special features than they did in bilingual education classes.
    A. The statement proves the conclusion.
    B. The statement supports the conclusion but does not prove it.
    C. The statement disproves the conclusion.
    D. The statement weakens the conclusion but does not disprove it.
    E. The statement has no relevance to the conclusion.

    11.____

12. In the academic year that begins after the Board's vote, Montgomery Burns Elementary, an Owyhee Mission District school, launches a new bilingual program for the children of Somali immigrants.
    A. The statement proves the conclusion.
    B. The statement supports the conclusion but does not prove it.
    C. The statement disproves the conclusion.
    D. The statement weakens the conclusion but does not disprove it.
    E. The statement has no relevance to the conclusion.

    12.____

13. In the previous academic year, under severe budget restraints, the Owyhee Mission District cut all physical education, music, and art classes, but its funding for bilingual education classes increased by 18%.
    A. The statement proves the conclusion.
    B. The statement supports the conclusion but does not prove it.
    C. The statement disproves the conclusion.
    D. The statement weakens the conclusion but does not disprove it.
    E. The statement has no relevance to the conclusion.

    13.____

14. Before the Board votes, a polling consultant conducts randomly sampled assessments of immigrant students who enrolled in Owyhee District schools at a time when they did not speak any English at all. Ten years after graduating from high school, 44% of those who received bilingual education were professionals – doctors, lawyers, educators, engineers, etc. Of those who did not receive bilingual education, 38% were professionals.
    A. The statement proves the conclusion.
    B. The statement supports the conclusion but does not prove it.
    C. The statement disproves the conclusion.
    D. The statement weakens the conclusion but does not disprove it.
    E. The statement has no relevance to the conclusion.

    14.____

15. Over the past several years, the scores of Owyhee District students have gradually declined, and enrollment numbers have followed as anxious parents transferred their children to other schools or applied for a state-funded voucher program.
    A. The statement proves the conclusion.
    B. The statement supports the conclusion but does not prove it.
    C. The statement disproves the conclusion.
    D. The statement weakens the conclusion but does not disprove it.
    E. The statement has no relevance to the conclusion.

15.____

16. California and Massachusetts, two of the most liberal states in the country, have each passed ballot measures banning bilingual education in public schools.
    A. The statement proves the conclusion.
    B. The statement supports the conclusion but does not prove it.
    C. The statement disproves the conclusion.
    D. The statement weakens the conclusion but does not disprove it.
    E. The statement has no relevance to the conclusion.

16.____

17. In the academic year that begins after the Board's vote, no Owyhee Mission Schools are conducting bilingual instruction.
    A. The statement proves the conclusion.
    B. The statement supports the conclusion but does not prove it.
    C. The statement disproves the conclusion.
    D. The statement weakens the conclusion but does not disprove it.
    E. The statement has no relevance to the conclusion.

17.____

Questions 18-25.

DIRECTIONS: Questions 18 through 25 each provide four factual statements and a conclusion based on these statements. After reading the entire question, you will decide whether:
  A. The conclusion is proved by Statements 1-4;
  B. The conclusion is disproved by Statements 1-4;
  C. The facts are not sufficient to prove or disprove the conclusion.

18. FACTUAL STATEMENTS:
    1) Gear X rotates in a clockwise direction if Switch C is in the OFF position.
    2) Gear X will rotate in a counter-clockwise direction if Switch C is ON.
    3) If Gear X is rotating in a clockwise direction, then Gear Y will not be rotating at all.
    4) Switch C is OFF.

    CONCLUSION: Gear Y is rotating.

    A. The conclusion is proved by Statements 1-4;
    B. The conclusion is disproved by Statements 1-4;
    C. The facts are not sufficient to prove or disprove the conclusion.

18.____

19. **FACTUAL STATEMENTS:**
    1) Mark is older than Jim but younger than Dan.
    2) Fern is older than Mark but younger than Silas.
    3) Dan is younger than Silas but older than Edward.
    4) Edward is older than Mark but younger than Fern.

    CONCLUSION: Dan is older than Fern.

    A. The conclusion is proved by Statements 1-4;
    B. The conclusion is disproved by Statements 1-4;
    C. The facts are not sufficient to prove or disprove the conclusion.

20. **FACTUAL STATEMENTS:**
    1) Each of Fred's three sofa cushions lies on top of four lost coins.
    2) The cushion on the right covers two pennies and two dimes.
    3) The middle cushion covers two dimes and two quarters.
    4) The cushion on the left covers two nickels and two quarters.

    CONCLUSION: To be guaranteed of retrieving at least one coin of each denomination, and without looking at any of the coins, Frank must take three coins each from under the cushions on the right and the left.

    A. The conclusion is proved by Statements 1-4;
    B. The conclusion is disproved by Statements 1-4;
    C. The facts are not sufficient to prove or disprove the conclusion.

21. **FACTUAL STATEMENTS:**
    1) The door to the hammer mill chamber is locked if light 6 is red.
    2) The door to the hammer mill chamber is locked only when the mill is operating.
    3) If the mill is not operating, light 6 is blue.
    4) The door to the hammer mill chamber is locked.

    CONCLUSION: The mill is in operation.

    A. The conclusion is proved by Statements 1-4;
    B. The conclusion is disproved by Statements 1-4;
    C. The facts are not sufficient to prove or disprove the conclusion.

22. **FACTUAL STATEMENTS:**
    1) In a five-story office building, where each story is occupied by a single professional, Dr. Kane's office is above Dr. Assad's.
    2) Dr. Johnson's office is between Dr. Kane's and Dr. Conlon's.
    3) Dr. Steen's office is between Dr. Conlon's and Dr. Assad's.
    4) Dr. Johnson is on the fourth story.

    CONCLUSION: Dr. Steen occupies the second story.

A. The conclusion is proved by Statements 1-4;
B. The conclusion is disproved by Statements 1-4;
C. The facts are not sufficient to prove or disprove the conclusion.

23. FACTUAL STATEMENTS:
    1) On Saturday, farmers Hank, Earl, Roy, and Cletus plowed a total of 520 acres.
    2) Hank plowed twice as many acres as Roy.
    3) Roy plowed half as much as the farmer who plowed the most.
    4) Cletus plowed 160 acres.

    CONCLUSION: Hank plowed 200 acres.
    A. The conclusion is proved by Statements 1-4;
    B. The conclusion is disproved by Statements 1-4;
    C. The facts are not sufficient to prove or disprove the conclusion.

24. FACTUAL STATEMENTS:
    1) Four travelers – Tina, Jodie, Alex, and Oscar – each traveled to a different island – Aruba, Jamaica, Nevis, and Barbados – but not necessarily respectively.
    2) Tina did not travel as far to Jamaica as Jodie traveled to her island.
    3) Oscar traveled twice as far as Alex, who traveled the same distance as the traveler who went to Aruba.
    4) Oscar went to Barbados.

    CONCLUSION: Oscar traveled the farthest.

    A. The conclusion is proved by Statements 1-4;
    B. The conclusion is disproved by Statements 1-4;
    C. The facts are not sufficient to prove or disprove the conclusion.

25. FACTUAL STATEMENT:
    1) In the natural history museum, every Native American display that contains pottery also contains beadwork.
    2) Some of the displays containing lodge replicas also contain beadwork.
    3) The display on the Choctaw, a Native American tribe, contains pottery.
    4) The display on the Modoc, a Native American tribe, contains only two of these items.

    CONCLUSION: If the Modoc display contains pottery, it does not contain lodge replicas.

    A. The conclusion is proved by Statements 1-4;
    B. The conclusion is disproved by Statements 1-4;
    C. The facts are not sufficient to prove or disprove the conclusion.

KEY (CORRECT ANSWERS)

1.	A		11.	B
2.	B		12.	C
3.	A		13.	B
4.	A		14.	D
5.	C		15.	E
6.	B		16.	E
7.	B		17.	A
8.	B		18.	B
9.	A		19.	C
10.	B		20.	A

21. A
22. A
23. C
24. A
25. A

TEST 2

DIRECTIONS: Each question or incomplete statement is followed by several suggested answers or completions. Select the one that BEST answers the question or completes the statement. *PRINT THE LETTER OF THE CORRECT ANSWER IN THE SPACE AT THE RIGHT.*

Questions 1-9.

DIRECTIONS: In Questions 1 through 9, you will read a set of facts and a conclusion drawn from them. The conclusion may be valid or invalid, based on the facts. It is your task to determine the validity of the conclusion.
For each question, select the letter before the statement that BEST expresses the relationship between the given facts and the conclusion that has been drawn from them. Your choices are:
- A. The facts prove the conclusion.
- B. The facts disprove the conclusion; or
- C. The facts neither prove nor disprove the conclusion.

1. FACTS: If the maximum allowable income for Medicaid recipients is increased, the number of Medicaid recipients will increase. If the number of Medicaid recipients increases, more funds must be allocated to the Medicaid program, which will require a tax increase. Taxes cannot be approved without the approval of the legislature. The legislature probably will not approve a tax increase.

    CONCLUSION: The maximum allowable income for Medicaid recipients will increase.

    A. The facts prove the conclusion.
    B. The facts disprove the conclusion; or
    C. The facts neither prove nor disprove the conclusion.

    1.____

2. FACTS: All the dentists on the baseball team are short. Everyone in the dugout is a dentist, but not everyone in the dugout is short. The baseball team is not made up of people of any particular profession.

    CONCLUSION: Some people who are not dentists are in the dugout.

    A. The facts prove the conclusion.
    B. The facts disprove the conclusion; or
    C. The facts neither prove nor disprove the conclusion.

    2.____

3. FACTS: A taxi company's fleet is divided into two fleets. Fleet One contains cabs A, B, C, and D. Fleet Two contains E, F, G, and H. Each cab is either yellow or green. Five of the cabs are yellow. Cabs A and E are not both yellow. Either Cab C or F, or both, are not yellow. Cabs B and H are either both yellow or both green.

    CONCLUSION: Cab H is green.

    3.____

A. The facts prove the conclusion.
B. The facts disprove the conclusion; or
C. The facts neither prove nor disprove the conclusion.

4. FACTS: Most people in the skydiving club are not afraid of heights. Everyone in the skydiving club makes three parachute jumps a month.

   CONCLUSION: At least one person who is afraid of heights makes three parachute jumps a month.

   A. The facts prove the conclusion.
   B. The facts disprove the conclusion; or
   C. The facts neither prove nor disprove the conclusion.

4.____

5. FACTS: If the Board approves the new rule, the agency will move to a new location immediately. If the agency moves, five new supervisors will be immediately appointed. The Board has approved the new proposal.

   CONCLUSION: No new supervisors were appointed.

   A. The facts prove the conclusion.
   B. The facts disprove the conclusion; or
   C. The facts neither prove nor disprove the conclusion.

5.____

6. FACTS: All the workers at the supermarket chew gum when they sack groceries. Sometimes Lance, a supermarket worker, doesn't chew gum at all when he works. Another supermarket worker, Jenny, chews gum the whole time she is at work.

   CONCLUSION: Jenny always sacks groceries when she is at work.

6.____

7. FACTS: Lake Lottawatta is bigger than Lake Tacomi. Lake Tacomi and Lake Ottawa are exactly the same size. All lakes in Montana are bigger than Lake Ottawa.

   CONCLUSION: Lake Lottawatta is in Montana.

   A. The facts prove the conclusion.
   B. The facts disprove the conclusion; or
   C. The facts neither prove nor disprove the conclusion.

7.____

8. FACTS: Two men, Cox and Taylor, are playing poker at a table. Taylor has a pair of aces in his hand. One man is smoking a cigar. One of them has no pairs in his hand and is wearing an eye patch. The man wearing the eye patch is smoking a cigar. One man is bald.

   CONCLUSION: Cox is smoking a cigar.

8.____

A. The facts prove the conclusion.
B. The facts disprove the conclusion; or
C. The facts neither prove nor disprove the conclusion.

9. FACTS: All Kwakiutls are Wakashan Indians. All Wakashan Indians originated on Vancouver Island. The Nootka also originated on Vancouver Island.

   CONCLUSION: Kwakiutls originated on Vancouver Island.

   A. The facts prove the conclusion.
   B. The facts disprove the conclusion; or
   C. The facts neither prove nor disprove the conclusion.

9.____

Questions 10-17.

DIRECTIONS: Questions 10 through 17 are based on the following reading passage. It is not your knowledge of the particular topic that is being tested, but your ability to reason based on what you have read. The passage is likely to detail several proposed courses of action and factors affecting these proposals. The reading passage is followed by a conclusion or outcome based on the facts in the passage, or a description of a decision taken regarding the situation. The conclusion is followed by a number of statements that have a possible connection to the conclusion. For each statement, you are to determine whether:
A. The statement proves the conclusion.
B. The statement supports the conclusion but does not prove it.
C. The statement disproves the conclusion.
D. The statement weakens the conclusion but does not disprove it.
E. The statement has no relevance to the conclusion.

Remember that the conclusion after the passage is to be accepted as the outcome of what actually happened, and that you are being asked to evaluate the impact each statement would have had on the conclusion.

PASSAGE

The World Wide Web portal and search engine, HipBot, is considering becoming a subscription-only service, locking out nonsubscribers from the content on its web site. HipBot currently relies solely on advertising revenues.

HipBot's content director says that by taking in an annual fee from each customer, the company can both increase profits and provide premium content that no other portal can match.

The marketing director disagrees, saying that there is no guarantee that anyone who now visits the web site for free will agree to pay for the privilege of visiting it again. Most will probably simply use the other major portals. Also, HipBot's advertising clients will not be happy when they learn that the site will be viewed by a more limited number of people.

4 (#2)

CONCLUSION: In January of 2016, the CEO of HipBot decides to keep the portal open to all web users, with some limited "premium content" available to subscribers who don't mind paying a little extra to access it. The company will aim to maintain, or perhaps increase, its advertising revenue.

10. In an independent marketing survey, 62% of respondents said they "strongly agree" with the following statement: "I almost never pay attention to advertisements that appear on the World Wide Web."
    A. The statement proves the conclusion.
    B. The statement supports the conclusion but does not prove it.
    C. The statement disproves the conclusion.
    D. The statement weakens the conclusion but does not disprove it.
    E. The statement has no relevance to the conclusion.

10.____

11. When it learns about the subscription-only debate going on at HipBot, Wernham Hogg Entertainment, one of HipBot's most reliable clients, says it will withdraw its ads and place them on a free web portal if HipBot decides to limit its content to subscribers. Wernham Hogg pays HipBot about $6 million annually – about 12% of HipBot's gross revenues – to run its ads online.
    A. The statement proves the conclusion.
    B. The statement supports the conclusion but does not prove it.
    C. The statement disproves the conclusion.
    D. The statement weakens the conclusion but does not disprove it.
    E. The statement has no relevance to the conclusion.

11.____

12. At the end of the second quarter of FY 2016, after continued stagnant profits, the CEO of HipBot assembles a blue ribbon commission to gather and analyze data on the costs, benefits, and feasibility of adding a limited amount of "premium" content to the HipBot portal.
    A. The statement proves the conclusion.
    B. The statement supports the conclusion but does not prove it.
    C. The statement disproves the conclusion.
    D. The statement weakens the conclusion but does not disprove it.
    E. The statement has no relevance to the conclusion.

12.____

13. In the following fiscal year, Wernham Hogg Entertainment, satisfied with the "hit counts" on HipBot's free web site, spends another $1 million on advertisements that will appear on web pages that are available to HipBot's "premium subscribers.
    A. The statement proves the conclusion.
    B. The statement supports the conclusion but does not prove it.
    C. The statement disproves the conclusion.
    D. The statement weakens the conclusion but does not disprove it.
    E. The statement has no relevance to the conclusion.

13.____

14. HipBot's information technology director reports that the engineers in his department have come up with a feature that will search not only individual web pages, but tie into other web-based search engines, as well, and then comb through all these results to find those most relevant to the user's search.

14.____

A. The statement proves the conclusion.
B. The statement supports the conclusion but does not prove it.
C. The statement disproves the conclusion.
D. The statement weakens the conclusion but does not disprove it.
E. The statement has no relevance to the conclusion.

15. In an independent marketing survey, 79% of respondents said they "strongly agree" with the following statement: "Many web sites are so dominated by advertisements these days that it is increasingly frustrating to find the content I want to read or see."
    A. The statement proves the conclusion.
    B. The statement supports the conclusion but does not prove it.
    C. The statement disproves the conclusion.
    D. The statement weakens the conclusion but does not disprove it.
    E. The statement has no relevance to the conclusion.

15.____

16. After three years of studies at the federal level, the Department of Commerce releases a report suggesting that, in general, the only private "subscriber-only" web sites that do well financially are those with a very specialized user population.
    A. The statement proves the conclusion.
    B. The statement supports the conclusion but does not prove it.
    C. The statement disproves the conclusion.
    D. The statement weakens the conclusion but does not disprove it.
    E. The statement has no relevance to the conclusion.

16.____

17. HipBot's own marketing research indicates that the introduction of premium content has the potential to attract new users to the HipBot portal.
    A. The statement proves the conclusion.
    B. The statement supports the conclusion but does not prove it.
    C. The statement disproves the conclusion.
    D. The statement weakens the conclusion but does not disprove it.
    E. The statement has no relevance to the conclusion.

17.____

Questions 18-25.

DIRECTIONS: Questions 18 through 25 each provide four factual statements and a conclusion based on these statements. After reading the entire question, you will decide whether:
A. The conclusion is proved by Statements 1-4;
B. The conclusion is disproved by Statements 1-4;
C. The facts are not sufficient to prove or disprove the conclusion.

6 (#2)

18. FACTUAL STATEMENTS:
    1) If the alarm goes off, Sam will wake up.
    2) If Tandy wakes up before 4:00, Linda will leave the bedroom and sleep on the couch.
    3) If Linda leaves the bedroom, she'll check the alarm to make sure it is working.
    4) The alarm goes off.

    CONCLUSION: Tandy woke up before 4:00.

    A. The conclusion is proved by Statements 1-4;
    B. The conclusion is disproved by Statements 1-4;
    C. The facts are not sufficient to prove or disprove the conclusion.

19. FACTUAL STATEMENTS:
    1) Four brothers are named Earl, John, Gary, and Pete.
    2) Earl and Pete are unmarried.
    3) John is shorter than the youngest of the four.
    4) The oldest brother is married, and is also the tallest.

    CONCLUSION: Pete is the youngest brother.

    A. The conclusion is proved by Statements 1-4;
    B. The conclusion is disproved by Statements 1-4;
    C. The facts are not sufficient to prove or disprove the conclusion.

20. FACTUAL STATEMENTS:
    1) Automobile engines are cooled either by air or by liquid.
    2) If the engine is small and simple enough, air from a belt-driven fan will cool it sufficiently.
    3) Most newer automobile engines are too complicated to be air-cooled.
    4) Air-cooled engines are cheaper and easier to build then liquid-cooled engines.

    CONCLUSION: Most newer automobile engines use liquid coolant.

    A. The conclusion is proved by Statements 1-4;
    B. The conclusion is disproved by Statements 1-4;
    C. The facts are not sufficient to prove or disprove the conclusion.

21. FACTUAL STATEMENTS:
    1) Erica will only file a lawsuit if she is injured while parasailing.
    2) If Rick orders Trip to run a rope test, Trip will check the rigging.
    3) If the rigging does not malfunction, Erica will not be injured.
    4) Rick orders Trip to run a rope test.

18.____

19.____

20.____

21.____

CONCLUSION: Erica does not file a lawsuit.

    A. The conclusion is proved by Statements 1-4;
    B. The conclusion is disproved by Statements 1-4;
    C. The facts are not sufficient to prove or disprove the conclusion.

22. FACTUAL STATEMENTS:
    1) On Maple Street, which is four blocks long, Bill's shop is two blocks east of Ken's shop.
    2) Ken's shop is one block west of the only shop on Maple Street with an awning.
    3) Erma's shop is one block west of the easternmost block.
    4) Bill's shop is on the easternmost block.

CONCLUSION: Bill's shop has an awning.

    A. The conclusion is proved by Statements 1-4;
    B. The conclusion is disproved by Statements 1-4;
    C. The facts are not sufficient to prove or disprove the conclusion.

23. FACTUAL STATEMENTS:
    1) Gear X rotates in a clockwise direction if Switch C is in the OFF position.
    2) Gear X will rotate in a counter-clockwise direction if Switch C is ON.
    3) If Gear X is rotating in a clockwise direction, then Gear Y will not be rotating at all.
    4) Gear Y is rotating.

CONCLUSION: Gear X is rotating in a counter-clockwise direction.

    A. The conclusion is proved by Statements 1-4;
    B. The conclusion is disproved by Statements 1-4;
    C. The facts are not sufficient to prove or disprove the conclusion.

24. FACTUAL STATEMENTS:
    1) The Republic of Garbanzo's currency system has four basic denominations: the pastor, the noble, the donner, and the rojo.
    2) A pastor is worth 2 nobles.
    3) 2 donners can be exchanged for a rojo.
    4) 3 pastors are equal in value to 2 donners.

CONCLUSION: The rojo is most valuable.

    A. The conclusion is proved by Statements 1-4;
    B. The conclusion is disproved by Statements 1-4;
    C. The facts are not sufficient to prove or disprove the conclusion.

8 (#2)

25. FACTUAL STATEMENTS:
   1) At Prickett's Nursery, the only citrus trees left are either Meyer lemons or Valencia oranges, and every citrus tree left is either a dwarf or a semidwarf.
   2) Half of the semidwarf trees are Meyer lemons.
   3) There are more semidwarf trees left than dwarf trees.
   4) A quarter of the dwarf trees are Valencia oranges.

   CONCLUSION: There are more Valencia oranges left at Prickett's Nursery than Meyer lemons.

   A. The conclusion is proved by Statements 1-4;
   B. The conclusion is disproved by Statements 1-4;
   C. The facts are not sufficient to prove or disprove the conclusion.

   25.____

KEY (CORRECT ANSWERS)

1. C
2. B
3. B
4. A
5. B

6. C
7. C
8. A
9. A
10. E

11. B
12. C
13. A
14. E
15. D

16. B
17. B
18. C
19. C
20. A

21. C
22. B
23. C
24. A
25. B

EXAMINATION SECTION

TEST 1

DIRECTIONS: Each question or incomplete statement is followed by several suggested answers or completions. Select the one that BEST answers the question or completes the statement. *PRINT THE LETTER OF THE CORRECT ANSWER IN THE SPACE AT THE RIGHT.*

Questions 1-9.

DIRECTIONS: Questions 1 through 9, inclusive, are based on the STATE MOTOR VEHICLE BUREAU'S POINT SYSTEM given below. Read this point carefully before answering these items.

STATE MOTOR VEHICLE BUREAU'S POINT SYSTEM

    The newly revised point system was effective April 1. After that date, a driver having offenses resulting in an accumulation of eight points within two years, ten points within three years, or twelve points within four years, is to be summoned for a hearing which may result in the loss of his license. Under the point system, three points are charged for speeding, two points for passing a red light or crossing a double line or failing to stop at a stop sign, one and a half points for inoperative horn or insufficient lights, and one point for improper turn or failure to notify Bureau of change of address. The Commissioner of Motor Vehicles is required to revoke a driver's license if he has three speeding violations in a period of 18 months, or drives while intoxicated or leaves the scene of an accident or makes a false statement in his application for a driver's license. This system is necessary because studies show violations of traffic laws cause four out of five fatal accidents in the state.

1. The traffic offense which calls for license revocation if repeated three times within a period of 1½ years is
   A. passing a red light
   B. passing a stop sign
   C. crossing a double line
   D. speeding

2. The individual who has the power to revoke a driver's license is the
   A. traffic officer
   B. motor vehicle inspector
   C. Commissioner of Motor Vehicles
   D. Traffic Commissioner

3. Crossing a double line has a penalty of twice as many points as for
   A. making an improper turn
   B. speeding
   C. passing a red light
   D. an inoperative horn

4. Failure of a driver to properly notify the Bureau of Motor Vehicles of a change in his address carries a penalty of _____ point(s).
   A. ½   B. 1   C. 1½   D. 2

5. The point system is specifically designed to penalize the driver who
   A. is inexperienced
   B. repeatedly violates traffic laws
   C. is overage
   D. ignores parking violations

6. A false statement on a driver's license application calls for a penalty of
   A. 10 points
   B. 8 points
   C. license suspension
   D. license revocation

7. Insufficient lights carries a penalty of _____ point(s).
   A. ½   B. 1   C. 1½   D. 2

8. A driver is summoned for a hearing if, within a period of three years, he accumulates _____ points.
   A. 6   B. 8   C. 10   D. 12

9. The percentage of fatal accidents caused by traffic violations is
   A. 80%   B. 70%   C. 60%   D. 50%

Questions 10-11.

DIRECTIONS: Questions 10 and 11 are to be answered ONLY according to the information given in the following passage.

The State Vehicle and Traffic law was changed effective October 1, 2005 to provide for all new driving licenses to be issued on a six-month probationary basis. The probationary license will be cancelled if during this six-month period the driver is found guilty of tailgating, speeding, reckless driving, or driving while his ability is impaired by alcohol. The license will also be cancelled if the driver is found guilty of two other moving violations. If a probationary license is cancelled, the driver must wait for sixty days after the date of cancellation before applying for another license; and if the application is approved, the applicant must meet certain additional requirements including a new road test before a new license will be issued.

10. It is MOST reasonable to assume that the main purpose of the change in the law referred to above was to
    A. find out who is responsible for most traffic accidents
    B. make the road tests more difficult for new drivers to pass
    C. make it harder to get a driver's license
    D. serve as a further check on the competence of new drivers

11. According to the above passage, we may assume that a probationary license will NOT be cancelled if a driver is found guilty of
    A. passing a red light and failing to keep to the right on a road
    B. following another vehicle too closely
    C. overtime parking at a meter on two or more occasions
    D. driving at 60 miles an hour on a road where the speed limit is 50 miles an hour

Questions 12-13.

DIRECTIONS: Questions 12 and 13 are to be answered ONLY on the basis of the following passage.

If a motor vehicle fails to pass inspection, the owner will be given a rejection notice by the inspection station. Repairs must be made within ten days after this notice is issued. It is not necessary to have the required adjustment or repairs made at the station where the inspection occurred. The vehicle may be taken to any other garage. Re-inspection after repairs may be made at any official inspection station, not necessarily the same station which made the initial inspection. The registration of any motor vehicle for which an inspection sticker has not been obtained as required, or which is not repaired and inspected within ten days after inspection indicates defects, is subject to suspension. A vehicle cannot be used on public highways while its registration is under suspension.

12. According to the above passage, the owner of a car which does NOT pass inspection must
    A. have repairs made at the same station which rejected this car
    B. take the car to another station and have it re-inspected
    C. have repairs made anywhere and then have the car re-inspected
    D. not use the car on a public highway until the necessary repairs have been made

13. According to the above passage, the one of the following which may be cause for suspension of the registration of a vehicle is that
    A. an inspection sticker was issued before the rejection notice had been in force for ten days
    B. it was not re-inspected by the station that rejected it originally
    C. it was not re-inspected either by the station that rejected it originally or by the garage which made the repairs
    D. it has not had defective parts repaired within ten days after inspection

Questions 14-18.

DIRECTIONS: Questions 14 through 18 are to be answered ONLY on the basis of the following passage.

Under the Vehicular Responsibility Law of a certain state, an insurance carrier who has previously furnished the Division of Roads and Vehicles with evidence of a vehicle registrant's financial responsibility (Form VR-1, VR-1A, VR-2B or VR-11) must, in case of termination of insurance, first notify the insured registrant at least 10 days in advance if the termination is due to failure to pay the insurance premium and at least 20 days if the termination is due to any other reason. The insurance carrier must then notify the Division not later than 30 days following the effective date of actual termination of insurance coverage. The only acceptable proof of such termination is Form VR-4.

Upon receipt of Form VR-4 by the Division, a search will be made for any superseding coverage or a record of voluntary surrender of plates and registration certificate on or prior to the effective date of termination. If such a record is found, no further action is taken by the

Division. If the Division finds no record of acceptable superseding coverage or timely surrender of plates and registration, Form Letter VR-7T is sent to the registrant with a photostatic copy of Form VR-4, providing him with an opportunity to invalidate the proceeding to cancel his registration by submitting additional evidence, which may take the form of proof of continuous financial responsibility, timely sale of the vehicle, or evidence of voluntary surrender of plates and registration certificate. Only after the registrant has failed to comply by one of the above three methods is an order to cancel registration (Form VR-8) issued.

Upon the issuance of a cancellation order, a copy of the order is mailed to the registrant directing him to immediately surrender his plates and registration certificate to a specified area office of the Division. At the same time, two copies of the cancellation order are sent to the area office, where they are held for 15 days. If the registrant complies with the order, he is issued a notice of compliance (Form VR-3). If he fails to comply within the 15 days, two more copies of the order are mailed to the Highway Patrol for enforcement of the cancellation order. No further action is taken for a period of 30 days. If no record of enforcement is received, another copy of the cancellation order is sent to the Police Department as a follow-up.

14. When the Division of Roads and Vehicles receives acceptable evidence that the insurance coverage on a particular registrant has been terminated, it is required FIRST to
    A. cancel the registration if the insurance was terminated because of failure to pay the insurance premium
    B. notify the registrant to voluntarily surrender his plates and registration certificate on or prior to a certain date
    C. determine whether the registrant has obtained other insurance for that vehicle
    D. send the registrant Form Letter VR-7T stating that he must submit evidence to prevent cancellation of his registration

14._____

15. In order to comply with the above procedure, the MINIMUM number of copies of the cancellation order that must be prepared, including one to be kept in the central Division of Roads and Vehicles file, is
    A. 3 B. 4 C. 5 d. 6

15._____

16. The one of the following which is required before steps
    A. the insurance carrier to notify the Division of Roads and Vehicles in writing (VR-11) that the insured registrant's premium payment is 30 days overdue
    B. the registrant to notify the Division of Roads and Vehicles that he either intends to sell or has sold his vehicle
    C. Form VR-8 to be sent to the insured registrant by the Division of Roads and Vehicles
    D. Form VR-4 to be sent by the insurance carrier to the Division of Roads and Vehicles

16._____

17. The MAXIMUM amount of time a vehicle registrant is allowed in which to comply with a cancellation order before the police are asked to enforce the order is _____ days.
    A. 30 B. 35 C. 40 D. 45

17._____

18. It would be MOST accurate to state with regard to the issuance of a certificate of compliance that the
    A. Division of Roads and Vehicles issues one to the registrant after he has submitted the additional evidence in response to Form Letter VR-7T
    B. Division of Roads and Vehicles may issue one to the registrant at any time after he has been mailed a copy of the cancellation order and before the Highway Patrol is notified
    C. Highway Patrol may issue one to the registrant if he surrenders his plates and registration to them during the 30 days following their receipt of the request for enforcement
    D. Highway Patrol may issue one to the registrant at any time before the Police Department is notified

18.____

Questions 19-22.

DIRECTIONS: Questions 19 through 22 are to be answered ONLY on the basis of the information given in the following passage.

All automotive accidents, no matter how slight, are to be reported to the Safety Division by the employee involved on Accident Report Form S-23 in duplicate. When the accident is of such a nature that it requires the filling out of the State Motor Vehicle Report Form MV-104, this form is also prepared by the employee in duplicate and sent to the Safety Division for comparison with Form S-23. The Safety Division forwards both copies of Form MV-104 to the Corporation Counsel, who sends one copy to the State Bureau of Motor Vehicles. When the information on the Form S-23 indicates that the employee may be at fault, an investigation is made by the Safety Division. If this investigation shows that the employee was at fault, the employee's dispatcher is asked to file a complaint on Form D-11. The foreman of mechanics prepares a damage report on Form D8 and an estimate of the cost of repairs on Form D-9. The dispatcher's complaint, the damage report, the repair estimate, and the employee's previous accident record are sent to the Safety Division where they are studied together with the accident report. The Safety Division then recommends whether or not disciplinary action should be taken against the employee.

19. According to the above passage, the Safety Division should be notified whenever an automotive accident has occurred by means of Form(s)
    A. S-23
    B. S-23 and MV-104
    C. S-23, MV-104, D-8, D-9, and D-11
    D. S-23, MV-104, D-8, D-9, D-11, and employee's accident report

19.____

20. According to the above passage, the forwarding of the Form MV-104 to the State Bureau of Motor Vehicles is done by the
    A. Corporation Counsel
    B. dispatcher
    C. employee involved in the accident
    D. Safety Division

20.____

21. According to the above passage, the Safety Division investigates an automotive accident if the
    A. accident is serious enough to be reported to the State Bureau of Motor Vehicles
    B. dispatcher files a complaint
    C. employee appears to have been at fault
    D. employee's previous accident report is poor

    21.____

22. Of the forms mentioned in the above passage, the dispatcher is responsible for preparing the
    A. accident report form
    B. complaint form
    C. damage report
    D. estimate cost of repairs

    22.____

Questions 23-25.

DIRECTIONS: Questions 23 through 25 are to be answered ONLY on the basis of the information given in the following passage.

One of the major problems in the control of city motor equipment, and especially passenger equipment, is keeping the equipment working for the city and for the city alone for as many hours of the day as is practical. Even when most city employees try to get the most out of the cars, a poor system of control will result in wasted car hours. Some city employees have a legitimate use for a car all day long while others use a car only a small part of the day and then let it stand. As a rule, trucks are easier to control than passenger cars because they are usually assigned to a specific job where a foreman continually oversees them. Even though trucks are usually fully utilized, there are times when the normal work assignment cannot be carried out because of weather conditions or seasonal changes. At such times, a control system could plan to make the trucks available for other uses.

23. According to the above passage, a problem connected with controlling the use of city motor equipment is
    A. increasing the life span of the equipment
    B. keeping the equipment working all hours of the day
    C. preventing the overuse of the equipment to avoid breakdowns
    D. preventing the private use of the equipment

    23.____

24. According to the above passage, a good control system for passenger equipment will MOST likely lead to
    A. better employees being assigned to operate the cars
    B. fewer city employees using city cars
    C. fewer wasted car hours for city cars
    D. insuring that city cars are used for legitimate purposes

    24.____

25. According to the above passage, a control system for trucks is useful because
    A. a foreman usually supervises each job
    B. special conditions sometimes prevent the planned use of a truck
    C. trucks are easier to control than passenger cars
    D. trucks are usually assigned to specific jobs where they cannot be fully utilized

    25.____

Question 26.

DIRECTIONS: Question 26 is to be answered SOLELY on the basis of the following passage.

Whereas automobile travel in general corresponds to the general motor vehicles index, as represented by total gas usage. Traffic trends on one particular road may vary from average. Comparison of the records of various main arteries indicates that automobile travel on some highways has gone up much faster than the general trend of gas usage. The conclusion is that the bulk of local travel remains stable, but a very large share of the total increase in travel is concentrated on main highways. This would be especially true on new highways which provide better means of travel and foster trips which would not have been made if the new route has not been constructed.

26. According to the above passage, which one of the following is MOST likely to result in increased automobile travel? 26._____
    A. A new roadway
    B. Stable local conditions
    C. A choice of routes
    D. Traffic trends

Questions 27-30.

DIRECTIONS: Questions 27 through 30 are to be answered ONLY on the basis of the following passage.

Analysis of current data reveals that motor vehicle transportation actually requires less space than was used for other types of transportation in the pre-automobile era, even including the substantial area taken by freeways. The reason is that when the fast-moving through traffic is put on built-for-the-purpose arterial roads, then the amount of ordinary space needed for strictly local movement and for access to property drops sharply. Even the amount of land taken for urban expressways turns out to be surprisingly small in terms either of total urban acreage or of the volume of traffic they carry. No existing or contemplated urban expressway system requires as much as 3 percent of the land in the areas it serves, and this would be exceptionally high. The Los Angeles freeway system, when complete, will occupy only 2 percent of the available land; the same is true of the District of Columbia, where only 0.75 percent will be pavement, with the remaining 1.25 percent as open space. California studies estimate that, in a typical California urban community, 1.6 to 2 percent of the area should be devoted to freeways, which will handle 50 to 60 percent of all traffic needs, and about ten time as much land to the ordinary roads and streets that carry the rest of the traffic. By comparison, when John A. Sutter laid out Sacramento in 1850, he provided 38 percent of the area for street and sidewalks. The French architect, Pierre L'Enfant, proposed 59 percent of the area of the District of Columbia for roads and streets; urban renewal in Southwest Washington, incorporating a modern street network, reduced the acreage of space for pedestrian and vehicular traffic in the renewal area from 48.2 to 41.5 percent of the total. If we are to have a reasonable consideration of the impact of highway transportation on contemporary urban development, it would be well to understand these relationships.

27. The author of this passage says that
    A. modern transportation uses less space than was used for transportation before the auto age
    B. expressways require more space than streets in terms of urban acreage
    C. typical urban communities were poorly designed in terms of relationship between space used for traffic and that used for other purposes
    D. the need for local and access roads would increase if the number of expressways were increased

28. According to the above passage, it was originally planned that the percent of the area to be used for roads and streets in the District of Columbia should be MOST NEARLY
    A. 40%   B. 45%   C. 50%   D. 60%

29. The above passage states that the amount of space needed for local traffic
    A. *increases* when arterial highways are constructed
    B. *decreases* when arterial highways are constructed
    C. *decreases* when there is more land available
    D. *increases* when there is more land available

30. According to the above passage, studies estimate that, land devoted to in a typical California urban community, the amount of ordinary roads and streets as compared with that devoted to freeways should be MOST NEARLY as much.
    A. One-half   B. One-tenth   C. Twice   D. Ten times

KEY (CORRECT ANSWERS)

1.	D	11.	C	21.	C
2.	C	12.	C	22.	B
3.	A	13.	D	23.	D
4.	B	14.	C	24.	C
5.	B	15.	B	25.	B
6.	D	16.	D	26.	A
7.	C	17.	D	27.	A
8.	C	18.	B	28.	D
9.	A	19.	A	29.	B
10.	D	20.	A	30.	D

TEST 2

DIRECTIONS: Each question or incomplete statement is followed by several suggested answers or completions. Select the one that BEST answers the question or completes the statement. *PRINT THE LETTER OF THE CORRECT ANSWER IN THE SPACE AT THE RIGHT.*

Questions 1-5.

DIRECTIONS: Questions 1 through 5 are to be answered ONLY on the basis of information given in the following passage.

    Fatigue can make a driver incompetent. He may become less vigilant. He may lose judgment as to the speed and distance of other cars. His reaction time is likely to be slowed down, and he is less able to resist glare. With increasing fatigue, driving efficiency falls. Finally, nodding at the wheel results, from which accidents follow almost invariably.

    Accidents that occur with the driver asleep at the wheel are generally very serious. With the driver unconscious, no effort is made either to prevent the accident or to lessen its seriousness. Accidents increase as day wears on and reach their peak in the early evening and during the first half of the night. Driver fatigue undoubtedly plays a significant part in causing these frequent night accidents.

1. Among the results of fatigue, the passage does NOT indicate
   A. lessened hearing effectiveness
   B. lessened vigilance
   C. loss of driving efficiency
   D. increased reaction time

2. According to the passage, accidents almost always follow as a result of
   A. fatigue
   B. slowed down reaction time
   C. nodding at the wheel
   D. lessened vigilance

3. According to the passage, accidents that occur in the early evening and during the first half of the night are
   A. always caused by driver fatigue
   B. very frequently the result of lessened resistance to glare
   C. usually due to falling asleep at the wheel
   D. more frequent than accidents in the afternoon

4. According to the passage, very serious accidents result from
   A. falling asleep at the wheel
   B. poor driving
   C. lack of judgment
   D. poor vision

5. Referring to the passage, which of the following conclusions is NOT correct?
   A. There are only two paragraphs in the entire passage.
   B. One paragraph contains four sentences.
   C. There are six words in the first sentence.
   D. There is no sentence of less than six words.

Questions 6-8.

DIRECTIONS: Questions 6 through 8 are to be answered ONLY according to the information given in the following passage.

Drivers and pedestrians face additional traffic hazards during the fall months. Changing autumn weather conditions, longer hours of darkness, and the abrupt nightfall during the evening rush hour can mean more traffic deaths and injuries unless drivers and pedestrians exercise greater care and alertness. Drivers must adjust to changing light conditions; they cannot use the same driving habits and attitudes at dusk as they do during daylight. Moderate speed and continual alertness are imperative for safe city driving at this time of year.

6. According to the above passage, two new traffic risks which motorists face in the fall are 6.____
   A. changing weather conditions and more traffic during the evening rush hour
   B. fewer hours of daylight and sudden nightfall
   C. less care by pedestrians and a change in autumn weather conditions
   D. more pedestrians on the street and longer hours of darkness

7. According to the above passage, there may be more traffic deaths and injuries in the fall MAINLY because both pedestrians and drivers are 7.____
   A. distracted by car lights being turned on earlier
   B. hurrying to get home from work in the evening
   C. confronted with more traffic dangers
   D. using the streets in greater numbers

8. According to the above passage, an ESSENTIAL requirement of driving safely in the city in the fall is 8.____
   A. eyes down on the road at all times
   B. very slow speed
   C. no passing
   D. reasonable speed

Questions 9-11.

DIRECTIONS: Questions 9 through 11 are to be answered ONLY according to the information given in the following passage.

A traffic sign is a device mounted on a fixed or portable support through which a specific message is conveyed by means of words or symbols. It is erected through which a specific purpose of regulating, warning, or guiding traffic.

A regulatory sign is used to indicate the required method of traffic movement or the permitted use of a highway. It gives notice of traffic regulations that apply only at specific places or at specific times that would not otherwise be apparent.

A warning sign is used to call attention to conditions on or near a road that are actually or potentially hazardous to the safe movement of traffic.

A guide sign is used to direct traffic along a route or toward a destination, or to give directions, distances, or information concerning places or points of interest.

9. According to the above passage, which one of the following is NOT a *regulatory* sign?
   A. Right turn on red signal permitted
   B. Trucks use right lane
   C. Slippery when wet
   D. Speed limit 60

9._____

10. According to the above passage, which one of the following LEAST fits the description of a *warning* sign?
    A. No right turn
    B. Falling rock zone
    C. Low clearance, 12 ft. 6 in.
    D. Merging traffic

10._____

11. According to the above passage, which one of the following messages is LEAST likely to be conveyed by a *guide* sign?
    A. Southbound
    B. Signal ahead
    C. Bridge next exit
    D. Entering city

11._____

Questions 12-14.

DIRECTIONS: Questions 12 through 14 are to be answered ONLY on the basis of the information given in the following passage.

A National Safety Council study of 685,000 traffic accidents reveals that most accidents happen under *safe* conditions—in clear, dry weather, on straight roads, and when traffic volumes are low. The point is most accidents can be attributed to lapses on the part of the drivers rather than traffic or road conditions or deliberate law violations. Most drivers try to avoid accidents. Why, then, do so many get into trouble? A major cause is the average motorist's failure to recognize a hazard soon enough to avoid it entirely. He does not, by habit, notice the clues that are there for him to see. He takes constant risks in traffic without even knowing it. These faulty seeing habits plus the common distractions that all drivers must deal with, such as hurry, worry daydreaming, impatience, concentration on route problems, add up to a guaranteed answer—an accident.

12. According to a study by the National Safety Council, MOST accidents can be blamed on
    A. curving, hilly roads
    B. errors made by drivers
    C. heavy streams of traffic
    D. wet, foggy weather

12._____

13. According to the above passage, an IMPORTANT reason why the average motorist gets into an accident is that he
    A. does not see the danger of an accident soon enough
    B. does not try to avoid accidents
    C. drives at too great a speed
    D. purposely takes reckless chances

13._____

14. According to the above passage, it is NOT reasonable to say that drivers are distracted from their driving and possibly involved in an accident because they
    A. are impatient about something
    B. concentrate on the road ahead
    C. hurry to get to where they are going
    D. worry about some problem

14.____

Questions 15-18.

DIRECTIONS: Questions 15 through 18 are to be answered ONLY on the basis of the information given in the following passage.

If a good automobile road map is studied thoroughly before a trip is started, much useful information can be learned. This information may help to decrease the cost of and the time required for the trip and, at the same time, increase the safety and comfort of the trip. The legend found on the face of the map explains symbols and markings and the kind of roads on various routes. The legend also explains how to tell by width, color, or type of line whether the road is dual- or multiple-lane, and whether it is paved, all-weather, graded, earth, under construction, or proposed for construction. Federal routes are usually shown by a number within a shield, and state routes by a number within a circle. The legend also shows scale of miles on a bar marked to indicate the distance each portion of the bar represents on the earth's surface. Distances between locations on the map are shown by plain numerals beside the route lines; they indicate mileage between marked points or intersections. Add the mileage numbers shown along a route to determine distances.

15. According to the above passage, the markings on the road map will show
    A. a different color for a road proposed for construction than for one under construction
    B. a double line if a road is a dual-lane road
    C. what part of a road is damaged or being repaired
    D. which roads on state routes have more than two lanes

15.____

16. The above passage does NOT mention as a possible advantage of studying a good road map before beginning a trip the
    A. increase in interest of the trip
    B. reduction in the chance of an accident on the trip
    C. saving of money
    D. saving of time

16.____

17. According to the above passage, in order to find the total mileage of a certain route, a motorist should add the numbers
    A. on the bar scale in the legend
    B. between marked points beside the route lines
    C. inside a shield along the route
    D. within a circle along the route

17.____

18. According to the above passage, the legend on a road map includes information   18._____
    which a motorist could use to
    A. choose the best paved route
    B. figure the toll charges
    C. find the allowable speed limits
    D. learn the location of bridges

Questions 19-30.

DIRECTIONS: The following is an accident report similar to those used by departments for reporting accidents. Questions 19 through 30 are to be answered ONLY on the basis of the information contained in this accident report.

ACCIDENT REPORT

Date of Accident: April 12, _____
Place of Accident: 17th Ave. & 22nd St.
Time of Accident: 10:15 A.M.
City Vehicle:
Operator's Name: John Smith
Title: Motor Vehicle Operator
Badge No.: 17-5427
Operator License No.: S2874-7513-3984
Vehicle Code No.: B7-8213
License Plate No.: BK-4782
Damage to Vehicle: Left front fender dented; broken left front headlight and parking light; windshield wipers not operating

Date of Report: April 15, _____ Friday
Vehicle No. 2:
Operator's Name: James Jones
Operator's Address: 427 E. 198th St.
Operator License No.: J0837-0882-7851
Owner's Name: Michael Greene
Owner's Address: 582 E. 92nd St.
License Plate No.: 6Y-3916
Damage to Vehicle: Left front bumper bent inward; broken left front headlight; grille broken in three places

DESCRIPTION OF ACCIDENT: I was driving on 17th Avenue, a southbound one-way street and made a slow, wide turn west into 22nd Street, a two-way street, because a moving van was parked near the corner of 22nd Street. As I completed my turn, a station wagon going east on 22nd Street hit me. The driver of the station wagon said he put on his brakes but he skidded on some oil that was on the street. The driver of the van saw the accident from his cab and told me that the station wagon skidded as he put on his brakes. Patrolman Jack Reed, Badge #24578, who was at the southeast corner of the intersection, saw what happened and made some notes in his memo book.

    Persons Injured – Names and Addresses. If none, state NONE:
    Witnesses – Names and Addresses: If none, state NONE:
      Jack Reed, 33-47 83rd Drive
      Thomas Quinn: 527 Flatlands Avenue

                              Report prepared by: John Smith
                              Title: Motor Vehicle Operator

19. According to the report, the accident happened on
    A. Friday, between 6:00 A.M. and 12:00 Noon
    B. Friday, between 12:00 Noon and 6:00 P.M.
    C. Tuesday, between 6:00 A.M. and 12:00 Noon
    D. Monday, between 12:00 Noon and 6:00 P.M.

20. Which one of the following numbers is part of the driver's license of the operator of the city vehicle?
    A. 3984   B. 5247   C. 4782   D. 7851

21. The address of the driver of the city vehicle is
    A. not given in the report
    B. 427 E. 198th Street
    C. 582 E. 92nd Street
    D. 33-47 83rd Drive

22. A section of the report that is NOT properly filled out is
    A. Witnesses
    B. Description of Accident
    C. Persons Injured
    D. Damage to Vehicle

23. According to the accident report, if the only witnesses were the patrolman and the van driver, then the van driver's name is
    A. Reed   B. Quinn   C. Jones   D. Greene

24. According to the report, the diagram that would BEST show where the cars collided and where the moving van ($\boxed{v}$) was parked at the time of the accident is

25. According to the information in the report, it would be MOST correct to say that Michael Greene was
    A. the driver of the station wagon
    B. a passenger in the station wagon
    C. the owner of the moving van
    D. the owner of the station wagon

26. According to the information in the report, a factor which contributed to the accident was 26.____
    A. a slippery road condition
    B. bad brakes of one car
    C. obstructed view of traffic light caused by parked van
    D. windshield wipers on the city car not operating properly

27. When a driver makes a report such as this, it is MOST important that he 27.____
    A. print the information so that his supervisor can read it quickly
    B. keep it short because a long report makes it look as though he is hiding a mistake behind many words
    C. show clearly why the accident isn't his fault
    D. give all the facts accurately and completely

28. The first two letters or numbers in the City Vehicle Code Number indicate the type of vehicle. Two letters indicate an 8 passenger 8-cylinder car; two numbers indicates a 6 passenger, 8-cylinder car; a letter followed by a number indicates a 6 passenger 6-cylinder car; a number followed by a letter indicate an 8-cylinder station wagon. 28.____
    The city car involved in this accident is, therefore, a(n)
    A. 8-cylinder station wagon   B. 6 passenger 6-cylinder car
    C. 6 passenger 8-cylinder car   D. 8 passenger 8-cylinder car

29. From the information in the report, the driver of the city vehicle may have been partially at fault because he 29.____
    A. appears to have begun his turn from the wrong lane
    B. appears to have entered the wrong lane of traffic
    C. did not blow his horn as he made the turn
    D. should have braked as he made the turn

30. What evidence is there in the report that the two vehicles collided in front, driver's side? 30.____
    A. The description of the accident
    B. There is no such evidence
    C. The type of damage to the vehicles
    D. The van driver's statement

KEY (CORRECT ANSWERS)

1.	A	11.	B	21.	A
2.	C	12.	B	22.	C
3.	D	13.	A	23.	B
4.	A	14.	B	24.	D
5.	D	15.	D	25.	D
6.	B	16.	A	26.	A
7.	C	17.	B	27.	D
8.	D	18.	A	28.	B
9.	C	19.	C	29.	B
10.	A	20.	A	30.	C

TEST 3

DIRECTIONS: Each question or incomplete statement is followed by several suggested answers or completions. Select the one that BEST answers the question or completes the statement. *PRINT THE LETTER OF THE CORRECT ANSWER IN THE SPACE AT THE RIGHT.*

Questions 1-7.

DIRECTIONS: Questions 1 through 7, inclusive, are to be answered on the basis of the following passage.

DRINKING AND DRIVING

In fatal traffic accidents, a drinking driver is involved more than 30% of the time; on holiday weekends, more than 50% of the fatal accidents involve drinking drivers. Drinking to any extent reduces the judgment, self-control, and driving ability of any driver. Social drinkers, especially those who think they drive better after a drink, are a greater menace than commonly believed, and they outnumber the obviously intoxicated. Two cocktails may reduce visual acuity as much as wearing dark glasses at night. Alcohol is not a stimulant; it is classified medically as a depressant. Coffee or other stimulants will not offset the effects of alcohol; only time can eliminate alcohol from the bloodstream. It takes at least three hours to eliminate one ounce of pure alcohol from the bloodstream.

1. Alcohol is classified by doctors as a
   A. stimulant B. sedative C. depressant D. medicine

2. Social drinkers
   A. never become obviously intoxicated
   B. always drink in large groups
   C. drive better after two cocktails
   D. are a greater menace than commonly believed

3. Alcohol will BEST be eliminated from the bloodstream by
   A. fresh air B. a stimulant C. coffee D. time

4. More than half of the fatal accidents on holiday weekends involve _____ drivers.
   A. inexperienced B. drinking C. fast D. slow

5. Drinking to any extent does NOT
   A. impair judgment B. decrease visual acuity
   C. reduce accident potential D. affect driving ability

6. In traffic accidents resulting in death, a drinking driver is involved
   A. about one-third of the time
   B. mainly at night
   C. more than 80% of the time
   D. practically all the time on weekends

7. After taking two alcoholic drinks, it is BEST not to drive until you have   7._____
   A. had a cup of black coffee   B. waited three hours
   C. eaten a full meal   D. taken a half-hour nap

Questions 8-12.

DIRECTIONS: Questions 8 through 12 are to be answered ONLY on the basis of the information contained in the following accident report.

REPORT OF ACCIDENT

Date of Accident: Nov. 27, _____   Time: 2:20 P.M.   Date of Report: 11/28

Department Vehicle
Operator's Name: John Doe
Title: Motor Vehicle Operator
Vehicle Code No.: 17-129
License Plate No.: IN-2345
Damage to Vehicle: Crumpled and torn front left fender, broken left headlight, front bumper bent outward on left side, hubcap dented badly and torn off

Vehicle No. 2
Operator's Name: Richard Roe
Operator's Address: 983 E. 84th St.
Owner's Name: Robert Roe
Owner's Address: 983 E. 84th St.
License Plate No.: 9Y-8765
Damage to Vehicle: Crumpled right front fender, broken right headlight and parking light, right left front side of front bumper badly bent

Place of Accident: 71st & 3rd Ave.

DESCRIPTION OF ACCIDENT: I was driving west on 71st St. and started to turn north into 3rd Avenue since the light was still green for me. I stopped at the crosswalk because a woman was in the middle of 3rd Avenue crossing from west to east. She had just cleared my car when a Ford sedan, going north, crashed into my left front fender. The light was green on 3rd Ave. when he hit me. The woman who had crossed the avenue in front of me, and whose name I got as a witness, was standing on the corner when I got out of the car.

Persons Injured

_____   _____
Mrs. Mary Brown   Witness   215 E. 71 St.

Report prepared by: John Doe
Title: Motor Vehicle Operator
Badge #17832

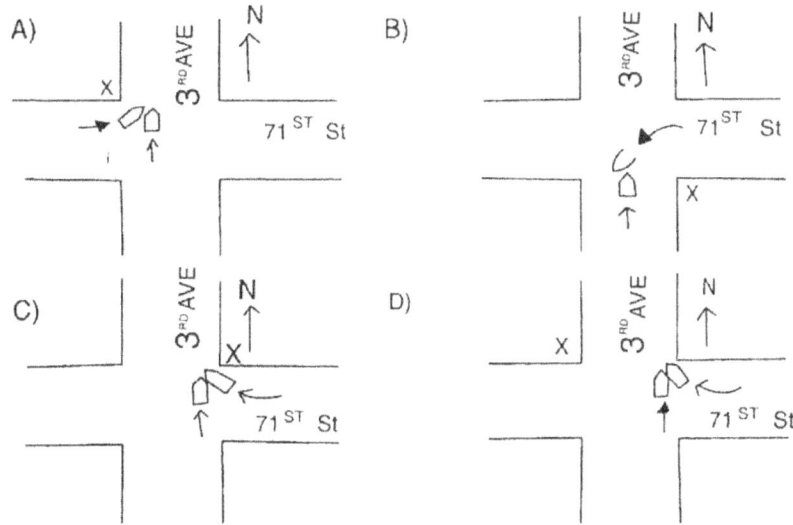

8. According to the description of the accident, the diagram that would BEST show how and where the vehicles crashed and the position of the witness (X) is
   A. A   B. B   C. C   D. D

9. The pedestrian mentioned in the description of the accident was
   A. an unknown woman   B. Mary Brown
   C. an unknown man   D. Robert Roe

10. According to the information in the report, the one of the following statements which is INCORRECT is:
    A. Both cars were moving when the accident happened
    B. One car was moving when the accident happened
    C. The Department car was headed northwest when the accident happened
    D. The traffic lights had changed just before the accident happened

11. From the description of the accident as given in the report, the accident would PROBABLY be classified as
    A. premeditated   B. calamitous   C. minor   D. fatal

12. From a reading of the accident report, it can be seen that
    A. the witness was completely unfamiliar with the neighborhood in which the accident took place
    B. the accident occurred in the early hours of the morning
    C. neither driver owned the vehicle he was driving
    D. it was raining when the accident took place

Questions 13-24.

DIRECTIONS: Questions 13 through 24 are based on the description of an automobile accident given below. Read the description carefully before answering these questions.

DESCRIPTION OF AUTOMOBILE ACCIDENT

Ten persons were injured, two critically, when a driverless auto—its accelerator jammed-up ran wild through the busy intersection at 8th Ave. and 42nd Street at 11:30 A.M. yesterday. The car struck a truck, overturned it, and mounted the sidewalk. Several persons were bowled over before the car was finally stopped by collision with a second truck. Police Officer Fred Black, Badge No. 82143, said that the freak accident occurred after the car's driver, Mrs. Mary Jones, 39, of Queens, got out of the car with her daughter, Gloria, aged 3, while the engine was still running. Mr. Herbert Field, 64, of the Bronx, a passenger in the car, accidentally stepped on the accelerator when he tried to get out. This caused the car to shoot forward because the shift was in *drive*, and 5 pedestrians were thrown to the ground.

13. This accident occurred
    A. late in the morning
    B. early in the morning
    C. early in the afternoon
    D. late in the evening

14. The number of persons who were injured, but not critically, is
    A. 2   B. 5   C. 8   D. 10

15. This accident occurred a block away from
    A. Grand Central Terminal
    B. Times Square
    C. Union Square
    D. Pennsylvania Station

16. The runaway car was finally stopped just after it
    A. mounted the sidewalk
    B. collided with a second truck
    C. crossed the intersection
    D. bowled over several persons

17. It can be inferred from the description that the driverless auto had
    A. power brakes
    B. power steering
    C. a turn indicator
    D. an automatic shift

18. The number on the police officer's badge is
    A. 82314   B. 82413   C. 82143   D. 82341

19. The first name of the driver of the car is
    A. Mary   B. Fred   C. Gloria   D. Herbert

20. According to the accident description, the adult passenger lives in
    A. the Bronx, and so does the driver
    B. Queens, and so does the driver
    C. the Bronx, and the driver in Queens
    D. Queens, and the driver in the Bronx

21. The number of pedestrians who were thrown to the ground is
    A. 2   B. 5   C. 7   D. 10

22. The person who made a statement about the runaway car was
    A. Herbert Field   B. Mary Jones
    C. Gloria Jones   D. Fred Black

23. Herbert Field is older than Mary Jones by about _____ years.
    A. 25   B. 35   C. 51   D. 61

24. The car shot forward immediately after
    A. Mrs. Jones placed the shift in *drive*
    B. Mr. Field stepped on the accelerator
    C. Mrs. Jones stepped out of the car
    D. Mr. Field got out of the car

Questions 25-28.

DIRECTIONS: Questions 25 through 28 are to be answered ONLY on the basis of the information given in the following passage.

ACCIDENT PRONESS

Accident proneness is a subject deserving much more attention than it has received. Studies have shown a high incidence of accidents to be associated with particular employees who are called accident prone. Such employees, according to these studies, behave on their jobs in ways which make them likely to have more accidents than would normally be expected.

It is important to point out the difference between the employee who is a *repeater* and the one who is truly accident prone. It is obvious that any person assigned to work about which he knows little will be liable to injury until he does learn the *how* of the job. Few workers left completely on their own will develop adequate safe practices. Therefore, they must be trained. Only those who fail to respond to proper training should be regarded as accident prone.

The dangers of an occupation should also be considered when judging an accident record. For a crane operator, a record of five accidents in a given period of time may not indicate accident proneness, while, in the case of a clerk, two accidents over the same period of time may be excessive. There are the reporters whose accident records can be explained by correctible physical defects, by correctible unsafe plant or machine conditions, or by assignment to work for which they are not suited because they cannot meet all the job's physical requirements. Such repeaters cannot be fairly called *accident prone*. A diagnosis of accident proneness should not be lightly made but should be based on all of these considerations.

25. According to the above passage, studies have shown that accident prone employees
    A. work under unsafe physical conditions
    B. act in unsafe ways on the job
    C. are not usually physically suited for their jobs
    D. work in the more dangerous occupations

26. According to the above passage, a person who is accident prone
    A. has received proper training which has not reduced his tendency toward accidents
    B. repeats the same accident several times over a short period of time
    C. experiences excessive anxiety about dangers in his occupation
    D. ignores unsafe but correctible machine conditions

27. According to the above passage, MOST persons who are given work they know little about
    A. will eventually learn on their own sufficient safety practices to follow
    B. work safely if they are not accident prone
    C. must be trained before they develop adequate safety methods
    D. should be regarded as accident prone until they become familiar with the job

28. According to the above passage, to effectively judge the accident record of an employee, one should consider
    A. the employee's age and physical condition
    B. that five accidents are excessive
    C. the type of dangers that are natural to his job
    D. the difficulty level of previous occupations held by the employee

Questions 29-30.

DIRECTIONS: Questions 29 and 30 are to be answered ONLY on the basis of the information given in the following passage.

When heavy rain beats on your windshield, it becomes hard for you to see ahead and even harder to see objects to the side—despite good windshield wipers. Also, the danger zone becomes longer when it is raining because the car takes longer to stop on wet streets. Remember that the danger zone of your car is the distance within which you can't stop after you have seen something on the road ahead of your car. The way to reduce the length of the danger zone of your car while driving is to reduce speed.

29. From the information in the above passage, you cannot tell if the danger zone of your car
    A. can be made smaller
    B. is greater on a rainy day
    C. is greater on cloudy days than on clear days
    D. is the distance in back of the car or in front of the car

30. According to the above passage, the danger zone of a moving car is affected by
    A. the condition of the street and the speed of the car
    B. many things which cannot be pinned down, in addition to the mechanical condition of the car
    C. the number of objects to the front and to the side
    D. visibility of the road and the reaction time of the driver

KEY (CORRECT ANSWERS)

1.	C	11.	C	21.	B
2.	D	12.	C	22.	D
3.	D	13.	A	23.	A
4.	B	14.	C	24.	B
5.	C	15.	B	25.	B
6.	A	16.	B	26.	A
7.	B	17.	D	27.	C
8.	C	18.	C	28.	C
9.	B	19.	A	29.	C
10.	A	20.	C	30.	A

PREPARING WRITTEN MATERIAL

PARAGRAPH REARRANGEMENT
COMMENTARY

The sentences that follow are in scrambled order. You are to rearrange them in proper order and indicate the letter choice containing the correct answer at the space at the right.

Each group of sentences in this section is actually a paragraph presented in scrambled order. Each sentence in the group has a place in that paragraph; no sentence is to be left out. You are to read each group of sentences and decide upon the best order in which to put the sentences so as to form a well-organized paragraph.

The questions in this section measure the ability to solve a problem when all the facts relevant to its solution are not given.

More specifically, certain positions of responsibility and authority require the employee to discover connection between events sometimes, apparently, unrelated. In order to do this, the employee will find it necessary to correctly infer that unspecified events have probably occurred or are likely to occur. This ability becomes especially important when action must be taken on incomplete information.

Accordingly, these questions require competitors to choose among several suggested alternatives, each of which presents a different sequential arrangement of the events. Competitors must choose the MOST logical of the suggested sequences.

In order to do so, they may be required to draw on general knowledge to infer missing concepts or events that are essential to sequencing the given events. Competitors should be careful to infer only what is essential to the sequence. The plausibility of the wrong alternatives will always require the inclusion of unlikely events or of additional chains of events which are NOT essential to sequencing the given events.

It's very important to remember that you are looking for the best of the four possible choices, and that the best choice of all may not even be one of the answers you're given to choose from.

There is no one right way to solve these problems. Many people have found it helpful to first write out the order of the sentences, as they would have arranged them, on their scrap paper before looking at the possible answers. If their optimum answer is there, this can save them some time. If it isn't, this method can still give insight into solving the problem. Others find it most helpful to just go through each of the possible choices, contrasting each as they go along. You should use whatever method feels comfortable and works for you.

While most of these types of questions are not that difficult, we've added a higher percentage of the difficult type, just to give you more practice. Usually there are only one or two questions on this section that contain such subtle distinctions that you're unable to answer confidently. And you then may find yourself stuck deciding between two possible choices, neither of which you're sure about.

PREPARING WRITTEN MATERIAL
PARAGRAPH REARRANGEMENT
EXAMINATION SECTION
TEST 1

DIRECTIONS: The sentences listed below are part of a meaningful paragraph, but they are not given in their proper order. You are to decide what would be the BEST order to put sentences to form a well-organized paragraph. Each sentence has a place in the paragraph; there are no extra sentences. *PRINT THE LETTER OF THE CORRECT ANSWER IN THE SPACE AT THE RIGHT.*

1.
   I. At first, I had very low enrollment, but then I started passing out flyers describing my services.
   II. Last summer I started a carwashing venture.
   III. I hope to save enough to buy my own carwash business one day.
   IV. I've been in business almost a year.
   V. After the advertising, I was booked every weekend during the summer.
   The CORRECT answer is:
   A. II, I, V, IV, III   B. I, II, IV, III, V   C. II, I, IV, V, III   D. V, III, IV, I, II

   1.____

2.
   I. Yesterday, John had to call work and tell them he wouldn't be able to come in.
   II. She wanted to eat at the new seafood restaurant in town.
   III. Two days ago, John and Sally went to dinner for Sally's birthday.
   IV. However, later John realized the sushi made him sick.
   V. They both tried the sushi and thought it tasted good.
   The CORRECT answer is:
   A. I, V, IV, III, II   B. III, II, V, IV, I   C. III, V, IV, I, II   D. V, IV, III, I, II

   2.____

3.
   I. Music programs should not be cut when school funds are tight.
   II. Some will argue that music programs are too costly.
   III. According to many experts, music programs have even shown the ability to re-engage student populations who have lost interest in scholastic endeavors.
   IV. There is a direct connection between school improvement and a student's connection to music.
   V. However, there are many different programs to choose from that are not as expensive.
   The CORRECT answer is:
   A. IV, II, V, I, III   B. I, III, IV, II, V   C. II, I, III, IV, V   D. I, IV, III, II, V

   3.____

4.
   I. The hockey team went undefeated in their tournament.
   II. Because the coach and their parents believed in them, the players played with great confidence.
   III. No one wanted to go home after they won the championship.
   IV. Their coach made them believe they could beat anyone they played.
   V. They were not expected to beat all of the teams in their bracket.
   The CORRECT answer is:
   A. III, II, V, IV, I   B. I, II, III, IV, V   C. I, V, IV, II, III   D. I, IV, V, II, III

   4.____

5.
   I. The problem started when my alarm clock was set for 6:00 P.M. not 6:00 A.M., so I woke up late.
   II. I guess a neighbor's dog got loose before practice started, so it was delayed and no one notices I was a little tardy.
   III. I rode my bike as fast as I could and thought I was going to be in trouble for sure.
   IV. This morning was crazy because if I was late, I would get cut from the team.
   V. When I got to the field, everyone was standing on the outside of the fence and there were policemen all on the field.
   The CORRECT answer is:
   A. I, IV, III, V, II   B. IV, III, I, II, V   C. I, V, II, III, IV   D. IV, I, III, V, II

6.
   I. Lastly, do not eat food off of your date's plate unless they have offered it to you first.
   II. Do not tell jokes that aren't funny and especially do not laugh at them yourself.
   III. Remember, there are many ways to screw up a date, but these are the worst ways.
   IV. When on a first date, there are many ways to screw it up, but here are the three worst.
   V. Do not forget to shower and groom yourself before showing up.
   The CORRECT answer is:
   A. IV, V, II, I, III   B. I, V, IV, II, III   C. IV, III, II, I, V   D. V, IV, II, I, III

7.
   I. We could prevent drunk drivers from harming themselves or others by by providing this service.
   II. Thousands each year die because of accidents caused by drugs or alcohol.
   III. Many are not willing to pay for a taxi and decide to drive themselves home instead.
   IV. While the cost may be a burden to the wallet, it would be small compared to the loss of a loved one because of drunk driving.
   V. Lives could be saved if the town started a free taxi service.
   The CORRECT answer is:
   A. I, III, V, IV, II   B. II, V, III, I, IV   C. II, III, I, V, IV   D. V, III, II, IV, I

8.
   I. These amazing animals are disappearing at a startling rate.
   II. Do people really want to explain to our grandchildren why they can only see these majestic animals in a book?
   III. Zoos all across the country do not want the Siberian tiger to vanish.
   IV. We can also make donations to charities and sanctuaries that protect the Siberian tiger.
   V. If we write to local governments, we could let them know we demand the preservation of this species.
   The CORRECT answer is:
   A. I, III, V, II, IV   B. V, II, I, III, IV   C. III, I, V, IV, II   D. II, IV, V, I, III

9. I. Often, they have been described as eating machines, and their design certainly matches perfectly for that activity.
    II. Of all the creatures that live in water, Orcas are the greediest eaters and killers.
    III. As soon as they finish a meal, Orcas are on the prowl for more food.
    IV. Orcas, better known as killer whales, are powerful swimmers, with sleek, muscled, stream-lined bodies.
    V. They suffer from continual hunger.
    The CORRECT answer is:
    A. II, V, III, I, IV   B. II, III, I, IV, V   C. V, II, III, IV, I   D. I, IV, II, III, V

10. I. Sleep researchers have recently concluded that high school students need more sleep than they currently get.
    II. In an attempt to aid high school students get more sleep, some schools have delayed start times so students can perform better.
    III. In addition to having difficulty with thinking, students who are sleep deprived often see more stress in their lives because of an increase in stress hormones like cortisol.
    IV. Consistent data has determined that sleep is necessary to help with creating memories and solving complex issues.
    V. At school, teens have difficulty with complex thought because many of them do not get enough sleep each night.
    The CORRECT answer is:
    A. I, V, III, II, IV   B. IV, III, I, V, II   C. I, IV, V, III, II   D. II, III, V, IV, I

11. I. It took me twice as long to pack because I was so excited.
    II. That all changed on the last day of school.
    III. Until last year, I had never been out of the state, let alone out of the country.
    IV. My sister decided to take me on a trip to London.
    V. Now I think I want to be a travel agent, so I can see the world.
    The CORRECT answer is:
    A. II, IV, I, V, III   B. III, II, IV, I, V   C. IV, V, I, III, II   D. III, IV, II, I, V

12. I. The owner felt that tattoos gave a negative image for the coffee shop.
    II. Furthermore, a clean cut appearance would attract better customers.
    III. Since then, the policy has seen few complaints from residents or employees.
    IV. In 2008, a coffee shop in Billings, Montana instituted a policy that banned employees from having tattoos that can be seen by customers.
    V. When one of the employees refused to wear a long sleeve shirt to cover up, he was told he could no longer work at the coffee shop.
    The CORRECT answer is:
    A. IV, II, III, I, V   B. V, I, II, IV, III   C. I, II, V, III, IV   D. IV, I, II, V, III

13. I. Our household might have been described as uncooperative.
    II. When the tide was high, she would be standing on the inlet bridge with her waders on.
    III. Everything was subservient to the disposal of the tides.
    IV. I grew up with buckets, shovels, and nets waiting by the back door.
    V. When the tide was low, Mom could be found down on the mudflats.
    The CORRECT answer is:
    A. I, V, IV, V, III   B. IV, I, III, V, II   C. V, IV, II, I, III   D. II, IV, I, III, V

14. I. A 2012 survey found that over 50% of those polled thought educators were prohibited from teaching about religion.
    II. The result is that many schools and teachers are hesitant to educate students about world religions.
    III. However, for many it is impossible to deny the role that religion plays in history and literature.
    IV. As many people know, the First Amendment guarantees the separation of church and state.
    V. Ultimately, this is a dilemma that will continue to plague Social Studies and World History educators.
    The CORRECT answer is:
    A. IV, I, III, V, II   B. I, III, V, II, IV   C. IV, III, II, I, V   D. II, III, V, IV, I

15. I. The Wampanoag religion was similar to that of the other Algonquin tribes.
    II. They also had spiritual beliefs about animals, and the forest.
    III. Then, they told their stories of the cycle of life and the Great Spirit.
    IV. They expressed their religious beliefs during festivals and at night when they sat at huge campfires.
    V. In those times, people believed in a Great Spirit and many other things that Nature had a part of the Great Spirit in them.
    The CORRECT answer is:
    A. I, V, II, IV, III   B. V, II, III, I, IV   C. I, II, III, IV, V   D. III, IV, II, V, I

16. I. Consumers spend an endless amount of money each year on cutting, lengthening, highlighting and curling hair.
    II. Brunettes want to be blonde, redheads long to be brunettes, and all cringe at the thought of gray hair.
    III. Why is everyone so obsessed with the hair on their heads?
    IV. These thoughts all crossed my mind as I examine the result of my most recent hair adventure.
    V. The result was not quite what I expected, but I resolved to live with it, as it's my hair and no one else's!
    The CORRECT answer is:
    A. I, IV, V, II, III   B. I, III, II, IV, V   C. IV, I, III, V, II   D. III, I, II, IV, V

17. I.   It was only years afterwards that he learned his ancestors were actually accomplished coppersmiths.
     II. He's an old-fashioned current day blacksmith that still practices manipulating metal over hot fires.
     III. This started him on his quest to collect and read any and every book concerning the nature and process of blacksmithing.
     IV. Beginning at age 30, Lee's attraction to metal work lay in creating an object out of such obstinate material such as iron.
     V.   While one will probably never read about him in a history book, Mr. Amos Lee contributes mightily to the preservation of America.
     The CORRECT answer is:
     A. II, III, I, IV, V   B. V, II, IV, III, I   C. III, I, V, II, IV   D. I, IV, III, V, II

17.____

18. I.   After she was stung, she killed the scorpion with a boot, and flushed it down the sink.
     II. My sister once told me about a scorpion that stung her in her bed.
     III. As she recounted her tale of horror, I could only wonder how she remained so calm.
     IV. Later, she realized she should've kept it to figure out what type of scorpion it was.
     V.   While she's lucky to be alive, it could've been a deadly scorpion that would've required medical attention immediately.
     The CORRECT answer is:
     A. II, III, I, IV, V   B. II, I, IV, V, III   C. I, IV, II, III, V   D. V, II, III, I, IV

18.____

19. I.   While the majority of people know this, it was not always the case.
     II. Many laws hold sponsors responsible to participants and courts are full of non-compliance lawsuits on both sides.
     III. Seven months after departure, she arrived at her destination, battered and tired, but the contest sponsors were nowhere to be found.
     IV. For anyone who has ever entered a contest, the rules and disclaimers that go along with each one are well known.
     V.   In 1896, a contest motivated a Norwegian immigrant to travel from New York City to the state of Washington.
     The CORRECT answer is:
     A. II, III, V, IV, I   B. V, I, IV, III, II   C. IV, II, I, V, III   D. I, IV, III, II, V

19.____

20. I.   One thought as to why this happens is due to a person's circadian rhythm being thrown off.
     II. While most people find traveling internationally to be exhilarating, those same people would probably agree that the worst part is the jet lag.
     III. It is considered a sleeping disorder, albeit one that is temporary and not as serious as other sleeping dysfunctions.
     IV. Normally, the body operates on a 24-hour time period in conjunction with the earth's 24-hour cycle of night and day.
     V.   When one adds or subtracts time while traveling, a condition known as desynchronosis likely affects them.
     The CORRECT answer is:
     A. I, II, III, IV, V   B. IV, I, III, V, II   C. III, IV, I, II, V   D. II, V, III, I, IV

20.____

21.
   I. The consumption rate is due to its ability to create cleaner fuel for electrical power.
   II. While cleaner burning fuel is optimal, the usage rate will mean the U.S. only has about a five-year supply of natural gas.
   III. Current research studies are showing that Americans use around 20 trillion cubic feet (TCF) on a yearly basis.
   IV. It is no wonder, then, that natural gas has become such a controversial and critical topic for politicians, businesses, and consumers.
   V. While gasoline is still a crucial energy source, natural gas actually supplies approximately one-fourth of America's energy needs.
   The CORRECT answer is:
   A. I, IV, II, III, V   B. IV, II, III, V, I   C. V, III, I, II, IV   D. III, V, IV, I, II

22.
   I. Their protection comes from bony plates covered by leathery skin.
   II. This desert wanderer has few worries and one can understand why: his "coat" of armor.
   III. What would be certain death for most animals, armadillos meander along highway shoulders and remains surprisingly unaffected.
   IV. While their shells are not impenetrable, the armadillo can relax knowing that he is safer than many animals who wander the roads of the southwest.
   V. While on the smaller side, armadillos are equipped to deal with aggressive and dangerous predators.
   The CORRECT answer is:
   A. III, II, V, I, IV   B. IV, I, II, V, III   C. I, III, IV, II, V   D. V, IV, I, III, II

23.
   I. Since its discovery in 1930, Pluto has had a troubled history concerning its acceptance as a planet.
   II. Anytime there is a controversial topic like this, it is sure to be debated for years to come.
   III. Some researchers believe that it is a planet arguing that Pluto is almost 1,000 times bigger than an average comet.
   IV. However, others argue that due to its icy composition and irregular orbit, Pluto more likely belongs to the Kuiper Belt, which features sizeable comets.
   V. They also argue that any would be planet must be large enough to be pulled into a spherical shape by its own gravity, which like the other eight, Pluto can lay claim to.
   The CORRECT answer is:
   A. IV, V, I, II, III   B. I, III, V, IV, II   C. III, I, IV, V, II   D. II, IV, V, III, I

24.
  I. When I found out I'd be traveling to France, I was so ecstatic.
  II. He told me that studying may be difficult because I will want to meet new friends and see all the landmarks associated with such a beautiful country.
  III. My brother has also been in an exchange before and he had some advice for me.
  IV. Despite his warnings to study hard, I know I would be disappointed if I didn't do any sightseeing at all.
  V. In the fall, I will be participating in a foreign exchange program.
  The CORRECT answer is:
  A. I, V, II, IV, III   B. IV, II, I, III, V   C. III, I, II, IV, IV   D. V, I, III, II, IV

25.
  I. Well over two hundred years ago, Lewis and Clark set forth on a journey at the request of President Thomas Jefferson.
  II. Their instructions were simple; they needed to find the fastest route across North America.
  III. Throughout it all, including long winters and harsh conditions, the travelers forged west in search of a trade route using only rivers.
  IV. The actual task was much more difficult as it would require them to set a course through dangerous territories replete with hostile natives and ferocious animals.
  V. While land travel ended up being faster, many still credit this group with "breaking through" into the unknown land and launching a movement for westward expansion.
  The CORRECT answer is:
  A. I, II, IV, III, V   B. II, I, III, IV, V   C. V, III, IV, II, I   D. IV, I, III, V, II

KEY (CORRECT ANSWERS)

1.	A	11.	B
2.	B	12.	D
3.	D	13.	B
4.	C	14.	C
5.	D	15.	A
6.	A	16.	D
7.	B	17.	B
8.	C	18.	A
9.	A	19.	C
10.	C	20.	D

21. C
22. A
23. B
24. D
25. A

TEST 2

DIRECTIONS: The sentences listed below are part of a meaningful paragraph, but they are not given in their proper order. You are to decide what would be the BEST order to put sentences to form a well-organized paragraph. Each sentence has a place in the paragraph; there are no extra sentences. *PRINT THE LETTER OF THE CORRECT ANSWER IN THE SPACE AT THE RIGHT.*

1. I. Whenever I start to feel sadness and disgust over a poor hair style, I ask myself why we are so obsessed with the hair on our heads.
    II. The answer always comes to me in a flash.
    III. Soon after this realization, I often cease my crying over how I look.
    IV. It's pure vanity; no other reason explains fully why we worry about how to style, color or cut our follicles.
    V. Instead, I focus on positive, kind thoughts towards myself and others, which usually allows me to overcome any negative feelings I had right after I looked in the mirror.
    The CORRECT answer is:
    A. III, I, V, IV, II   B. I, II, IV, III, V   C. IV, III, II, V, I   D. V, IV, I, II, III

2. I. The riverboat director was our captain and our host.
    II. We affectionately watched him with his back toward us, as he stood at the helm, looking toward the sea.
    III. Within all of the Mississippi River, nothing looked nearly as nautical and trustworthy as our pilot as he surveyed the waters before him.
    IV. What we had not realized at the time was that his work was not out there in the estuaries, but rather behind him, within the gloom of the vessel.
    V. We would realize soon enough, however, how difficult the next few days would get, and why he was so ponderous on that ship deck.
    The CORRECT answer is:
    A. III, I, IV, II, V   B. IV, II, III, V, I   C. V, II, I, IV, III   D. I, III, II, IV, V

3. I. Ultimately, no new qualities are added to an object, person, or action when it becomes good.
    II. Whenever one examines the word "good", there is always an implied end to be reached.
    III. The good is useful, and it must be used for something.
    IV. However, good is a relative term.
    V. So in that light, whether good is spoken out loud or silently assumed, it is a mental exercise to something else that puts all meaning into it.
    The CORRECT answer is:
    A. V, II, I, IV, III   B. III, I, V, II, IV   C. I, V, IV, III, II   D. II, IV, III, V, I

4. I. There are specific temperature ranges for petroleum gas, kerosene, oil stocks and also residue.
    II. Called fractional distillation, the oil is heated and drawn off at different points, which leads to the various products.
    III. To start, the oil is heated up to around 600 degrees Celsius, which vaporizes it.
    IV. From there, the vapors cool and condense as they move upwards and eventually turn back into liquid and flows into various tanks.
    V. Crude oil is refined when it is split into different by-products.
    The CORRECT answer is:
    A. II, III, I, V, IV   B. IV, I, IV, III, V   C. V, II, I, III, IV   D. I, IV, II, III, V

5. I. With that said, x-ray distortion has more than one use regarding planets.
    II. The higher "bend" in an x-ray would seemingly indicate a larger planet, while lower bending would most likely mean a smaller planet.
    III. Distortion can also help determine how a planet orbits its star.
    IV. Releasing x-rays by distant stars can help reveal the presence of planets orbiting these stars.
    V. The distortion of the x-rays, which is how scientists would tell if planets are near, would be caused by gravitational pull exerted from planets.
    The CORRECT answer is:
    A. IV, V, II, I, III   B. V, IV, III, I, II   C. II, III, I, IV, V   D. I, V, II, III, IV

6. I. Some feel that this fact reflects the rise of English as an accepted language of business around the world, and, therefore, that foreign languages are lessening in importance.
    II. Foreign language instruction is dropping in U.S. public high schools.
    III. They feel that this drop is actually a threat to the nation's vitality in what is an ever-increasing multicultural marketplace.
    IV. Others feel that the reduction in language study is a U.S. failure to integrate with the rest of the world.
    V. The question then becomes this, should greater support be given to foreign language programs in U.S. public schools?
    The CORRECT answer is:
    A. V, IV, III, I, II   B. III, IV, V, II, I   C. II, I, IV, III, V   D. IV, II, III, V, I

7. I. The owner, Nate, still runs the joint, which means it doesn't usually close until he's served the last customer.
    II. The alley might dissuade visitors from finding this local gem, but if one can get past the masking tape and yellowing paint that line the door, they will be in for a real treat.
    III. The Shack, as the locals call it, is located in a nondescript alley across from beautiful City Park.
    IV. While I'd love for Nate to get more publicity, I'm just fine with knowing that the Shack will have a short line and a great ambience each time I stop in.
    V. Nathan's Crab Shack serves up some of the best sandwiches I've ever eaten.
    The CORRECT answer is:
    A. III, II, V, IV, I   B. I, IV, II, III, V   C. II, V, I, IV, III   D. V, I, III, II, IV

8.
   I. All activity halted, however, at the onset of World War II, so construction did not officially begin until the early 1950s.
   II. In total, it took almost three years to build, cost five men their lives, and cost the state of Michigan more than $40 million.
   III. In the 1930's, the Mackinac Bridge Authority sought funding from the federal government to construct a bridge.
   IV. Even though they were denied, the MBA plotted a route and studied the lake bed and rock below.
   V. Despite numerous setbacks, the Mackinac Bridge opened to traffic on November 1, 1957, and for years it was the longest suspension bridge in the world.
   The CORRECT answer is:
   A. II, I, V, IV, III   B. III, IV, I, II, V   C. V, III, IV, I, II   D. I, II, III, V, IV

   8.____

9.
   I. It also teaches them to bargain and trade for cards to complete their sets.
   II. Collecting cards is a rewarding experience not only for kids, but also adults.
   III. It teaches important skills, such as patience and organization.
   IV. Lastly, card collecting is a social activity that encourages the old and the young to swap stories, cards, and knowledge in a fun and engaging way.
   V. For younger collectors, it enhances fine motor skills such as developing a more careful touch.
   The CORRECT answer is:
   A. III, IV, I, II, V   B. II, V, III, IV, I   C. I, II, V, III, IV   D. II, III, V, I, IV

   9.____

10.
   I. Spyware can cripple unsecured computers and data around the world.
   II. Even when computer users experience program crashes and warnings about missing system files, they tend to wait until these problems get too ad to manage.
   III. Sometimes it is used for marketing agencies, but just as often there is a more malicious intent behind spyware stored on an unsecured computer.
   IV. Much of the time, the cause of these problems rests with the biggest online threat there is: spyware.
   V. While most people do not realize it, those who use a personal computer to connect to the internet expose themselves to many risks.
   The CORRECT answer is:
   A. II, IV, V, III, I   B. V, II, IV, I, III   C. III, II, I, IV, V   D. V, IV, I, II, III

   10.____

11.
   I. When people have parties at their homes, Susan cooks for them, and she is a fabulous cook.
   II. My friend, Susan, owns her own catering business.
   III. Once everything has been planned, Susan will hire servers to wait on the people.
   IV. One of the things that makes her so good is that she asks the customer lots of questions like how many people will be there and what food the customer would like to serve.
   V. All in all, she loves the work involved with her catering business and it does not hurt that she's really good at it.

   11.____

The CORRECT answer is:
A. II, I, IV, III, V   B. I, III, V, II, IV   C. IV, II, I, III, V   D. V, IV, I, III, II

12. I.   "To be, or not to be...." is an extremely well-known phrase that has been the source of both mystery and wonderment since the turn of the 16th century.
     II. Where did it come from and what does it mean?
     III. As for the meaning of the phrase, a complete answer would necessitate a deeper, more comprehensive look into Shakespeare culture and nuance.
     IV. The first question is easy enough to answer: from Shakespeare's famous play, *Hamlet*.
     V.   The issue, however, is that despite the fact that everyone knows the phrase, few actually know the context of this well-worn saying.
     The CORRECT answer is:
     A. V, I, III, II, IV   B. II, III, IV, V, I   C. I, V, II, IV, III   D. IV, II, I, III, V

12.____

13. I.   For example, it was recently discovered that we were connected to a Civil War ancestor that we previously had not known about.
     II. He maintains the records of births, deaths, marriages, and even divorces, and he takes the job very seriously.
     III. This ancestor bestowed his beautiful and antique furniture to his children, who then passed the items down to their descendants.
     IV. My Uncle Mike is the genealogist of our family.
     V.   In fact, he will even send out letters to our family whenever something noteworthy occurs.
     The CORRECT answer is:
     A. II, III, I, IV, V   B. V, IV, II, III, I   C. I, II, IV, V, III   D. IV, II, V, I, III

13.____

14. I.   He was part of a team that performed complicated experiments during the 1940s.
     II. However, he is most likely known for his creation of "Murphy's Law."
     III. While many Americans do not know the name Edward Murphy, they owe a considerable debt to this member of the Air Force.
     IV. This somewhat funny observation has actually inspired similar "laws" such as Hofstadter's Law.
     V.   This "law" states that "if anything can go wrong, it will."
     The CORRECT answer is:
     A. I, III, V, II, IV   B. III, IV, V, I, II   C. III, I, II, V, IV   D. V, II, IV, I, III

14.____

15. I.   During winter months, its white coat is ideal to camouflage and the insulation provided by its unbeatable fur lining allows the fox to hunt all winter long.
     II. While this strategy could be fruitful, it also carries risk because of the possibility that the polar bear might consume the fox if it catches it.
     III. One of the Snow Fox's unique traits is the ability to adapt to extreme weather conditions.

15.____

5 (#2)

IV. When food becomes scarce, the Arctic fox can follow polar bears as they attack seals on the sea ice.
V. Often referred to as the "Snow Fox," the Arctic fox is comparable in size to a domestic cat.
The CORRECT answer is:
A. V, III, I, IV, II   B. II, IV, III, I, V   C. III, I, V, II, IV   D. IV, III, II, V, I

16.
I. The venerable professor, aged 85, encouraged his audience to show compassion for the poor and homeless in the city.
II. Students flocked to hear the returning professor, Dr. Willis, give a speech.
III. He abhors opulence and urges people to be charitable through frugality.
IV. Dr. Willis, a kind and empathetic activist for the poor, spoke to a full auditorium on Tuesday.
V. Much of his work is due to his personal memories stemming from the Great Depression.
The CORRECT answer is:
A. I, II, III, IV, V   B. V, IV, III, II, I   C. III, I, IV, II, V   D. II, IV, I, V, III

16._____

17.
I. As some of his friends have noted, this antisocial attitude is an aberration for him, as he is normally quite extroverted and cheerful.
II. Many people have tried to evoke some of his normal geniality, but it has not worked, which is disconcerting.
III. It is now a commonly held belief that the only antidote to Johnny's stressful situation would be complete and total success on his exam.
IV. Upon learning of his pending exam, his roommates have agreed that his current mood is directly correlated to the test.
V. Upon being informed of an upcoming test in statistics, Johnny has started to act aloof and uninterested in social activities.
The CORRECT answer is:
A. I, V, II, III, IV   B. IV, III, I, V, II   C. II, IV, I, III, V   D. V, I, IV, II, III

17._____

18.
I. When viewing a star formation through the Spitzer Space Telescope, a person has a view of disruption.
II. The Spitzer Space Telescope challenges the commonly held thought that smooth gas clouds gracefully facilitate the creation of new stars.
III. The relative few stars can be attributed to the turbulence that these processes bring to the heavens.
IV. Through the telescope's lens, one can see the creation of a star that disrupts nearby space.
V. Recent models of star formation, aided by telescopes like Spitzer, recognize that stars interact with one another in their stellar neighborhood.
The CORRECT answer is:
A. IV, II, I, III, V   B. I, IV, II, V, III   C. III, I, V, IV, II   D. II, V, III, I, IV

18._____

19.
   I. In addition, models predicting the placement of electrons within the cloud describe one probability among many, instead of showing planet-like electrons orbiting a sun-like nucleus.
   II. Although the majority of us think of an atom's nucleus being orbited by electrons, the reality differs considerably from the stereotypical depiction.
   III. Oddly enough, it is mostly composed of empty space: its nucleus, made of protons and neutrons, makes up only about a billionth of the atom itself.
   IV. As many people know, the atom is the basic building block of matter.
   V. Researchers prefer to describe the electron movement as a "wave-pattern cloud."
   The CORRECT answer is:
   A. III, I, V, IV, II   B. V, III, IV, I, II   C. IV, III, II, V, I   D. II, V, I, III, IV

20.
   I. These buildings were thought to have been constructed upwards in order to thwart would-be attackers.
   II. Ancient Yemeni architects created a walled city that they called Shibam.
   III. Nowadays, with the planning of mile-high skyscrapers planned for construction, Shibam does not seem as impressive, but given their tools and knowledge at the time, the city will be held in esteem in architecturfal history books.
   IV. This wonder of the old world is now dubbed "Manhattan of the Desert".
   V. The city was composed of 500 buildings, ranging from five to eight stories high.
   The CORRECT answer is:
   A. II, IV, V, I, III   B. V, III, I, IV, II   C. IV, V, II, III, I   D. III, I, IV, II, V

21.
   I. Almost 2,000 years after being buried by falling ash from a volcanic eruption, the residents of Pompeii do reveal fascinating details about daily life in the Roman Empire.
   II. Pompeii's population, roughly 20,000 inhabitants, practiced several different religions.
   III. This is evidenced by temples dedicated to Egyptian gods, as well as Jewish temples and worshippers of Cybele.
   IV. While radically different in beliefs, Pompeii's citizens practiced all of these religions in peaceful co-existence with followers of the state religion.
   V. These people worshipped Jupiter and the Roman emperor.
   The CORRECT answer is:
   A. I, III, V, II, IV   B. II, IV, I, III, V   C. IV, I, III, V, II   D. III, II, IV, I, V

22. I.   Instead of driving there, I may just stay home and cook myself a big breakfast with toast, fruit, eggs, and bacon.
    II.   I was going to take a jog around the neighborhood to train for my race.
    III. As I woke up today, I realized that it would be yet another rainy day.
    IV.   Now, I will have to drive to the gymnasium that is on the opposite side of town.
    V.   After I eat, hopefully the rain will have gone away so I can train successfully.
    The CORRECT answer is:
    A. IV, I, II, V, III   B. III, II, IV, I, V   C. II, IV, I, III, V   D. V, III, II, I, IV

22._____

23. I.   Yesterday, he received a call from an H.R. representative of a firm in Chicago.
    II.   The H.R. rep asked William to fly out to Chicago for an interview and he even offered to pay for William's plane ticket.
    III. Having received such a generous offer, William could not say no to the interview.
    IV.   The interview will take place in one week, so William will spend the next few days researching the company's history.
    V.   William has been searching for a full-time job for the last few months.
    The CORRECT answer is:
    A. IV, II, III, I, V   B. V, II, I, IV, III   C. I, II, III, IV, V   D. V, I, II, III, IV

23._____

24. I.   I wonder when I'll feel well enough to go back to work.
    II.   I've tried eating chicken soup, drinking orange juice, taking Benadryl since the weekend.
    III. I finally decided to visit the doctor to see if I can get any stronger medicine to help me.
    IV.   My allergies have been terrible the last several days.
    V.   I've been blowing my nose, sneezing, and coughing the entire time.
    The CORRECT answer is:
    A. V, II, IV, III, I   B. I, III, II, IV, V   C. IV, V, II, III, I   D. II, III, V, I, IV

24._____

25. I.   Myrta is a sophomore in college and she's working on her degree in Special Education.
    II.   In order to prepare herself for her career, she works at a camp in the summer.
    III. All of the children who attend this camp have physical and mental disabilities.
    IV.   Myrta helps the kids get exercise and increase their social skills.
    V.   At the end of each summer, she cannot wait to start her career in Special Education.
    The CORRECT answer is:
    A. V, I, II, III, IV   B. I, II, III, IV, V   C. III, IV, V, I, II   D. V, IV, III, II, I

25._____

KEY (CORRECT ANSWERS)

1.	B	11.	A
2.	A	12.	C
3.	D	13.	D
4.	C	14.	C
5.	A	15.	A
6.	C	16.	D
7.	D	17.	D
8.	B	18.	B
9.	D	19.	C
10.	B	20.	A

21. A
22. B
23. D
24. C
25. B

PREPARING WRITTEN MATERIAL
PARAGRAPH REARRANGEMENT

EXAMINATION SECTION
TEST 1

DIRECTIONS: The sentences listed below are part of a meaningful paragraph, but they are not given in their proper order. You are to decide what would be the BEST order to put sentences to form a well-organized paragraph. Each sentence has a place in the paragraph; there are no extra sentences. *PRINT THE LETTER OF THE CORRECT ANSWER IN THE SPACE AT THE RIGHT.*

Questions 1-3.

DIRECTIONS: Questions 1 through 3 are to be answered on the basis of the following paragraph.

The CDC estimates that food-borne pathogens cause approximately 48 million illnesses, 3,000 deaths, and 128,000 hospitalizations in the United States each year. Contamination with disease-causing microbes called pathogens is usually due to improper food handling or storage. Other causes of food-borne diseases are toxic chemicals or other harmful substances in food and beverages. Food-borne diseases are illnesses caused when people consume contaminated food or beverages. More than 250 food-borne illnesses have been described, according to the United States Centers for Disease Control and Prevention (CDC).

1. When the five sentences are arranged in proper order, the paragraph starts with the sentence that begins:
   A. "Food-borne diseases..."
   B. "More than 250..."
   C. "Other causes of..."
   D. The CDC estimates..."

2. If the above paragraph were correctly organized, which of the following transition words would be appropriate to place at the beginning of the sentence that starts "The CDC estimates..."?
   A. With that said
   B. However
   C. To start off
   D. Ultimately

3. When the above paragraph is properly arranged, it ends with the words:
   A. "...Disease Control and Prevention (CDC).
   B. "...improper food handling or storage."
   C. "...United States each year."
   D. "...in food and beverages."

Questions 4-7.

DIRECTIONS: Questions 4 through 7 are to be answered on the basis of the following passage.

113

Her father, Abraham Quintanilla, who worked in the shipping department of a chemical plant and later opened a restaurant, had fronted a moderately successful band called Los Dinos ("The Guys") as a young man. Among them, her murder evoked an outpouring of grief comparable to that experienced by other Americans after the deaths of such major cultural figures as President John F. Kennedy. Selena had become an icon in the Hispanic community.

Selena Quintanilla was born in Lake Jackson, Texas, near Houston, on April 16, 1971. She had turned into a beloved figure to whom Mexican-Americans attached their aspirations and their feelings about their cultural identities. The violent death of beloved Tejano vocalist Selena on Mach 31, 1995 brought to an end more than just a promising musical career.

4. When arranged properly, the paragraph's opening sentence should start with:
   A. "Among them…"
   B. "The violent death…"
   C. "Her father, Abraham…"
   D. "Selena had become…"

4.____

5. In the second sentence listed above, "them" refers to
   A. Selena and her fans
   B. other non-Mexican Americans
   C. Selena and John F. Kennedy
   D. Mexican-Americans

5.____

6. After correctly organizing the paragraph, the author decides to split it into two separate paragraphs. Which of the following would begin the newly made second paragraph?
   A. "Selena had become…"
   B. "Selena Quintanilla was…"
   C. "The violent death…"
   D. "Her father, Abraham…"

6.____

7. When correctly organized, the final sentence of the paragraph should end end with the words:
   A. "…as a young man."
   B. "…on April 16, 1971."
   C. "…in the Hispanic community."
   D. "…a promising music career."

7.____

Questions 8-10.

DIRECTIONS: Questions 8 through 10 are to be answered on the basis of the following paragraph.

Whether Death takes the form of a decrepit old man, a grim reaper, or a ferryman, his visit is almost never welcome by the poor mortal who finds him at the door. Such is not the case in "Because I Could Not Stop for Death." Knowing that the woman has been keeping herself too busy in her daily life to remember Death, he "kindly" comes by to get her. Perhaps Dickinson's most famous work, "Because I Could Not Stop for Death" is generally considered to be one of the great masterpieces of American poetry. Here, Death is a gentleman, perhaps handsome and well-groomed, who makes a call at the home of a naïve young woman. The poem begins with a comment upon Death's politeness, although he surprises the woman with his visit. While most people would try to bar the door once they recognized his identity, this woman gives the impression that she is quite flattered to find herself in even this gentleman's favor. Death is personified, or described in terms of human characteristics, throughout literature. Figuratively speaking, this poem is about one woman's "date with death." Dickinson uses the personification of Death as a metaphor throughout the poem.

8. Which of the following sentence beginnings indicate the opening sentence of this paragraph?
   A. "Perhaps Dickinson's most..."
   B. "The poem begins with..."
   C. "Death is personified..."
   D. "Whether Death takes..."

   8.____

9. To whom does "his" refer to in the sentence that starts "While most people would..."?
   A. A gentleman
   B. Death
   C. People trying to avoid death
   D. Ms. Dickinson

   9.____

10. If the paragraph were correctly organized, the second to last sentence would end with:
    A. "...gentleman's favor."
    B. "...a naive young woman."
    C. "...of American poetry."
    D. "...throughout literature."

    10.____

Questions 11-13.

DIRECTIONS: Questions 11 through 13 are to be answered on the basis of the following paragraph.

Reformers such as Jacob Riis, author of *The Children of the Tenements* (1903), and George Creel, who with the assistance of Denver's juvenile court judge, Ben Lindsey, wrote *Children in Bondage* (1913), helped broaden awareness of the conditions under which many of the nation's poor children were reared. At the same time, changes were taking place in the way the childhood years were perceived. More and more Americans began to regard children as a national resource that deserved society's protection and guidance. In sharp contrast to these images of child workers worn down by the toil of their labor were the children of the middle class, who led quite different lives and whose progress was measured not in industrial output, but in ways increasingly seen as being vital to their development as productive citizens. Exhibitions of photographs of children employed in all sorts of economic pursuits, including those considered among the most dangerous and grueling, proved equally successful in pricking the public's conscience. When the United States was a nation of farms, shops, and small mills, the use of children to supplement a family's income was so common that it attracted little notice and even less concern. The nation's rapid and dramatic transformation into an industrialized society, however, changed the environment in which children labored and the conditions to which they were exposed.

11. When organized correctly, the third sentence in the above paragraph would start:
    A. "The nation's rapid..."
    B. "In sharp contrast..."
    C. "At the same time..."
    D. "Exhibitions of photographs..."

    11.____

12. If the author wanted to change the beginning of the topic sentence for this paragraph to "In the past," they would need to change which of the following?
    A. "Reformers such as..."
    B. "Exhibitions of photographs..."
    C. "More and more Americans..."
    D. "When the United States..."

    12.____

13. If the above paragraph was organized correctly, its ending words of the last sentence would be:

    13.____

A. "...as productive citizens."
B. "...and even less concern."
C. "...in pricking the public's conscience."
D. "...poor children were reared."

Questions 14-16.

DIRECTIONS: Questions 14 through 16 are to be answered on the basis of the following paragraph.

Here we outline a unique bivariate flood hazard assessment framework that accounts for the interactions between a primary oceanic flooding hazard, coastal water level, and fluvial flooding hazards. Common flood hazard assessment practices typically focus on one flood driver at a time and ignore potential compounding impacts. The results show that, in a warming climate, future sea level rise not only increases the failure probability, but also exacerbates the compounding effects of flood drivers. Using the notion of "failure probability," we also assess coastal flood hazard under different future sea level rise scenarios. Population and assets in coastal regions are threatened by both oceanic and fluvial flooding hazards.

14. When the sentences above are organized correctly, the paragraph starts with the sentence that begins:
    A. "The results show..."
    B. "Here we outline..."
    C. "Population and assets..."
    D. "Using the notion..."

14.____

15. If the author wanted to add the phrase "To sum up" to the above paragraph, he would insert it in front of the sentence that begins:
    A. "Using the notion..."
    B. "Common flood hazard..."
    C. "Here we outline..."
    D. "The results show..."

15.____

16. Assuming the paragraph were organized correctly, the second to last sentence would end:
    A. "...of flood drivers."
    B. "...level rise scenarios."
    C. "...fluvial flooding hazards."
    D. "...compounding impacts."

16.____

Questions 17-19.

DIRECTIONS: Questions 17 through 19 are to be answered on the basis of the following paragraph.

The adhesive stuck to a pig heart even when the surface was coated in blood, the team reported in the July 28 Science. Li, who did the research while at Harvard University, and colleagues also tested the glue in live rats with liver lacerations. A solution might be found under wet leaves on a forest floor, recent research suggests. For surgeons closing internal incisions, that's more than an annoyance. The right glue could hold wounds together as effectively as stitches and staples with less damage to the surrounding soft tissue, enabling safer surgical procedures. It stopped the rats' bleeding, and the animals didn't appear to suffer any bad reaction from the adhesive. Finding a great glue is a sticky task — especially if you want to attach to something as slick as the inside of the human body. Jianyu Li of McGill University in Montreal and colleagues have created a surgical glue that mimics the chemical recipe of goopy slime that slugs exude when they're startled. Using the glue to plug a hole in the pig heart worked so well that the heart still held in liquid after being inflated and deflated tens of thousands of times. Even the strongest human-made adhesives don't work well on wet surfaces like tissues and organs.

17. The above paragraph, when organized correctly, should begin with the words: 17.____
    A. "Finding a great..." B. "Using the glue..."
    C. "The adhesive stuck..." D. "It stopped the rats..."

18. If the author wanted to split the paragraph into two separate paragraphs, the   18.____
    first sentence of the second paragraph would begin:
    A. "For surgeons closing..." B. "Even the strongest..."
    C. "A solution might be..." D. "Jianyu Li of McGill..."

19. If the above paragraph were organized correctly, the final sentence would   19.____
    end with:
    A. "...recent research suggests." B. "...from the adhesive."
    C. "...like tissues and organs." D. "...thousands of times."

Questions 20-22.

DIRECTIONS: Questions 20 to 22 are to be answered on the basis of the following paragraph.

The signal from the spacecraft is gone, and within the next 45 seconds, so will be the spacecraft," Cassini project manager Earl Maize announced from the mission control center at NASA's Jet Propulsion Lab. The signal that Cassini had reached its destination arrived at Earth at 4:54 A.M., and cut out about a minute later as the spacecraft lost its battle with Saturn's atmosphere. I'm going to call this the end of mission. Project manager, off the net." With that, the mission control team erupted in applause, hugs and some tears. This has been an incredible mission, an incredible spacecraft, and you're all an incredible team. The spacecraft entered Saturn's atmosphere at about 3:31 A.M. PDT on September 15 and immediately began running through all of its stabilizing procedures to try to keep itself upright. Cassini went down fighting. After 20 years in space and 13 years orbiting Saturn, the veteran spacecraft spent its last 90 seconds or so firing its thrusters as hard as it could to keep sending Saturnian secrets back to Earth for as long as possible.

20. In the above paragraph, who does "you all" refer to in the sentence that begins   20.____
    "Congratulations"?
    A. All Americans B. Cassini
    C. Earl Maize D. The mission control team

21. If the sentence were organized correctly, the fourth sentence's last words   21.____
    would be:
    A. "...as long as possible." B. "...this amazing accomplishment."
    C. "...Saturn's atmosphere." D. "...off the net."

22. When organized correctly, the final sentence would end with the following: 22.____
    A. "...and some tears." B. "...went down fighting."
    C. "...Jet Propulsion Lab." D. "...keep itself upright."

Questions 23-25.

DIRECTIONS: Questions 23 through 25 are to be answered on the basis of the following paragraph.

As the first African-American woman to carry mail, she stood out on the trail — and became a Wild West legend. Born Mary Fields in around 1832, Fields was born into slavery, and like many other enslaved people, her exact date of birth is not known. Rumor had it that she'd fending off an angry pack of wolves with her rifle, had "the temperament of a grizzly bear," and was not above a gunfight. Bandits beware: In 1890s Montana, would-be mail thieves didn't stand a chance against Stagecoach Mary. Even the place of her birth is questionable, though historians have pinpointed Hickman County, Tennessee as the most likely location. At the time, slaves were treated like pieces of property; their numbers were recorded in record books, their names were not. But how much of Stagecoach Mary's story is myth? The hard-drinking, quick-shooting mail carrier sported two guns, men's clothing, and a bad attitude.

23. Who does "she'd" refer to in the sentence that begins "Rumor had it..."? 23.____
    A. An anonymous African-American   B. Hickman County
    C. A mail thief   D. Stagecoach Mary

24. If the author were interested in splitting this paragraph into two separate paragraphs, the topic sentence of the second paragraph would begin: 24.____
    A. "At the time..."   B. "Born Mary Fields..."
    C. "Bandits beware..."   D. "As the first..."

25. When organized correctly, the final sentence of the paragraph would end with the words: 25.____
    A. "...their names were not."   B. "...above a gunfight."
    C. "...against Stagecoach Mary."   D. "...a Wild West legend."

KEY (CORRECT ANSWERS)

1.	A	11.	C
2.	D	12.	D
3.	C	13.	A
4.	B	14.	C
5.	D	15.	D
6.	B	16.	B
7.	A	17.	A
8.	C	18.	C
9.	B	19.	B
10.	A	20.	D

21. C
22. A
23. D
24. B
25. A

TEST 2

DIRECTIONS: Each question or incomplete statement is followed by several suggested answers or completions. Select the one that BEST answers the question or completes the statement. *PRINT THE LETTER OF THE CORRECT ANSWER IN THE SPACE AT THE RIGHT.*

Questions 1-3.

DIRECTIONS: Questions 1 through 3 are to be answered on the basis of the following paragraph.

The majority of people who develop these issues are athletes who participate in popular high-impact sports, especially football. Although most people who suffer a concussion experience initial bouts of dizziness, nausea, and drowsiness, these symptoms often disappear after a few days. Although both new sports regulations and improvements in helmet technology can help protect players, the sports media and fans alike bear some of the responsibility for reducing the incidence of these devastating injuries. These psychological problems can include depression, anxiety, memory loss, inability to concentrate, and aggression. In extreme cases, people suffering from CTE have even committed suicide or homicide. The long-term effects of concussions, however, are less understood and far more severe. Recent studies suggest that people who suffer multiple concussions are at a significant risk for developing chronic traumatic encephalopathy (CTE), a degenerative brain disorder that causes a variety of dangerous mental and emotional problems to arise weeks, months, or even years after the initial injury. Chronic Traumatic Encephalopathy Concussions are brain injuries that occur when a person receives a blow to the head, face, or neck.

1. When organized correctly, the first sentence of the paragraph begins with: 1.____
   A. "Recent studies suggest..."   B. "The long-term effects..."
   C. "Although both new..."   D. "Chronic Traumatic..."

2. Upon ordering the paragraph correctly, the author wishes to substitute for a 2.____
   word in sentence four that means "progressive irreversible deterioration."
   Which word does the author wish to replace?
   A. Anxiety   B. Degenerative
   C. Responsibility   D. Devastating

3. If put in the right order, the paragraph's last words would be: 3.____
   A. "...to the head, face, or neck."
   B. "...committed suicide or homicide."
   C. "...these devastating injuries."
   D. "...far more severe."

2 (#2)

Questions 4-8.

DIRECTIONS: Questions 4 through 8 are to be answered on the basis of the following paragraph.

These controversies were settled by the 1977 treaty, which provided for a twenty-two-year period of U.S. withdrawal and turnover of the canal to Panama. For its first 85 years the canal was operate exclusively by the United States government as an international maritime passage, according to the 1903 Hay-Buneau-Varilla Treaty and the 1977 Carter-Torrijos Treaty that replaced it. Panamanian and other critics pointed out that the United States took unfair advantage of the newly independent republic (separated from Colombia in 1903, with the help of the United States) to impose conditions for near-sovereign ownership; complained that it exceeded its original concession by creating a strategic military complex with fourteen bases and numerous intelligence sites; and asserted that it created a virtual state within a state by establishing public agencies and enterprises in the 500-plus square miles of territory it controlled in the Canal Zone. One of the world's great engineering projects, the canal was controversial because of the method by which the United States gained the concession (by negotiating a treaty with a French shareholder temporarily representing Panama) and its operation of the utility with regard to the interests of Panama. Built between 1904 and 1914, the canal shortened maritime voyages considerably. The Panama Canal is a 51-mile ship canal with six pairs of locks that crosses the Isthmus of Panama and allows vessels to transit between the Caribbean Sea and the Pacific Ocean. Under the latter treaty, the canal was turned over in 1999 to the Republic of Panama, which has operated it ever since.

4. When organized correctly, the sentence AFTERs the topic sentence should begin: 4.____
   A. "Built between 1904…"   B. "The Panama Canal…"
   C. "These controversies…"   D. "Panamanian and other…"

5. If the author ordered the sentences correctly, one sentence that provides evidence of controversy surrounding the Panama Canal would be Sentence 5.____
   A. 7   B. 5   C. 1   D. 2

6. When correctly ordered, the last words of the paragraph would be: 6.____
   A. "…the canal to Panama."   B. "…in the Canal Zone."
   C. "…and the Pacific Ocean."   D. "…to the interests of Panama."

7. What "latter treaty" is the sentence that begins "Under the latter treaty…" referring to in the paragraph? 7.____
   A. The Treaty of Panama   B. The Hay-Buneau-Varilla Treaty
   C. The Carter-Torrijos Treaty   D. Both B and C

8. When organized correctly, the sentence that ends "…in the Canal Zone" would be preceded by the sentence that begins: 8.____
   A. "The Panama Canal…"   B. "These controversies were…"
   C. "For its first…"   D. "One of the world's great…"

Questions 9-11.

DIRECTIONS: Questions 9 through 11 are to be answered on the basis of the following paragraph.

Such incidents revolved around many issues, including, among others, job security, wages, occupational safety, and, especially, the eight-hour day. The Haymarket Riot of 1886 grew out of a long string of circumstances that eventually culminated in an unfortunate incident. Not only were skilled craftsmen seeing their professions disappear in the face of machines operated by unskilled labor, but the length of hours in the workday lengthened and could range from ten to twelve and even longer in some specific instances. It was this last issue that was particularly important as the Industrial Revolution truly swept over America. Regardless of who might have been at fault in a labor struggle, each moment of violent upheaval had serious consequences. During the post-Civil War era, there were periods of labor upheaval both in Chicago and across the nation. Each of these topics played an important role in labor unrest as the climate in the country between workers and the state reached fever pitch. At issue were several key points: the continued growth of the Industrial Revolution and its impact on society, the movement for the eight-hour workday, worker dissatisfaction, suppression of labor activities by various government authorities, and the growth of radicalism in the United States.

9. If the author were to put the paragraph in the correct order, the third sentence would begin with the words:
    A. "Each of these…"
    B. "It was this last…"
    C. "Not only were skilled…"
    D. "The Haymarket Riot…"

10. The author has determined that one paragraph is too long, so they wish to split it into two paragraphs and change the start of the new paragraph to "Dating back to". The sentence that the author would need to alter slightly currently begins:
    A. "The Haymarket Riot…"
    B. "Each of these topics…"
    C. "During the post-Civil…"
    D. "Not only were…"

11. When organized correctly, the last sentence of the paragraph would end with the words:
    A. "…an unfortunate incident."
    B. "…some specific instances."
    C. "…in the United States."
    D. "…across the nation."

Questions 12-14.

DIRECTIONS: Questions 12 through 14 are to be answered on the basis of the following paragraph.

Using an experimental design, they find no evidence that the use of Twitter improves students' learning. The authors assess students across three different institutions to see if the use of Twitter improves learning outcomes relative to a traditional Learning Management System. Ever since Becker and Watts (1996) found that economic educators rely heavily on "chalk and talk" as a primary teaching method, economic educators have been seeking new ways to engage students and improve learning outcomes. Recently, the use of social media as a pedagogical tool in economics has received increasing interest.

12. When organized correctly, the paragraph would begin with the words: 12.____
    A. "Using an…"   B. "Recently, the…"
    C. "The authors…"   D. "Ever since…"

13. In the sentence that begins "Using an experimental…", to whom does "they"   13.____
    refer?
    A. Social media users   B. Becker and Watts
    C. Economic educators   D. Different institutions

14. If the author wanted to start the last sentence with "With that said…", they   14.____
    would be adding it to the sentence that currently starts:
    A. "Using an…"   B. "The authors…"
    C. "Recently, the…" D. "Ever since…"

Questions 15-17.

DIRECTIONS: Questions 15 through 17 are to be answered on the basis of the following paragraph.

Teaching the topic of genetics in relationship to ancestry and race generates many questions, and requires a teaching strategy that encourages perspective-based exploration and discussion. We have developed a set of dialogues for discussing the complex science of genetics, ancestry, and race that is contextualized in real human interactions and that contends with the social and ethical implications of this science. This article provides some brief historical and scientific context for these dialogues, describes their development, and relates how we have used them in different ways to engage diverse groups of science learners. The dialogue series can be incorporated into classroom or informal science education settings. After listening to or performing the dialogues and participating in a discussion, students will: (1) recognize misunderstandings about the relationship between DNA and race; (2) describe how DNA testing services assign geographic ancestry; (3) explain how scientific findings have been used historically to promote institutionalized racism and the role personal biases can play in science; (4) identify situations in their own life that have affected their understanding of genetics and race; and (5) discuss the potential consequences of the racialization of medicine as well as other fallacies about the connection of science and race.

15. If the author organized the above paragraph correctly, the fourth sentence   15.____
    would end with the words:
    A. "…connection of science and race."
    B. "…implications of this science."
    C. "…exploration and discussion."
    D. "…science education settings."

16. The author wishes to split the paragraph into two distinct paragraphs. When   16.____
    organized, the last sentence of the first paragraph would begin:
    A. "We have developed…"   B. "This article proves…"
    C. "The dialogue series…" D. "Teaching the topic…"

17. When organized correctly, the last sentence would begin with the words: 17._____
    A. "After listening to..." B. "Teaching the topic..."
    C. "We have developed..." D. "This article provides..."

Questions 18-20.

DIRECTIONS: Questions 18 through 20 are to be answered on the basis of the following paragraph.

For example, Canadian Immigration officers have the power to deny persons with OWI convictions from crossing the border into Canada. Individuals who have been acquitted of an OWI can still be stopped at the border and denied entry. Some restrictions, however, are not known to individuals that have been charged with an OWI. In fact, if you have been arrested or convicted for driving under the influence of drugs or alcohol, regardless of whether it was a felony or a misdemeanor, you may be criminally inadmissible to Canada or denied entry. In order to receive an eTA, individuals have to disclose their criminal convictions, which may bar them from entering Canada. The restrictions imposed by an OWI conviction can be quite burdensome. Even if you will not be driving in Canada, you can still be denied entry. This stringent border patrol comes as a surprise to many U.S. citizens. Canadian Immigration Officials have introduced a new entry requirement, known as an Electronic Travel Authorization (eTA).

18. When organized correctly, the topic sentence of the paragraph would begin with the words: 18._____
    A. "This stringent border..." B. "In fact, if..."
    C. "Canadian Immigration Officials..." D. "The restrictions imposed..."

19. Once properly ordered, it would make the most sense to insert the words "With that being the case..." in front of the sentence that currently begins: 19._____
    A. "The restrictions imposed..." B. "For example..."
    C. "Canadian Immigration Officials..." D. "Even if you will..."

20. If the author were to put the paragraph in correct order, the second to last sentence would end with the words: 20._____
    A. "...border into Canada." B. "...from entering Canada."
    C. "...to many U.S. citizens." D. "...to Canada or denied entry."

Questions 21-25.

DIRECTIONS: Questions 21 through 25 are to be answered on the basis of the following paragraph.

Many instructors at the college level require that you use scholarly articles as sources when writing a research paper. Scholarly or peer-reviewed articles are written by experts in academic or professional fields. They are excellent sources for finding out what has been studied or researched on a topic as well as to find bibliographies that point to other relevant sources of information. Peer-reviewed journals require that articles are read and evaluated by experts in the field before they are accepted for publication. Although most scholarly articles are refereed or peer reviewed, some are not. Generally, instructors are happy with either peer-reviewed or scholarly articles, but if your article HAS to be peer-reviewed, you will need to find that information in the front of the journal, or use Ulrich's Periodicals Directory (Reference Z6941 U5) located behind the Reference Desk on the 2nd floor of the library. Look up your title and look for the Document Type: Journal, Academic/Scholarly. Articles that are peer-reviewed will have an arrow to the left of the title.

21. When organized correctly, the introductory sentence would begin with the words: 21.____
    A. "They are excellent..." B. "Peer-reviewed journals..."
    C. "Many instructors at..." D. "Look up your..."

22. In the sentence that begins "They are", to what/whom does "They" refer? 22.____
    A. Scholarly articles B. Instructors
    C. Peers D. Library directory

23. If the author were interested in splitting up the paragraph into two separate paragraphs, the topic sentence of the second paragraph would begin: 23.____
    A. "Many instructors at..." B. "Peer-reviewed journals..."
    C. "Generally instructors are..." D. "Scholarly or peer-reviewed..."

24. When organized correctly, the third sentence of the paragraph would end with the words: 24.____
    A. "...a research paper." B. "...of the title."
    C. "...of the library." D. "...sources of information."

25. If the author were to organize the paragraph correctly, the paragraph would end with the words: 25.____
    A. "...some are not." B. "...a research paper."
    C. "...or professional fields." D. "...of the title."

KEY (CORRECT ANSWERS)

1.	D	11.	B
2.	B	12.	D
3.	C	13.	B
4.	A	14.	A
5.	B	15.	D
6.	A	16.	C
7.	C	17.	A
8.	D	18.	D
9.	A	19.	C
10.	C	20.	B

21. C
22. A
23. B
24. D
25. D

PREPARING WRITTEN MATERIAL
EXAMINATION SECTION
TEST 1

DIRECTIONS: Each question or incomplete statement is followed by several suggested answers or completions. Select the one that BEST answers the question or completes the statement. *PRINT THE LETTER OF THE CORRECT ANSWER IN THE SPACE AT THE RIGHT.*

1. The one of the following sentences which is LEAST acceptable from the viewpoint of correct usage is:
    A. The police thought the fugitive to be him.
    B. The criminals set a trap for whoever would fall into it.
    C. It is ten years ago since the fugitive fled from the city.
    D. The lecturer argued that criminals are usually cowards.
    E. The police removed four bucketfuls of earth from the scene of the crime.

1.____

2. The one of the following sentences which is LEAST acceptable from the viewpoint of correct usage is:
    A. The patrolman scrutinized the report with great care.
    B. Approaching the victim of the assault, two bruises were noticed by the patrolman.
    C. As soon as I had broken down the door, I stepped into the room.
    D. I observed the accused loitering near the building, which was closed at the time.
    E. The storekeeper complained that his neighbor was guilty of violating a local ordinance.

2.____

3. The one of the following sentences which is LEAST acceptable from the viewpoint of correct usage is:
    A. I realized immediately that he intended to assault the woman, so I disarmed him.
    B. It was apparent that Mr. Smith's explanation contained many inconsistencies.
    C. Despite the slippery condition of the street, he managed to stop the vehicle before injuring the child.
    D. Not a single one of them wish, despite the damage to property, to make a formal complaint.
    E. The body was found lying on the floor.

3.____

4. The one of the following sentences which contains NO error in usage is:
    A. After the robbers left, the proprietor stood tied in his chair for about two hours before help arrived.
    B. In the cellar I found the watchman's hat and coat.
    C. The persons living in adjacent apartments stated that they had heard no unusual noises.

4.____

D. Neither a knife or any firearms were found in the room.
E. Walking down the street, the shouting of the crowd indicated that something was wrong.

5. The one of the following sentences which contains NO error in usage is: 5.____
   A. The policeman lay a firm hand on the suspect's shoulder.
   B. It is true that neither strength nor agility are the most important requirement for a good patrolman.
   C. Good citizens constantly strive to do more than merely comply the restraints imposed by society.
   D. No decision was made as to whom the prize should be awarded.
   E. Twenty years is considered a severe sentence for a felony.

6. Which of the following sentences is NOT expressed in standard English usage?   5.____
   A. The victim reached a pay-phone booth and manages to call police headquarters.
   B. By the time the call was received, the assailant had left the scene.
   C. The victim has been a respected member of the community for the past eleven years.
   D. Although the lighting was bad and the shadows were deep, the storekeeper caught sight of the attacker.
   E. Additional street lights have since been installed, and the patrols have been strengthened.

7. Which of the following sentences is NOT expressed in standard English usage?   7.____
   A. The judge upheld the attorney's right to question the witness about the missing glove.
   B. To be absolutely fair to all parties is the jury's chief responsibility.
   C. Having finished the report, a loud noise in the next room startled the sergeant.
   D. The witness obviously enjoyed having played a part in the proceedings.
   E. The sergeant planned to assign the case to whoever arrived first.

8. In which of the following sentences is a word misused?   8.____
   A. As a matter of principle, the captain insisted that the suspect's partner be brought for questioning.
   B. The principle suspect had been detained at the station house for most of the day.
   C. The principal in the crime had no previous criminal record, but his closest associate had been convicted of felonies on two occasions.
   D. The interest payments had been made promptly, but the firm had been drawing upon the principal for these payments.
   E. The accused insisted that his high school principal would furnish him a character reference.

9. Which of the following statements is ambiguous?
    A. Mr. Sullivan explained why Mr. Johnson had been dismissed from his job.
    B. The storekeeper told the patrolman he had made a mistake.
    C. After waiting three hours, the patients in the doctor's office were sent home.
    D. The janitor's duties were to maintain the building in good shape and to answer tenants' complaints.
    E. The speed limit should, in my opinion, be raised to sixty miles an hour on that stretch of road.

9.____

10. In which of the following is the punctuation or capitalization faulty?
    A. The accident occurred at an intersection in the Kew Gardens section of Queens, near the bus stop.
    B. The sedan, not the convertible, was struck in the side.
    C. Before any of the patrolmen had left the police car received an important message from headquarters.
    D. The dog that had been stolen was returned to his master, John Dempsey, who lived in East Village.
    E. The letter had been sent to 12 Hillside Terrace, Rutland, Vermont 05702.

10.____

Questions 11-25.

DIRECTIONS: Questions 11 through 25 are to be answered in accordance with correct English usage; that is, standard English rather than nonstandard or substandard. Nonstandard and substandard English includes words or expressions usually classified as slang, dialect, illiterate, etc., which are not generally accepted as correct in current written communication. Standard English also requires clarity, proper punctuation and capitalization and appropriate use of words. Write the letter of the sentence NOT expressed in standard English usage in the space at the right.

11. A. There were three witnesses to the accident.
    B. At least three witnesses were found to testify for the plaintiff.
    C. Three of the witnesses who took the stand was uncertain about the defendant's competence to drive.
    D. Only three witnesses came forward to testify for the plaintiff.
    E. The three witnesses to the accident were pedestrians.

11.____

12. A. The driver had obviously drunk too many martinis before leaving for home.
    B. The boy who drowned had swum in these same waters many times before.
    C. The petty thief had stolen a bicycle from a private driveway before he was apprehended.
    D. The detectives had brung in the heroin shipment they intercepted.
    E. The passengers had never ridden in a converted bus before.

12.____

13. A. Between you and me, the new platoon plan sounds like a good idea.
    B. Money from an aunt's estate was left to his wife and he.
    C. He and I were assigned to the same patrol for the first time in two months.
    D. Either you or he should check the front door of that store.
    E. The captain himself was not sure of the witness's reliability.

13.____

14. A. The alarm had scarcely begun to ring when the explosion occurred.
    B. Before the firemen arrived at the scene, the second story had been destroyed.
    C. Because of the dense smoke and heat, the firemen could hardly approach the now-blazing structure.
    D. According to the patrolman's report, there wasn't nobody in the store when the explosion occurred.
    E. The sergeant's suggestion was not at all unsound, but no one agreed with him.

14.____

15. A. The driver and the passenger they were both found to be intoxicated.
    B. The driver and the passenger talked slowly and not too clearly.
    C. Neither the driver nor his passengers were able to give a coherent account of the accident.
    D. In a corner of the room sat the passenger, quietly dozing.
    E. the driver finally told a strange and unbelievable story, which the passenger contradicted.

15.____

16. A. Under the circumstances I decided not to continue my examination of the premises.
    B. There are many difficulties now not comparable with those existing in 1960.
    C. Friends of the accused were heard to announce that the witness had better been away on the day of the trial.
    D. The two criminals escaped in the confusion that followed the explosion.
    E. The aged man was struck by the considerateness of the patrolman's offer.

16.____

17. A. An assemblage of miscellaneous weapons lay on the table.
    B. Ample opportunities were given to the defendant to obtain counsel.
    C. The speaker often alluded to his past experience with youthful offenders in the armed forces.
    D. The sudden appearance of the truck aroused my suspicions.
    E. Her studying had a good affect on her grades in high school.

17.____

18. A. He sat down in the theater and began to watch the movie.
    B. The girl had ridden horses since she was four years old.
    C. Application was made on behalf of the prosecutor to cite the witness for contempt.
    D. The bank robber, with his two accomplices, were caught in the act.
    E. His story is simply not credible.

18.____

19. A. The angry boy said that he did not like those kind of friends.
    B. The merchant's financial condition was so precarious that he felt he must avail himself of any offer of assistance.
    C. He is apt to promise more than he can perform.
    D. Looking at the messy kitchen, the housewife felt like crying.
    E. A clerk was left in charge of the stolen property.

19.____

20. A. His wounds were aggravated by prolonged exposure to sub-freezing temperatures.
    B. The prosecutor remarked that the witness was not averse to changing his story each time he was interviewed.
    C. The crime pattern indicated that the burglars were adapt in the handling of explosives.
    D. His rigid adherence to a fixed plan brought him into renewed conflict with his subordinates.
    E. He had anticipated that the sentence would be delivered by noon.

20.____

21. A. The whole arraignment procedure is badly in need of revision.
    B. After his glasses were broken in the fight, he would of gone to the optometrist if he could.
    C. Neither Tom nor Jack brought his lunch to work.
    D. He stood aside until the quarrel was over.
    E. A statement in the psychiatrist's report disclosed that the probationer vowed to have his revenge.

21.____

22. A. His fiery and intemperate speech to the striking employees fatally affected any chance of a future reconciliation.
    B. The wording of the statute has been variously construed.
    C. The defendant's attorney, speaking in the courtroom, called the official a demagogue who contempuously disregarded the judge's orders.
    D. The baseball game is likely to be the most exciting one this year.
    E. The mother divided the cookies among her two children.

22.____

23. A. There was only a bed and a dresser in the dingy room.
    B. John was one of the few students that have protested the new rule.
    C. It cannot be argued that the child's testimony is negligible; it is, on the contrary, of the greatest importance.
    D. The basic criterion for clearance was so general that officials resolved any doubts in favor of dismissal.
    E. Having just returned from a long vacation, the officer found the city unbearably hot.

23.____

24. A. The librarian ought to give more help to small children.
    B. The small boy was criticized by the teacher because he often wrote careless.
    C. It was generally doubted whether the women would permit the use of her apartment for intelligence operations.
    D. The probationer acts differently every time the officer visits him.
    E. Each of the newly appointed officers has 12 years of service.

24.____

25. A. The North is the most industrialized region in the country.
    B. L. Patrick Gray 3d, the bureau's acting director, stated that, while "rehabilitation is fine" for some convicted criminals, "it is a useless gesture for those who resist every such effort."
    C. Careless driving, faulty mechanism, narrow or badly kept roads all play their part in causing accidents.
    D. The childrens' books were left in the bus.
    E. It was a matter of internal security; consequently, he felt no inclination to rescind his previous order.

25.____

KEY (CORRECT ANSWERS)

1. C
2. B
3. D
4. C
5. E

6. A
7. C
8. B
9. B
10. C

11. C
12. D
13. B
14. D
15. A

16. C
17. E
18. D
19. A
20. C

21. B
22. E
23. B
24. B
25. D

TEST 2

DIRECTIONS: Each question or incomplete statement is followed by several suggested answers or completions. Select the one that BEST answers the question or completes the statement. *PRINT THE LETTER OF THE CORRECT ANSWER IN THE SPACE AT THE RIGHT.*

Questions 1-6.

DIRECTIONS: Each of Questions 1 through 6 consists of a statement which contains a word (one of those underlined) that is either incorrectly used because it is not in keeping with the meaning the quotation is evidently intended to convey, or is misspelled. There is only one INCORRECT word in each quotation. Of the four underlined words, determine if the first one should be replaced by the word lettered A, the second replaced by the word lettered B, the third replaced by the word lettered C, or the fourth replaced by the word lettered D.

1. Whether one depends on <u>fluorescent</u> or artificial light or both, adequate <u>standards</u> should be <u>maintained</u> by means of <u>systematic</u> tests. 1.____
   A. natural   B. safeguards   C. established   D. routine

2. A police officer has to be <u>prepared</u> to assume his <u>knowledge</u> as a social <u>scientist</u> in the <u>community</u>. 2.____
   A. forced   B. role   C. philosopher   D. street

3. It is <u>practically</u> impossible to <u>indicate</u> whether a sentence is <u>too</u> long simply by <u>measuring</u> its length. 3.____
   A. almost   B. tell   C. very   D. guessing

4. Strong <u>leaders</u> are <u>required</u> to organize a community for delinquency prevention and for <u>dissemination</u> of organized <u>crime</u> and drug addiction. 4.____
   A. tactics   B. important   C. control   D. meetings

5. The <u>demonstrators</u> who were taken to the Criminal Courts building in <u>Manhattan</u> (because it was large enough to <u>accommodate</u> them), contended that the arrests were <u>unwarranted</u>. 5.____
   A. demonstraters   B. Manhatten
   C. accomodate   D. unwarranted

6. They were <u>guaranteed</u> a calm <u>atmosphere</u>, free from <u>harassment</u>, which would be conducive to quiet consideration of the <u>indictments</u>. 6.____
   A. guarenteed   B. atmspher
   C. harassment   D. inditements

Questions 7-11.

DIRECTIONS: Each of Questions 7 through 11 consists of a statement containing four words in capital letters. One of these words in capital letters is not in keeping with the meaning which the statement is evidently intended to carry. The four words in capital letters in each statement are reprinted after the statement. Print the capital letter preceding the one of the four words which does MOST to spoil the true meaning of the statement in the space at the right.

7. Retirement and pension systems are essential not only to provide employees with with a means of support in the future, but also to prevent longevity and CHARITABLE considerations from UPSETTING the PROMOTIONAL opportunities RETIRED members of the career service. 7.____
   A. charitable   B. upsetting   C. promotional   D. retired

8. Within each major DIVISION in a properly set up public or private organization, provision is made so that each NECESSARY activity is CARED for and lines of authority and responsibility are clear-cut and INFINITE. 8.____
   A. division   B. necessary   C. cared   D. infinite

9. In public service, the scale of salaries paid must be INCIDENTAL to the services rendered, with due CONSIDERATION for the attraction of the desired MANPOWER and for the maintenance of a standard of living COMMENSURATE with the work to be performed. 9.____
   A. incidental   B. consideration
   C. manpower   D. commensurate

10. An understanding of the AIMS of an organization by the staff will AID greatly in increasing the DEMAND of the correspondence work of the office, and will to a large extent DETERMINE the nature of the correspondence. 10.____
    A. aims   B. aid   C. demand   D. determine

11. BECAUSE the Civil Service Commission strongly feels that the MERIT system is a key factor in the MAINTENANCE of democratic government, it has adopted as one of its major DEFENSES the progressive democratization of its own procedures in dealing with candidates for positions in the public service. 11.____
    A. Because   B. merit   C. maintenance   D. defenses

Questions 12-14.

DIRECTIONS: Questions 12 through 14 consist of one sentence each. Each sentence contains an incorrectly used word. First, decide which is the incorrectly used word. Then, from among the options given, decide which word, when substituted for the incorrectly used word, makes the meaning of the sentence clear.
EXAMPLE:
The U.S. national income exhibits a pattern of long term deflection.
   A. reflection   B. subjection   C. rejoicing   D. growth

The word *deflection* in the sentence does not convey the meaning the sentence evidently intended to convey. The word *growth* (Answer D), when substituted for the word *deflection*, makes the meaning of the sentence clear. Accordingly, the answer to the question is D.

12. The study commissioned by the joint committee fell compassionately short of the mark and would have to be redone.
    A. successfully   B. insignificantly
    C. experimentally   D. woefully

13. He will not idly exploit any violation of the provisions of the order.
    A. tolerate   B. refuse   C. construe   D. guard

14. The defendant refused to be virile and bitterly protested service.
    A. irked   B. feasible   C. docile   D. credible

Questions 15-25.

DIRECTIONS: Questions 15 through 25 consist of short paragraphs. Each paragraph contains one word which is INCORRECTLY used because it is NOT in keeping with the meaning of the paragraph. Find the word in each paragraph which is INCORRECTLY used and then select as the answer the suggested word which should be substituted for the incorrectly used word.

SAMPLE QUESTION:
In determining who is to do the work in your unit, you will have to decide just who does what from day to day. One of your lowest responsibilities is to assign work so that everybody gets a fair share and that everyone can do his part well.
    A. new   B. old   C. important   D. performance

EXPLANATION:
The word which is NOT in keeping with the meaning of the paragraph is *lowest*. This is the INCORRECTLY used word. The suggested word *important* would be in keeping with the meaning of the paragraph and should be substituted for *lowest*. Therefore, the CORRECT answer is choice C.

15. If really good practice in the elimination of preventable injuries is to be achieved and held in any establishment, top management must refuse full and definite responsibility and must apply a good share of its attention to the task.
    A. accept   B. avoidable   C. duties   D. problem

16. Recording the human face for identification is by no means the only service performed by the camera in the field of investigation. When the trial of any issue takes place, a word picture is sought to be distorted to the court of incidents, occurrences, or events which are in dispute.
    A. appeals   B. description   C. portrayed   D. deranged

4 (#2)

17. In the collection of physical evidence, it cannot be emphasized too strongly that a haphazard systematic search at the scene of the crime is vital. Nothing must be overlooked. Often the only leads in a case will come from the results of this search.
    A. important
    B. investigation
    C. proof
    D. thorough

    17.____

18. If an investigator has reason to suspect that the witness is mentally stable, or a habitual drunkard, he should leave no stone unturned in his investigation to determine if the witness was under the influence of liquor or drugs, or was mentally unbalanced either at the time of the occurrence to which he testified or at the time of the trial.
    A. accused
    B. clue
    C. deranged
    D. question

    18.____

19. The use of records is a valuable step in crime investigation and is the main reason every department should maintain accurate reports. Crimes are not committed through the use of departmental records alone but from the use of all records, of almost every type, wherever they may be found and whenever they give any incidental information regarding the criminal.
    A. accidental
    B. necessary
    C. reported
    D. solved

    19.____

20. In the years since passage of the Harrison Narcotic Act of 1914, making the possession of opium amphetamines illegal in most circumstances, drug use has become a subject of considerable scientific interest and investigation. There is at present a voluminous literature on drug use of various kinds.
    A. ingestion
    B. derivatives
    C. addiction
    D. opiates

    20.____

21. Of course, the fact that criminal laws are extremely patterned in definition does not mean that the majority of persons who violate them are dealt with as criminals. Quite the contrary, for a great many forbidden acts are voluntarily engaged in within situations of privacy and go unobserved and unreported.
    A. symbolic
    B. casual
    C. scientific
    D. broad-gauged

    21.____

22. The most punitive way to study punishment is to focus attention on the pattern of punitive action: to study how a penalty is applied, too study what is done to or taken from an offender.
    A. characteristic
    B. degrading
    C. objective
    D. distinguished

    22.____

23. The most common forms of punishment in times past have been death, physical torture, mutilation, branding, public humiliation, fines, forfeits of property, banishment, transportation, and imprisonment. Although this list is by no means differentiated, practically every form of punishment has had several variations and applications.
    A. specific
    B. simple
    C. exhaustive
    D. characteristic

    23.____

24. There is another important line of inference between ordinary and professional criminals, and that is the source from which they are recruited. The professional criminal seems to be drawn from legitimate employment and, in many instances, from parallel vocations or pursuits. 24._____
    A. demarcation   B. justification   C. superiority   D. reference

25. He took the position that the success of the program was insidious on getting additional revenue. 25._____
    A. reputed   B. contingent   C. failure   D. indeterminate

KEY (CORRECT ANSWERS)

1.	A		11.	D
2.	B		12.	D
3.	B		13.	A
4.	C		14.	C
5.	D		15.	A
6.	C		16.	C
7.	D		17.	D
8.	D		18.	C
9.	A		19.	D
10.	C		20.	B

21. D
22. C
23. C
24. A
25. B

TEST 3

DIRECTIONS: Each question or incomplete statement is followed by several suggested answers or completions. Select the one that BEST answers the question or completes the statement. *PRINT THE LETTER OF THE CORRECT ANSWER IN THE SPACE AT THE RIGHT.*

Questions 1-5.

DIRECTIONS: Questions 1 through 5 are to be answered on the basis of the following.

    You are a supervising officer in an investigative unit. Earlier in the day, you directed Detectives Tom Dixon and Sal Mayo to investigate a reported assault and robbery in a liquor store within your area of jurisdiction.
    Detective Dixon has submitted to you a preliminary investigative report containing the following information:

- At 1630 hours on 2/20, arrived at Joe's Liquor Store at 350 SW Avenue with Detective Mayo to investigate A & R.
- At store interviewed Rob Ladd, store manager, who stated that he and Joe Brown (store owner) had been stuck up about ten minutes prior to our arrival.
- Ladd described the robbers as male whites in their late teens or early twenties. Further stated that one of the robbers displayed what appeared to be an automatic pistol as he entered the store, and said, *Give us the money or we'll kill you.* Ladd stated that Brown then reached under the counter where he kept a loaded .38 caliber pistol. Several shots followed, and Ladd threw himself to the floor.
- The robbers fled, and Ladd didn't know if any money had been taken.
- At this point, Ladd realized that Brown was unconscious on the floor and bleeding from a head wound.
- Ambulance called by Ladd, and Brown was removed by same to General Hospital.
- Personally interviewed John White, 382 Dartmouth Place, who stated he was inside store at the time of occurrence. White states that he hid behind a wine display upon hearing someone say, *Give us the money.* He then heard shots and saw two young men run from the store to a yellow car parked at the curb. White was unable to further describe auto. States the taller of the two men drove the car away while the other sat on passenger side in front.
- Recovered three spent .38 caliber bullets from premises and delivered them to Crime Lab.
- To General Hospital at 1800 hours but unable to interview Brown, who was under sedation and suffering from shock and a laceration of the head.
- Alarm #12487 transmitted for car and occupants.
- Case Active.

    Based solely on the contents of the preliminary investigation submitted by Detective Dixon, select one sentence from the following groups of sentences which is MOST accurate and is grammatically correct.

1. A. Both robbers were armed.
    B. Each of the robbers were described as a male white.
    C. Neither robber was armed.
    D. Mr. Ladd stated that one of the robbers was armed.

    1.____

2. A. Mr. Brown fired three shots from his revolver.
    B. Mr. Brown was shot in the head by one of the robbers.
    C. Mr. Brown suffered a gunshot wound of the head during the course of the robbery.
    D. Mr. Brown was taken to General Hospital by ambulance.

    2.____

3. A. Shots were fired after one of the robbers said, *Give us the money or we'll kill you.*
    B. After one of the robbers demanded the money from Mr. Brown, he fired a shot.
    C. The preliminary investigation indicated that although Mr. Brown did not have a license for the gun, he was justified in using deadly physical force.
    D. Mr. Brown was interviewed at General Hospital.

    3.____

4. A. Each of the witnesses were customers in the store at the time of occurrence.
    B. Neither of the witnesses interviewed was the owner of the liquor store.
    C. Neither of the witnesses interviewed were the owner of the store.
    D. Neither of the witnesses was employed by Mr. Brown.

    4.____

5. A. Mr. Brown arrived at General Hospital at about 5:00 P.M.
    B. Neither of the robbers was injured during the robbery.
    C. The robbery occurred at 3:30 P.M. on February 10.
    D. One of the witnesses called the ambulance.

    5.____

Questions 6-10.

DIRECTIONS: Each of Questions 6 through 10 consists of information given in outline form and four sentences labeled A, B, C, and D. For each question, choose the one sentence which CORRECTLY expresses the information given in outline form and which also displays PROPER English usage.

6. Client's Name: Joanna Jones
    Number of Children: 3
    Client's Income: None
    Client's Marital Status: Single

    6.____

    A. Joanna Jones is an unmarried client with three children who have no income.
    B. Joanna Jones, who is single and has no income, a client she has three children.
    C. Joanna Jones, whose three children are clients, is single and has no income.
    D. Joanna Jones, who has three children, is an unmarried client with no income.

7. Client's Name: Bertha Smith
   Number of Children: 2
   Client's Rent: $1050 per month
   Number of Rooms: 4

   A. Bertha Smith, a client, pays $1050 per month for her four rooms with two children.
   B. Client Bertha Smith has two children and pays $1050 per month for four rooms.
   C. Client Bertha Smith is paying $1050 per month for two children with four rooms.
   D. For four rooms and two children client Bertha Smith pays $1050 per month.

7.____

8. Name of Employee: Cynthia Dawes
   Number of Cases Assigned: 9
   Date Cases were Assigned: 12/16
   Number of Assigned Cases Completed: 8

   A. On December 16, employee Cynthia Dawes was assigned nine cases; she has completed eight of these cases.
   B. Cynthia Dawes, employee on December 16, assigned nine cases, completed eight.
   C. Being employed on December 16, Cynthia Dawes completed eight of nine assigned cases.
   D. Employee Cynthia Dawes, she was assigned nine cases and completed eight, on December 16.

8.____

9. Place of Audit: Broadway Center
   Names of Auditors: Paul Cahn, Raymond Perez
   Date of Audit: 11/20
   Number of Cases Audited: 41

   A. On November 20, at the Broadway Center 41 cases was audited by auditors Paul Cahn and Raymond Perez.
   B. Auditors Raymond Perez and Paul Cahn has audited 41 cases at the Broadway Center on November 20.
   C. At the Broadway Center, on November 20, auditors Paul Cahn and Raymond Perez audited 41 cases.
   D. Auditors Paul Cahn and Raymond Perez at the Broadway Center, on November 20, is auditing 41 cases.

9.____

10. Name of Client: Barbra Levine
    Client's Monthly Income: $2100
    Client's Monthly Expenses: $4520

    A. Barbra Levine is a client, her monthly income is $2100 and her monthly expenses is $4520.
    B. Barbra Levine's monthly income is $2100 and she is a client, with whose monthly expenses are $4520.

10.____

C. Barbra Levine is a client whose monthly income is $2100 and whose monthly expenses are $4520.
D. Barbra Levine, a client, is with a monthly income which is $2100 and monthly expenses which are $4520.

Questions 11-13.

DIRECTIONS: Questions 11 through 13 involve several statements of fact presented in a very simple way. These statements of fact are followed by 4 choices which attempt to incorporate all of the facts into one logical statement which is properly constructed and grammatically correct.

11. I. Mr. Brown was sweeping the sidewalk in front of his house. 11.____
    II. He was sweeping it because it was dirty.
    III. He swept the refuse into the street.
    IV. Police Officer gave him a ticket.

    Which one of the following BEST presents the information given above?
    A. Because his sidewalk was dirty, Mr. Brown received a ticket from Officer Green when he swept the refuse into the street.
    B. Police Officer Green gave Mr. Brown a ticket because his sidewalk was dirty and he swept the refuse into the street.
    C. Police Officer Green gave Mr. Brown a ticket for sweeping refuse into the street because his sidewalk was dirty.
    D. Mr. Brown, who was sweeping refuse from his dirty sidewalk into the street, was given a ticket by Police Officer Green.

12. I. Sergeant Smith radioed for help. 12.____
    II. The sergeant did so because the crowd was getting larger.
    III. It was 10:00 A.M. when he made his call.
    IV. Sergeant Smith was not in uniform at the time of occurrence.

    Which one of the following BEST presents the information given above?
    A. Sergeant Smith, although not on duty at the time, radioed for help at 10 o'clock because the crowd was getting uglier.
    B. Although not in uniform, Sergeant Smith called for help at 10:00 A.M. because the crowd was getting uglier.
    C. Sergeant Smith radioed for help at 10:00 A.M. because the crowd was getting larger.
    D. Although he was not in uniform, Sergeant Smith radioed for help at 10:00 A.M. because the crowd was getting larger.

13. I. The payroll office is open on Fridays. 13.____
    II. Paychecks are distributed from 9:00 A.M. to 12 Noon.
    III. The office is open on Fridays because that's the only day the payroll staff is available.
    IV. It is open for the specified hours in order to permit employees to cash checks at the bank during lunch hour.

The choice below which MOST clearly and accurately presents the above idea is:
   A. Because the payroll office is open on Fridays from 9:00 A.M. to 12 Noon, employees can cash their checks when the payroll staff is available.
   B. Because the payroll staff is only available on Fridays until noon, employees can cash their checks during their lunch hour.
   C. Because the payroll staff is available only on Fridays, the office is open from 9:00 A.M. to 12 Noon to allow employees to cash their checks.
   D. Because of payroll staff availability, the payroll office is open on Fridays. It is open from 9:00 A.M. to 12 Noon so that distributed paychecks can be cashed at the bank while employees are on their lunch hour.

Questions 14-16.

DIRECTIONS: In each of Questions 14 through 6, the four sentences are from a paragraph in a report. They are not in the right order. Which of the following arrangements is the BEST one?

14. I. An executive may answer a letter by writing his reply on the face of the letter itself instead of having a return letter typed.
    II. This procedure is efficient because it saves the executive's time, the typist's time, and saves office file space.
    III. Copying machines are used in small offices as well as large offices to save time and money in making brief replies to business letters.
    IV. A copy is made on a copy machine to go into the company files, while the original is mailed back to the sender.

   The CORRECT answer is:
      A. I, II, IV, III   B. I, IV, II, III   C. III, I, IV, II   D. III, IV, II, I   14.____

15. I. Most organizations favor one of the types but always include the others to a lesser degree.
    II. However, we can detect a definite trend toward greater use of symbolic control.
    III. We suggest that our local police agencies are today primarily utilizing material control.
    IV. Control can be classified into three types: physical, material, and symbolic.

   The CORRECT answer is:
      A. IV, II, III, I   B. II, I, IV, III   C. III, IV, II, I   D. IV, I, III, II   15.____

16. I. They can and do take advantage of ancient political and geographical boundaries, which often give them sanctuary from effective policy activity.
    II. This country is essentially a country of small police forces, each operating independently within the limits of its jurisdiction.
    III. The boundaries that define and limit police operations do not hinder the movement of criminals, of course.
    IV. The machinery of law enforcement in America is fragmented, complicated, and frequently overlapping.   16.____

The CORRECT answer is:
A. III, I, IV   B. II, IV, I, III   C. IV, II, III, I   D. IV, III, II, I

17. Examine the following sentence, and then choose from below the words which should be inserted in the blank spaces to produce the best sentence.
The unit has exceeded _____ goals and the employees are satisfied with _____ accomplishments.
A. their; it's   B. it's; it's   C. its; there   D. its; their

18. Examine the following sentence, and then choose from below the words which should be inserted in the blank spaces to produce the best sentence.
Research indicates that employees who _____ no opportunity for close social relationships often find their work unsatisfying, and this _____ of satisfaction often reflects itself in low production.
A. have; lack   B. have; excess   C. has; lack   D. has; excess

19. Words in a sentence must be arranged properly to make sure that the intended meaning of the sentence is clear.
The sentence below that does NOT make sense because a clause has been separated from the word on which its meaning depends is:
A. To be a good writer, clarity is necessary.
B. To be a good writer, you must write clearly.
C. You must write clearly to be a good writer.
D. Clarity is necessary to good writing.

Questions 20-21.

DIRECTIONS: Each of Questions 20 and 21 consists of a statement which contains a word (one of those underlined) that is either incorrectly used because it is not in keeping with the meaning the quotation is evidently intended to convey, or is misspelled. There is only one INCORRECT word in each quotation. Of the four underlined words, determine if the first one should be replaced by the word lettered A, the second one replaced by the word lettered B, the third one replaced by the word lettered C, or the fourth one replaced by the word lettered D.

20. The alleged killer was occasionally permitted to excercise in the corridor.
A. alledged   B. ocasionally   C. permited   D. exercise

21. Defense counsel stated, in affect, that their conduct was permissible under the First Amendment.
A. council   B. effect   C. there   D. permissable

Question 22.

DIRECTIONS: Question 22 consists of one sentence. This sentence contains an incorrectly used word. First, decide which is the incorrectly used word. Then, from among the options given, decide which word, when substituted for the incorrectly used word, makes the meaning of the sentence clear.

22. As today's violence has no single cause, so its causes have no single scheme. 22._____
    A. deference B. cure C. flaw D. relevance

23. In the sentence, *A man in a light-grey suit waited thirty-five minutes in the ante-room for the all-important document*, the word IMPROPERLY hyphenated is 23._____
    A. light-grey   B. thirty-five
    C. ante-room   D. all-important

24. In the sentence, *The candidate wants to file his application for preference before it is too late*, the word *before* is used as a(n) 24._____
    A. preposition   B. subordinating conjunction
    C. pronoun   D. adverb

25. In the sentence, *The perpetrators ran from the scene*, the word *from* is a 25._____
    A. preposition   B. pronoun   C. verb   D. conjunction

KEY (CORRECT ANSWERS)

1.	D		11.	D
2.	D		12.	D
3.	A		13.	D
4.	B		14.	C
5.	D		15.	D
6.	D		16.	C
7.	B		17.	D
8.	A		18.	A
9.	C		19.	A
10.	C		20.	D

21. B
22. B
23. C
24. B
25. A

PREPARING WRITTEN MATERIAL
EXAMINATION SECTION
TEST 1

Questions 1-15.

DIRECTIONS: For each of Questions 1 through 15, select from the options given below the MOST applicable choice, and mark your answer accordingly.
    A. The sentence is correct.
    B. The sentence contains a spelling error only.
    C. The sentence contains an English grammar error only.
    D. The sentence contains both a spelling error and an English grammar error.

1. He is a very dependible person whom we expect will be an asset to this division.   1.____

2. An investigator often finds it necessary to be very diplomatic when conducting an interview.   2.____

3. Accurate detail is especially important if court action results from an investigation.   3.____

4. The report was signed by him and I since we conducted the investigation jointly.   4.____

5. Upon receipt of the complaint, an inquiry was begun.   5.____

6. An employee has to organize his time so that he can handle his workload eficiantly.   6.____

7. It was not apparent that anyone was living at the address given by the client.   7.____

8. According to regulations, there is to be at least three attempts made to locate the client.   8.____

9. Neither the inmate nor the correction officer was willing to sign a formal statement.   9.____

10. It is our opinion that one of the persons interviewed were lying.   10.____

11. We interviewed both clients and departmental personel in the course of this investigation.   11.____

12. It is concievable that further research might produce additional evidence.   12.____

13. There are too many occurences of this nature to ignore.   13.____

14. We cannot accede to the candidate's request. 14.____

15. The submission of overdue reports is the reason that there was a delay in completion of this investigation. 15.____

Questions 16-25.

DIRECTIONS: Each of Questions 16 through 25 may be classified under one of the following four categories:
    A. Faulty because of incorrect grammar or sentence structure.
    B. Faulty because of incorrect punctuation.
    C. Faulty because of incorrect spelling.
    D. Correct

Examine each sentence carefully to determine under which of the above four options it is best classified. Then, in the space at the right, write the letter preceding the option which is the BEST of the four suggested above. Each incorrect sentence contains but one type of error. Consider a sentence to be correct if it contains none of the types of errors mentioned, even though there may be other correct ways of expressing the same thought.

16. Although the department's supply of scratch pads and stationary have diminished considerably, the allotment for our division has not been reduced. 16.____

17. You have not told us whom you wish to designate as your secretary. 17.____

18. Upon reading the minutes of the last meeting, the new proposal was taken up for consideration. 18.____

19. Before beginning the discussion, we locked the door as a precautionery measure. 19.____

20. The supervisor remarked, "Only those clerks, who perform routine work, are permitted to take a rest period." 20.____

21. Not only will this duplicating machine make accurate copies, but it will also produce a quantity of work equal to fifteen transcribing typists. 21.____

22. "Mr. Jones," said the supervisor, "we regret our inability to grant you an extention of your leave of absence. 22.____

23. Although the employees find the work monotonous and fatigueing, they rarely complain. 23.____

24. We completed the tabulation of the receipts on time despite the fact that Miss Smith our fastest operator was absent for over a week. 24.____

25. The reaction of the employees who attended the meeting, as well as the reaction of those who did not attend, indicates clearly that the schedule is satisfactory to everyone concerned.

25.____

KEY (CORRECT ANSWERS)

1.	D	11.	B
2.	A	12.	B
3.	A	13.	B
4.	C	14.	A
5.	A	15.	C
6.	B	16.	A
7.	B	17.	D
8.	C	18.	A
9.	A	19.	C
10.	C	20.	B

21.	A
22.	C
23.	C
24.	B
25.	D

TEST 2

Questions 1-15.

DIRECTIONS: Questions 1 through 15 consist of two sentences. Some are correct according to ordinary formal English usage. Others are incorrect because they contain errors in English usage, spelling, or punctuation. Consider a sentence correct if it contains no errors in English usage, spelling, or punctuation, even if there may be other ways of writing the sentence correctly. Mark your answer:
A. If only sentence I is correct.
B. If only sentence II is correct.
C. If sentences 1 and II are correct.
D. If neither sentence I nor II is correct.

1.
   I. The influence of recruitment efficiency upon administrative standards is readily apparant.
   II. Rapid and accurate thinking are an essential quality of the police officer.

2.
   I. The administrator of a police department is constantly confronted by the demands of subordinates for increased personnel in their respective units.
   II. Since a chief executive must work within well-defined fiscal limits, he must weigh the relative importance of various requests.

3.
   I. The two men whom the police arrested for a parking violation were wanted for robbery in three states.
   II. Strong executive control from the top to the bottom of the enterprise is one of the basic principals of police administration.

4.
   I. When he gave testimony unfavorable to the defendant loyalty seemed to mean very little.
   II. Having run off the road while passing a car, the patrolman gave the driver a traffic ticket.

5.
   I. The judge ruled that the defendant's conversation with his doctor was a privileged communication.
   II. The importance of our training program is widely recognized; however, fiscal difficulties limit the program's effectiveness.

6.
   I. Despite an increase in patrol coverage, there were less arrests for crimes against property this year.
   II. The investigators could hardly have expected greater cooperation from the public.

7.
   I. Neither the patrolman nor the witness could identify the defendant as the driver of the car.
   II. Each of the officers in the class received their certificates at the completion of the course.

8. I. The new commander made it clear that those kind of procedures would no longer be permitted.
    II. Giving some weight to performance records is more advisable than making promotions solely on the basis of test scores.

9. I. A deputy sheriff must ascertain whether the debtor, has any property.
    II. A good deputy sheriff does not cause histerical excitement when he executes a process.

10. I. Having learned that he has been assigned a judgment debtor, the deputy sheriff should call upon him.
    II. The deputy sheriff may seize and remove property without requiring a bond.

11. I. If legal procedures are not observed, the resulting contract is not enforseable.
    II. If the directions from the creditor's attorney are not in writing, the deputy sheriff should request a letter of instructions from the attorney.

12. I. The deputy sheriff may confer with the defendant and enter this defendants' place of business.
    II. A deputy sheriff must ascertain from the creditor's attorney whether the debtor has any property against which he may proceede.

13. I. The sheriff has a right to do whatever is necessary for the purpose of executing the order of the court.
    II. The written order of the court gives the sheriff general authority and he is governed in his acts by a very simple principal.

14. I. Either the patrolman or his sergeant are always ready to help the public.
    II. The sergeant asked the patrolman when he would finish the report.

15. I. The injured man could not hardly talk.
    II. Every officer had ought to had in their reports on time.

Questions 16-26.

DIRECTIONS: For each of the sentences given below, numbered 16 through 25, select from the following choices the MOST correct choice and print your choice in the space at the right. Select as your answer:
A. If the statement contains an unnecessary word or expression
B. If the statement contains a slang term or expression ordinarily not acceptable in government report writing.
C. If the statement contains an old-fashioned word or expression, where a concrete, plain term would be more useful.
D. If the statement contains no major faults.

16. Every one of us should try harder.

17. Yours of the first instant has been received.

3 (#2)

18. We will have to do a real snow job on him. 18._____
19. I shall contact him next Thursday. 19._____
20. None of us were invited to the meeting with the community. 20._____
21. We got this here job to do. 21._____
22. She could not help but see the mistake in the checkbook. 22._____
23. Don't bug the Director about the report. 23._____
24. I beg to inform you that your letter has been received. 24._____
25. This project is all screwed up. 25._____

KEY (CORRECT ANSWERS)

1.	D	11.	B
2.	C	12.	D
3.	A	13.	A
4.	D	14.	D
5.	B	15.	D
6.	B	16.	D
7.	A	17.	C
8.	D	18.	B
9.	D	19.	D
10.	C	20.	D

21.	B
22.	D
23.	B
24.	C
25.	B

TEST 3

DIRECTIONS: Questions 1 through 25 are sentences taken from reports. Some are correct according to ordinary English usage. Others are incorrect because they contain errors in English usage, spelling, or punctuation. Consider a sentence correct if it contains no errors in English usage, spelling, or punctuation, even if there may be other ways of writing the sentence correctly. Mark your answer:
- A. If only sentence I is correct
- B. If only sentence II is correct
- C. If sentences I and II are correct
- D. If neither sentence I nor II is correct

1.
   I. The Neighborhood Police Team Commander and Team Patrolmen are encouraged to give to the public the widest possible verbal and written disemination of information regarding the existence and purposes of the program.
   II. The police must be vitally interelated with every segment of the public they serve.

   1.____

2.
   I. If social gambling, prostitution, and other vices are to be prohibited, the law makers should provide the manpower and method for enforcement.
   II. In addition to checking on possible crime locations such as hallways, roofs yards and other similar locations, Team Patrolmen are encouraged to make known their presence to members of the community.

   2.____

3.
   I. The Neighborhood Police Team Commander is authorized to secure, the cooperation of local publications, as well as public and private agencies, to further the goals of the program.
   II. Recruitment from social minorities is essential to effective police work among minorities and meaningful relations with them.

   3.____

4.
   I. The Neighborhood Police Team Commander and his men have the responsibility for providing patrol service within the sector territory on a twenty-four hour basis.
   II. While the patrolman was walking his beat at midnight he noticed that the clothing stores' door was partly open.

   4.____

5.
   I. Authority is granted to the Neighborhood Police Team to device tactics for coping with the crime in the sector.
   II. Before leaving the scene of the accident, the patrolman drew a map showing the positions of the automobiles and indicated the time of the accident as 10 M. in the morning.

   5.____

6.
   I. The Neighborhood Police Team Commander and his men must be kept apprised of conditions effecting their sector.
   II. Clear, continuous communication with every segment of the public served based on the realization of mutual need and founded on trust and confidence is the basis for effective law enforcement.

   6.____

7. I. The irony is that the police are blamed for the laws they enforce when they are doing their duty.
   II. The Neighborhood Police Team Commander is authorized to prepare and distribute literature with pertinent information telling the public whom to contact for assistance.

7._____

8. I. The day is not far distant when major parts of the entire police compliment will need extensive college training or degrees.
   II. Although driving under the influence of alcohol is a specific charge in making arrests, drunkenness is basically a health and social problem.

8._____

9. I. If a deputy sheriff finds that property he has to attach is located on a ship, he should notify his supervisor.
   II. Any contract that tends to interfere with the administration of justice is illegal.

9._____

10. I. A mandate or official order of the court to the sheriff or other officer directs it to take into possession property of the judgment debtor.
    II. Tenancies from month-to-month, week-to-week, and sometimes year-to-year are termenable.

10._____

11. I. A civil arrest is an arrest pursuant to an order issued by a court in civil litigation.
    II. In a criminal arrest, a defendant is arrested for a crime he is alleged to have committed.

11._____

12. I. Having taken a defendant into custody, there is a complete restraint of personal liberty.
    II. Actual force is unnecessary when a deputy sheriff makes an arrest.

12._____

13. I. When a husband breaches a separation agreement by failing to supply to the wife the amount of money to be paid to her periodically under the agreement, the same legal steps may be taken to enforce his compliance as in any other breach of contract.
    II. Having obtained the writ of attachment, the plaintiff is then in the advantageous position of selling the very property that has been held for him by the sheriff while he was obtaining a judgment.

13._____

14. I. Being locked in his desk, the investigator felt sure that the records would be safe.
    II. The reason why the witness changed his statement was because he had been threatened.

14._____

15. I. The investigation had just began then an important witness disappeared.
    II. The check that had been missing was located and returned to its owner, Harry Morgan, a resident of Suffolk County, New York.

15._____

16. I. A supervisor will find that the establishment of standard procedures enables his staff to work more efficiently.
    II. An investigator hadn't ought to give any recommendations in his report if he is in doubt.

16.____

17. I. Neither the investigator nor his supervisor is ready to interview the witness.
    II. Interviewing has been and always will be an important asset in investigation.

17.____

18. I. One of the investigator's reports has been forwarded to the wrong person.
    II. The investigator stated that he was not familiar with those kind of cases.

18.____

19. I. Approaching the victim of the assault, two large bruises were noticed by me.
    II. The prisoner was arrested for assault, resisting arrest, and use of a deadly weapon.

19.____

20. I. A copy of the orders, which had been prepared by the captain, was given to each patrolman.
    II. It's always necessary to inform an arrested person of his constitutional rights before asking him any questions.

20.____

21. I. To prevent further bleeding, I applied a tourniquet to the wound.
    II. John Rano a senior officer was on duty at the time of the accident.

21.____

22. I. Limiting the term "property" to tangible property, in the criminal mischief setting, accords with prior case law holding that only tangible property came within the purview of the offense of malicious mischief.
    II. Thus, a person who intentionally destroys the property of another, but under an honest belief that he has title to such property, cannot be convicted of criminal mischief under the Revised Penal Law.

22.____

23. I. Very early in it's history, New York enacted statutes from time to time punishing, either as a felony or as a misdemeanor, malicious injuries to various kinds of property: piers, boos, dams, bridges, etc.
    II. The application of the statute is necessarily restricted to trespassory takings with larcenous intent: namely with intent permanently or virtually permanently to "appropriate" property or "deprive" the owner of its use.

23.____

24. I. Since the former Penal Law did not define the instruments of forgery in a general fashion, its crime of forgery was held to be narrower than the common law offense in this respect and to embrace only those instruments explicitly specified in the substantive provisions.
    II. After entering the barn through an open door for the purpose of stealing, it was closed by the defendants.

24.____

25. I. The use of fire or explosives to destroy tangible property is proscribed by the criminal mischief provisions of the Revised Penal Law.
   II. The defendant's taking of a taxicab for the immediate purpose of affecting his escape did not constitute grand larceny.

25.____

KEY (CORRECT ANSWERS)

1. D	11. C
2. D	12. B
3. B	13. C
4. A	14. D
5. D	15. B
6. D	16. A
7. C	17. C
8. D	18. A
9. C	19. B
10. D	20. C

21. A
22. C
23. B
24. A
25. A

TEST 4

Questions 1-4.

DIRECTIONS: Each of the two sentences in Questions 1 through 4 may be correct or may contain errors in punctuation, capitalization, or grammar. Mark your answer:
- A. If there is an error only in sentence I
- B. If there is an error only in sentence II
- C. If there is an error in both sentences I and II
- D. If both sentences are correct.

1. I. It is very annoying to have a pencil sharpener, which is not in working order. 1.____
    II. Patrolman Blake checked the door of Joe's Restaurant and found that the lock has been jammed.

2. I. When you are studying a good textbook is important. 2.____
    II. He said he would divide the money equally between you and me.

3. I. Since he went on the city council a year ago, one of his primary concerns has been safety in the streets. 3.____
    II. After waiting in the doorway for about 15 minutes, a black sedan appeared.

Questions 4-8.

DIRECTIONS: Each of the sentences in Questions 4 through 8 may be classified under one of the following four categories:
- A. Faulty because of incorrect grammar
- B. Faulty because of incorrect punctuation
- C. Faulty because of incorrect capitalization or incorrect spelling
- D. Correct

Examine each sentence carefully to determine under which of the above four options it is BEST classified. Then, in the space at the right, print the capitalized letter preceding the option which is the BEST of the four suggested above. Each faulty sentence contains but one type of error. Consider a sentence to be correct if it contains none of the types of errors mentioned, even though there may be other correct ways of expressing the same thought.

4. They told both he and I that the prisoner had escaped. 4.____

5. Any superior officer, who, disregards the just complaints of his subordinates, is remiss in the performance of his duty. 5.____

6. Only those members of the national organization who resided in the Middle west attended the conference in Chicago. 6.____

7. We told him to give the investigation assignment to whoever was available. 7.____

8. Please do not disappoint and embarass us by not appearing in court. 8.____

Questions 9-13

DIRECTIONS: Each of Questions 9 through 13 consists of three sentences lettered A, B, and C. In each of these questions, one of the sentences may contain an error in grammar, sentence structure, or punctuation, or all three sentences may be correct. If one of the sentence in a question contains an error in grammar, sentence structure, or punctuation, print in the space at the right the capital letter preceding the sentence which contains the error. If all three sentences are correct, print the letter D.

9. A. Mr. Smith appears to be less competent than I in performing these duties. 9.____
    B. The supervisor spoke to the employee, who had made the error, but did not reprimand him.
    C. When he found the book lying on the table, he immediately notified the owner.

10. A. Being locked in the desk, we were certain that the papers would not be taken. 10.____
    B. It wasn't I who dictated the telegram; I believe it was Eleanor.
    C. You should interview whoever comes to the office today.

11. A. The clerk was instructed to set the machine on the table before summoning the manager. 11.____
    B. He said that he was not familiar with those kind of activities.
    C. A box of pencils, in addition to erasers and blotters, was included in the shipment of supplies.

12. A. The supervisor remarked, "Assigning an employee to the proper type of work is not always easy." 12.____
    B. The employer found that each of the applicants were qualified to perform the duties of the position.
    C. Any competent student is permitted to take this course if he obtains the consent of the instructor.

13. A. The prize was awarded to the employee whom the judges believed to be most deserving. 13.____
    B. Since the instructor believes his book is the better of the two, he is recommending it for use in the school.
    C. It was obvious to the employees that the completion of the task by the scheduled date would require their working overtime.

Questions 14-20.

DIRECTIONS: In answering Questions 14 through 20, choose the sentence which is BEST from the point of view of English usage suitable for a business report.

14. A. The client's receiving of public assistance checks at two different addresses were disclosed by the investigation.
    B. The investigation disclosed that the client was receiving public assistance checks at two different addresses.
    C. The client was found out by the investigation to be receiving public assistance checks at two different addresses.
    D. The client has been receiving public assistance checks at two different addresses, disclosed the investigation.

14.____

15. A. The investigation of complaints are usually handled by this unit, which deals with internal security problems in the department.
    B. This unit deals with internal security problems in the department usually investigating complaints.
    C. Investigating complaints is this unit's job, being that it handles internal security problems in the department.
    D. This unit deals with internal security problems in the department and usually investigates complaints.

15.____

16. A. The delay in completing this investigation was caused by difficulty in obtaining the required documents from the candidate.
    B. Because of difficulty in obtaining the required documents from the candidate is the reason that there was a delay in completing this investigation.
    C. Having had difficulty in obtaining the required documents from the candidate, there was a delay in completing this investigation.
    D. Difficulty in obtaining the required documents from the candidate had the affect of delaying the completion of this investigation.

16.____

17. A. This report, together with documents supporting our recommendation, are being submitted for your approval.
    B. Documents supporting our recommendation is being submitted with the report for your approval.
    C. This report, together with documents supporting our recommendation, is being submitted for your approval.
    D. The report and documents supporting our recommendation is being submitted for your approval.

17.____

18. A. The chairman himself, rather than his aides, has reviewed the report.
    B. The chairman himself, rather than his aides, have reviewed the report.
    C. The chairmen, not the aide, has reviewed the report.
    D. The aide, not the chairmen, have reviewed the report.

18.____

19. A. Various proposals were submitted but the decision is not been made. 19.____
    B. Various proposals has been submitted but the decision has not been made.
    C. Various proposals were submitted but the decision is not been made.
    D. Various proposals have been submitted but the decision has not been made.

20. A. Everyone were rewarded for his successful attempt. 20.____
    B. They were successful in their attempts and each of them was rewarded.
    C. Each of them are rewarded for their successful attempts.
    D. The reward for their successful attempts were made to each of them.

21. The following is a paragraph from a request for departmental recognition consisting of five numbered sentences submitted to a Captain for review. These sentences may or may not have errors in spelling, grammar, and punctuation: 21.____
    (1) The officers observed the subject Mills surreptitiously remove a wallet from the woman's handbag and entered his automobile. (2) As they approached Mills, he looked in their direction and drove away. (3) The officers pursued in their car. (4) Mills executed a series of complicated manuvers to evade the pursuing officers. (5) At the corner of Broome and Elizabeth Streets, Mills stopped the car, got out, raised his hands and surrendered to the officers.
    Which one of the following BEST classifies the above with regard to spelling, grammar, and punctuation?
    A. 1, 2, and 3 are correct, but 4 and 5 have errors.
    B. 2, 3, and 5 are correct, but 1 and 4 have errors.
    C. 3, 4, and 5 are correct, but 1 and 2 have errors.
    D. 1, 2, 3, and 5 are correct, but 4 has errors.

22. The one of the following sentences which is grammatically PREFERABLE to the others is: 22.____
    A. Our engineers will go over your blueprints so that you may have no problems in construction.
    B. For a long time he had been arguing that we, not he, are to blame for the confusion.
    C. I worked on his automobile for two hours and still cannot find out what is wrong with it.
    D. Accustomed to all kinds of hardships, fatigue seldom bothers veteran policemen.

23. The MOST accurate of the following sentences is: 23.____
    A. The commissioner, as well as his deputy and various bureau heads, were present.
    B. A new organization of employers and employees have been formed.
    C. One or the other of these men have been selected.
    D. The number of pages in the book is enough to discourage a reader.

24. The MOST accurate of the following sentences is:
    A. Between you and me, I think he is the better man.
    B. He was believed to be me.
    C. Is it us that you wish to see?
    D. The winners are him and her.

24.____

KEY (CORRECT ANSWERS)

1.	C		11.	B
2.	A		12.	B
3.	C		13.	D
4.	A		14.	B
5.	B		15.	D
6.	C		16.	A
7.	D		17.	C
8.	C		18.	A
9.	B		19.	D
10.	A		20.	B

21. B
22. A
23. D
24. A

PRINCIPLES AND PRACTICES, OF ADMINISTRATION, SUPERVISION AND MANAGEMENT

TABLE OF CONTENTS

	Page
GENERAL ADMINISTRATION	1
SEVEN BASIC FUNCTIONS OF THE SUPERVISOR	2
I. Planning	2
II. Organizing	3
III. Staffing	3
IV. Directing	3
V. Coordinating	3
VI. Reporting	3
VII. Budgeting	3
PLANNING TO MEET MANAGEMENT GOALS	4
I. What is Planning	4
II. Who Should Make Plans	4
III. What are the Results of Poor Planning	4
IV. Principles of Planning	4
MANAGEMENT PRINCIPLES	5
I. Management	5
II. Management Principles	5
III. Organization Structure	6
ORGANIZATION	8
I. Unity of Command	8
II. Span of Control	8
III. Uniformity of Assignment	9
IV. Assignment of Responsibility and Delegation of Authority	9
PRINCIPLES OF ORGANIZATION	9
I. Definition	9
II. Purpose of Organization	9
III. Basic Considerations in Organizational Planning	9
IV. Bases for Organization	10
V. Assignment of Functions	10
VI. Delegation of Authority and Responsibility	10
VII. Employee Relationships	11

DELEGATING		11
I.	WHAT IS DELEGATING:	11
II.	TO WHOM TO DELEGATE	11
REPORTS		12
I.	DEFINITION	12
II.	PURPOSE	12
III.	TYPES	12
IV.	FACTORS TO CONSIDER BEFORE WRITING REPORT	12
V.	PREPARATORY STEPS	12
VI.	OUTLINE FOR A RECOMMENDATION REPORT	12
MANAGEMENT CONTROLS		13
I.	Control	13
II.	Basis for Control	13
III.	Policy	13
IV.	Procedure	14
V.	Basis of Control	14
FRAMEWORK OF MANAGEMENT		14
I.	Elements	14
II.	Manager's Responsibility	15
III.	Control Techniques	16
IV.	Where Forecasts Fit	16
PROBLEM SOLVING		16
I.	Identify the Problem	16
II.	Gather Data	17
III.	List Possible Solutions	17
IV.	Test Possible Solutions	18
V.	Select the Best Solution	18
VI.	Put the Solution into Actual Practice	19
COMMUNICATION		19
I.	What is Communication?	19
II.	Why is Communication Needed?	19
III.	How is Communication Achieved?	20
IV.	Why Does Communication Fail?	21
V.	How to Improve Communication	21
VI.	How to Determine If You Are Getting Across	21
VII.	The Key Attitude	22
HOW ORDERS AND INSTRUCTIONS SHOULD BE GIVEN		22
I.	Characteristics of Good Orders and Instructions	22
FUNCTIONS OF A DEPARTMENT PERSONNEL OFFICE		23

SUPERVISION	23
I. Leadership	23
A. The Authoritarian Approach	23
B. The Laissez-Faire Approach	24
C. The Democratic Approach	24
II. Nine Points of Contrast Between Boss and Leader	25
EMPLOYEE MORALE	25
I. Some Ways to Develop and Maintain Good Employee Morale	25
II. Some Indicators of Good Morale	26
MOTIVATION	26
EMPLOYEE PARTICIPATION	27
I. WHAT IS PARTICIPATION	27
II. WHY IS IT IMPORTANT?	27
III. HOW MAY SUPERVISORS OBTAIN IT?	28
STEPS IN HANDLING A GRIEVANCE	28
DISCIPLINE	29
I. THE DISCIPLINARY INTERVIEW	29
II. PLANNING THE INTERVIEW	29
III. CONDUCTING THE INTERVIEW	30

PRINCIPLES AND PRACTICES, OF ADMINISTRATION, SUPERVISION AND MANAGEMENT

Most people are inclined to think of administration as something that only a few persons are responsible for in a large organization. Perhaps this is true if you are thinking of Administration with a capital *A*, but administration with a lower case *a* is a responsibility of supervisors at all levels each working day.

All of us feel we are pretty good supervisors and that we do a good job of administering the workings of our agency. By and large, this is true, but every so often it is good to check up on ourselves. Checklists appear from time to time in various publications which psychologists say tell whether or not a person will make a good wife, husband, doctor, lawyer, or supervisor.

The following questions are an excellent checklist to test yourself as a supervisor and administrator.

Remember, Administration gives direction and points the way but administration carries the ideas to fruition. Each is dependent on the other for its success. Remember, too, that no unit is too small for these departmental functions to be carried out. These statements apply equally as well to the Chief Librarian as to the Department Head with but one or two persons to supervise.

GENERAL ADMINISTRATION: General Responsibilities of Supervisors

1. Have I prepared written statements of functions, activities, and duties for my organizational unit?

2. Have I prepared procedural guides for operating activities?

3. Have I established clearly in writing, lines of authority and responsibility for my organizational unit?

4. Do I make recommendations for improvements in organization, policies, administrative and operating routines and procedures, including simplification of work and elimination of non-essential operations?

5. Have I designated and trained an understudy to function in my absence?

6. Do I supervise and train personnel within the unit to effectively perform their assignments?

7. Do I assign personnel and distribute work on such a basis as to carry out the organizational unit's assignment or mission in the most effective and efficient manner?

8. Have I established administrative controls by:

    a. Fixing responsibility and accountability on all supervisors under my direction for the proper performance of their functions and duties.

b. Preparations and submitting periodic work load and progress reports covering the operations of the unit to my immediate superior.

c. Analysis and evaluation of such reports received from subordinate units.

d. Submission of significant developments and problems arising within the organizational unit to my immediate superior.

e. Conducting conferences, inspections, etc., as to the status and efficiency of unit operations.

9. Do I maintain an adequate and competent working force?

10. Have I fostered good employee-department relations, seeing that established rules, regulations, and instructions are being carried out properly?

11. Do I collaborate and consult with other organizational units performing related functions to insure harmonious and efficient working relationships?

12. Do I maintain liaison through prescribed channels with city departments and other governmental agencies concerned with the activities of the unit?

13. Do I maintain contact with and keep abreast of the latest developments and techniques of administration (professional societies, groups, periodicals, etc.) as to their applicability to the activities of the unit?

14. Do I communicate with superiors and subordinates through prescribed organizational channels?

15. Do I notify superiors and subordinates in instances where bypassing is necessary as soon thereafter as practicable?

16. Do I keep my superior informed of significant developments and problems?

SEVEN BASIC FUNCTIONS OF THE SUPERVISOR

I. PLANNING
This means working out goals and means to obtain goals. <u>What</u> needs to be done, <u>who</u> will do it, <u>how</u>, <u>when</u>, and <u>where</u> it is to be done.

SEVEN STEPS IN PLANNING

A. Define job or problem clearly.
B. Consider priority of job.
C. Consider time-limit—starting and completing.
D. Consider minimum distraction to, or interference with, other activities.
E. Consider and provide for contingencies—possible emergencies.
F. Break job down into components.

G. Consider the 5 W's and H:
   - WHY..........is it necessary to do the job? (Is the purpose clearly defined?)
   - WHAT........needs to be done to accomplish the defined purpose?
   - ....is needed to do the job? (Money, materials, etc.)
   - WHO..........is needed to do the job?
   - ....will have responsibilities?
   - WHERE......is the work to be done?
   - WHEN........is the job to begin and end? (Schedules, etc.)
   - HOW..........is the job to bed done? (Methods, controls, records, etc.)

II. ORGANIZING

This means dividing up the work, establishing clear lines of responsibility and authority and coordinating efforts to get the job done.

III. STAFFING

The whole personnel function of bringing in and <u>training</u> staff, getting the right man and fitting him to the right job—the job to which he is best suited.

In the normal situation, the supervisor's responsibility regarding staffing normally includes providing accurate job descriptions, that is, duties of the jobs, requirements, education and experience, skills, physical, etc.; assigning the work for maximum use of skills; and proper utilization of the probationary period to weed out unsatisfactory employees.

IV. DIRECTING

Providing the necessary leadership to the group supervised. Important work gets done to the supervisor's satisfaction.

V. COORDINATING

The all-important duty of inter-relating the various parts of the work.
The supervisor is also responsible for controlling the coordinated activities. This means measuring performance according to a time schedule and setting quotas to see that the goals previously set are being reached. Reports from workers should be analyzed, evaluated, and made part of all future plans.

VI. REPORTING

This means proper and effective communication to your superiors, subordinates, and your peers (in definition of the job of the supervisor). Reports should be read and information contained therein should be used, not be filed away and forgotten. Reports should be written in such a way that the desired action recommended by the report is forthcoming.

VII. BUDGETING
This means controlling current costs and forecasting future costs. This forecast Is based on past experience, future plans and programs, as well as current costs.

You will note that these seven functions can fall under three topics:

Planning) Make a plan
Organizing)

Staffing)
Directing) Get things done
Controlling)

Reporting) Watch it work
Budgeting)

PLANNING TO MEET MANAGEMENT GOALS

I. WHAT IS PLANNING?

   A. Thinking a job through before new work is done to determine the best way to do it
   B. A method of doing something
   C. Ways and means for achieving set goals
   D. A means of enabling a supervisor to deliver with a minimum of effort, all details involved in coordinating his work

II. WHO SHOULD MAKE PLANS?

   Everybody!
   All levels of supervision must plan work. (Top management, heads of divisions or bureaus, first line supervisors, and individual employees.) The higher the level, the more planning required.

III. WHAT ARE THE RESULTS OF POOR PLANNING?

   A. Failure to meet deadline
   B. Low employee morale
   C. Lack of job coordination
   D. Overtime is frequently necessary
   E. Excessive cost, waste of material and manhours

IV. PRINCIPLES OF PLANNING

   A. Getting a clear picture of your objectives. What exactly are you trying to accomplish?
   B. Plan the whole job, then the parts, in proper sequence.
   C. Delegate the planning of details to those responsible for executing them.
   D. Make your plan flexible.
   E. Coordinate your plan with the plans of others so that the work may be processed with a minimum of delay.
   F. Sell your plan before you execute it.
   G. Sell your plan to your superior, subordinate, in order to gain maximum participation and coordination.
   H. Your plan should take precedence. Use knowledge and skills that others have brought to a similar job.
   I. Your plan should take account of future contingencies; allow for future expansion.
   J. Plans should include minor details. Leave nothing to chance that can be anticipated.
   K. Your plan should be simple and provide standards and controls. Establish quality and quantity standards and set a standard method of doing the job. The controls will indicate whether the job is proceeding according to plan.
   L. Consider possible bottlenecks, breakdowns, or other difficulties that are likely to arise.

V. Q. WHAT ARE THE YARDSTICKS BY WHICH PLANNING SHOULD BE MEASURED?
    A. Any plan should:
       —Clearly state a definite course of action to be followed and goal to be achieved, with consideration for emergencies.
       — Be realistic and practical.
       — State what's to be done, when it's to be done, where, how, and by whom.
       — Establish the most efficient sequence of operating steps so that more is accomplished in less time, with the least effort, and with the best quality results.
       — Assure meeting deliveries without delays.
       — Establish the standard by which performance is to be judged.

    Q. WHAT KINDS OF PLANS DOES EFFECTIVE SUPERVISION REQUIRE?
    A. Plans should cover such factors as:
       — Manpower: right number of properly trained employees on the job
       — Materials: adequate supply of the right materials and supplies
       — Machines: full utilization of machines and equipment, with proper maintenance
       — Methods: most efficient handling of operations
       — Deliveries: making deliveries on time
       — Tools: sufficient well-conditioned tools
       — Layout: most effective use of space
       — Reports: maintaining proper records and reports
       — Supervision: planning work for employees and organizing supervisor's own time

MANAGEMENT PRINCIPLES

I. MANAGEMENT
    Q. What do we mean by management?
    A. Getting work done through others.

    Management could also be defined as planning, directing, and controlling the operations of a bureau or division so that all factors will function properly and all persons cooperate efficiently for a common objective.

II. MANAGEMENT PRINCIPLES

    A. There should be a hierarchy—wherein authority and responsibility run upward and downward through several levels—with a broad base at the bottom and a single head at the top.

    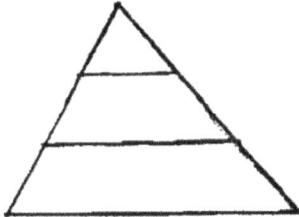

    B. Each and every unit or person in the organization should be answerable ultimately to the manager at the apex. In other words, *The buck stops here!*

C. Every necessary function involved in the bureau's objectives is assigned to a unit in that bureau.

D. Responsibilities assigned to a unit are specifically clear-cut and understood.

E. Consistent methods of organizational structure should be applied at each level of the organization.

F. Each member of the bureau from top to bottom knows: to whom he reports and who reports to him.

G. No member of one bureau reports to more than one supervisor. No dual functions.

H. Responsibility for a function is matched by authority necessary to perform that function. Weight of authority.

I. Individuals or units reporting to a supervisor do not exceed the number which can be feasibly and effectively coordinated and directed. Concept of *span of control*.

J. Channels of command (management) are not violated by staff units, although there should be staff services to facilitate and coordinate management functions.

K. Authority and responsibility should be decentralized to units and individuals who are responsible for the actual performance of operations.
Welfare – down to Welfare Centers
Hospitals – down to local hospitals

L. Management should exercise control through attention to policy problems of exceptional performance, rather than through review of routine actions of subordinates.

M. Organizations should never be permitted to grow so elaborate as to hinder work accomplishments.

III. ORGANIZATION STRUCTURE

Types of Organizations
The purest form is a leader and a few followers, such as:

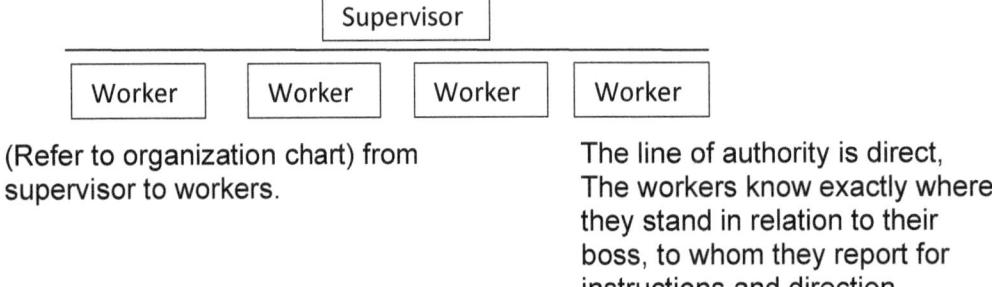

(Refer to organization chart) from supervisor to workers.

The line of authority is direct, The workers know exactly where they stand in relation to their boss, to whom they report for instructions and direction.

Unfortunately, in our present complex society, few organizations are similar to this example of a pure line organization. In this era of specialization, other people are often needed in the simplest of organizations. These specialists are known as staff. The sole purpose for their existence (staff) is to assist, advise, suggest, help or counsel line organizations. Staff has no authority to direct line people—nor do they give them direct instructions.

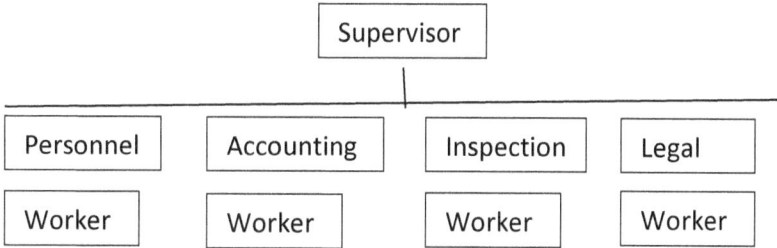

Line Functions
1. Directs
2. Orders
3. Responsibility for carrying out activities from beginning to end
4. Follows chain of command
5. Is identified with what it does
6. Decides when and how to use staff advice
7. Line executes

Staff Functions
1. Advises
2. Persuades and sells
3. Staff studies, reports, recommends but does not carry out
4. May advise across department lines
5. May find its ideas identified with others
6. Has to persuade line to want its advice
7. Staff: Conducts studies and research. Provides advice and instructions in technical matters. Serves as technical specialist to render specific services.

Types and Functions of Organization Charts
An organization chart is a picture of the arrangement and inter-relationship of the subdivisions of an organization.

A. Types of Charts:
   1. Structural: basic relationships only
   2. Functional: includes functions or duties
   3. Personnel: positions, salaries, status, etc.
   4. Process Chart: work performed
   5. Gantt Chart: actual performance against planned
   5. Flow Chart: flow and distribution of work

B. Functions of Charts:
   1. Assist in management planning and control
   2. Indicate duplication of functions
   3. Indicate incorrect stressing of functions
   4. Indicate neglect of important functions
   5. Correct unclear authority
   6. Establish proper span of control

C. Limitations of Charts:
1. Seldom maintained on current basis
2. Chart is oversimplified
3. Human factors cannot adequately be charted

D. Organization Charts should be:
1. Simple
2. Symmetrical
3. Indicate authority
4. Line and staff relationship differentiated
5. Chart should be dated and bear signature of approving officer
6. Chart should be displayed, not hidden

ORGANIZATION

There are four basic principles of organization:
1. Unity of command
2. Span of control
3. Uniformity of assignment
4. Assignment of responsibility and delegation of authority

I. UNITY OF COMMAND

Unity of command means that each person in the organization should receive orders from one, and only one, supervisor. When a person has to take orders from two or more people, (a) the orders may be in conflict and the employee is upset because he does not know which he should obey, or (b) different orders may reach him at the same time and he does not know which he should carry out first.

Equally as bad as having two bosses is the situation where the supervisor is bypassed. Let us suppose you are a supervisor whose boss bypasses you (deals directly with people reporting to you). To the worker, it is the same as having two bosses; but to you, the supervisor, it is equally serious. Bypassing on the part of your boss will undermine your authority, and the people under you will begin looking to your boss for decisions and even for routine orders.

You can prevent bypassing by telling the people you supervise that if anyone tries to give them orders, they should direct that person to you.

II. SPAN OF CONTROL

Span of control on a given level involves:
A. The number of people being supervised
B. The distance
C. The time involved in supervising the people. (One supervisor cannot supervise too many workers effectively.)

Span of control means that a supervisor has the right number (not too many and not too few) of subordinates that he can supervise well.

III. UNIFORMITY OF ASSIGNMENT

In assigning work, you as the supervisor should assign to each person jobs that are similar in nature. An employee who is assigned too many different types of jobs will waste time in going from one kind of work to another. It takes time for him to get to top production in one kind of task and, before he does so, he has to start on another.
When you assign work to people, remember that:

A. Job duties should be definite. Make it clear from the beginning what they are to do, how they are to do it, and why they are to do it. Let them know how much they are expected to do and how well they are expected to do it.
B. Check your assignments to be certain that there are no workers with too many unrelated duties, and that no two people have been given overlapping responsibilities. Your aim should be to have every task assigned to a specific person with the work fairly distributed and with each person doing his part.

IV. ASSIGNMENT OF RESPONSIBILITY AND DELEGATION OF AUTHORITY

A supervisor cannot delegate his final responsibility for the work of his department. The experienced supervisor knows that he gets his work done through people. He can't do it all himself. So he must assign the work and the responsibility for the work to his employees. Then they must be given the authority to carry out their responsibilities.

By assigning responsibility and delegating authority to carry out the responsibility, the supervisor builds in his workers initiative, resourcefulness, enthusiasm, and interest in their work. He is treating them as responsible adults. They can find satisfaction in their work, and they will respect the supervisor and be loyal to the supervisor.

PRINCIPLES OF ORGANIZATION

I. DEFINITION

Organization is the method of dividing up the work to provide the best channels for coordinated effort to get the agency's mission accomplished.

II. PURPOSE OF ORGANIZATION

A. To enable each employee within the organization to clearly know his responsibilities and relationships to his fellow employees and to organizational units
B. To avoid conflicts of authority and overlapping of jurisdiction.
C. To ensure teamwork.

III. BASIC CONSIDERATIONS IIN ORGANIZATIONAL PLANNING

A. The basic plans and objectives of the agency should be determined, and the organizational structure should be adapted to carry out effectively such plans and objectives.
B. The organization should be built around the major functions of the agency and not individuals or groups of individuals.

C. The organization should be sufficiently flexible to meet new and changing conditions which may be brought about from within or outside the department.
D. The organizational structure should be as simple as possible and the number of organizational units kept at a minimum.
E. The number of levels of authority should be kept at a minimum. Each additional management level lengthens the chain of authority and responsibility and increases the time for instructions to be distributed to operating levels and for decisions to be obtained from higher authority.
F. The form of organization should permit each executive to exercise maximum initiative within the limits of delegated authority.

IV. BASES FOR ORGANIZATION

A. Purpose (Examples: education, police, sanitation)
B. Process (Examples: accounting, legal, purchasing)
C. Clientele (Examples: welfare, parks, veteran)
D. Geographic (Examples: borough offices, precincts, libraries)

V. ASSIGNMENTS OF FUNCTIONS

A. Every function of the agency should be assigned to a specific organizational unit. Under normal circumstances, no single function should be assigned to more than one organizational unit.
B. There should be no overlapping, duplication, or conflict between organizational elements.
C. Line functions should be separated from staff functions, and proper emphasis should be placed on staff activities.
D. Functions which are closely related or similar should normally be assigned to a single organizational unit.
E. Functions should be properly distributed to promote balance, and to avoid overemphasis of less important functions and underemphasis of more essential functions.

VI. DELEGATION OF AUTHORITY AND RESPONSIBILITY

A. Responsibilities assigned to a specific individual or organizational unit should carry corresponding authority, and all statements of authority or limitations thereof should be as specific as possible.
B. Authority and responsibility for action should be decentralized to organizational units and individuals responsible for actual performance to the greatest extent possible, without relaxing necessary control over policy or the standardization of procedures. Delegation of authority will be consistent with decentralization of responsibility but such delegation will not divest an executive in higher authority of his overall responsibility.
C. The heads of organizational units should concern themselves with important matters and should delegate to the maximum extent details and routines performed in the ordinary course of business.
D. All responsibilities, authorities, and relationships should be stated in simple language to avoid misinterpretation.
E. Each individual or organizational unit charged with a specific responsibility will be held responsible for results.

VII. EMPLOYEE RELATIONSHIPS

   A. The employees reporting to one executive should not exceed the number which can be effectively directed and coordinated. The number will depend largely upon the scope and extent of the responsibilities of the subordinates.
   B. No person should report to more than one supervisor. Every supervisor should know who reports to him, and every employee should know to whom he reports. Channels of authority and responsibility should not be violated by staff units.
   C. Relationships between organizational units within the agency and with outside organizations and associations should be clearly stated and thoroughly understood to avoid misunderstanding.

DELEGATING

I. WHAT IS DELEGATING?
Delegating is assigning a job to an employee, giving him the authority to get that job done, and giving him the responsibility for seeing to it that the job is done.

   A. What To Delegate
      1. Routine details
      2. Jobs which may be necessary and take a lot of time, but do not have to be done by the supervisor personally (preparing reports, attending meetings, etc.)
      3. Routine decision-making (making decisions which do not require the supervisor's personal attention)

   B. What Not To Delegate
      1. Job details which are *executive functions* (setting goals, organizing employees into a good team, analyzing results so as to plan for the future)
      2. Disciplinary power (handling grievances, preparing service ratings, reprimands, etc.)
      3. Decision-making which involves large numbers of employees or other bureaus and departments
      4. Final and complete responsibility for the job done by the unit being supervised

   C. Why Delegate?
      1. To strengthen the organization by developing a greater number of skilled employees
      2. To improve the employee's performance by giving him the chance to learn more about the job, handle some responsibility, and become more interested in getting the job done
      3. To improve a supervisor's performance by relieving him of routine jobs and giving him more time for *executive functions* (planning, organizing, controlling, etc.) which cannot be delegated

II. TO WHOM TO DELEGATE
People with abilities not being used. Selection should be based on ability, not on favoritism.

REPORTS

I. **DEFINITION**
   A report is an orderly presentation of factual information directed to a specific reader for a specific purpose

II. **PURPOSE**
   The general purpose of a report is to bring to the reader useful and factual information about a condition or a problem. Some specific purposes of a report may be:

   A. To enable the reader to appraise the efficiency or effectiveness of a person or an operation
   B. To provide a basis for establishing standards
   C. To reflect the results of expenditures of time, effort, and money
   D. To provide a basis for developing or altering programs

III. **TYPES**

   A. Information Report: Contains facts arranged in sequence
   B. Summary (Examination) Report: Contains facts plus an analysis or discussion of the significance of the facts. Analysis may give advantages and disadvantages or give qualitative and quantitative comparisons
   C. Recommendation Report: Contains facts, analysis, and conclusion logically drawn from the facts and analysis, plus a recommendation based upon the facts, analysis, and conclusions

IV. **FACTORS TO CONSIDER BEFORE WRITING REPORT**

   A. _Why_ write the report?: The purpose of the report should be clearly defined.
   B. _Who_ will read the report?: What level of language should be used? Will the reader understand professional or technical language?
   C. _What_ should be said?: What does the reader need or want to know about the subject?
   D. _How_ should it be said?: Should the subject be presented tactfully? Convincingly? In a stimulating manner?

V. **PREPARATORY STEPS**

   A. Assemble the facts: Find out who, why, what, where, when, and how.
   B. Organize the facts: Eliminate unnecessary information
   C. Prepare an outline: Check for orderliness, logical sequence
   D. Prepare a draft: Check for correctness, clearness, completeness, conciseness, and tone
   E. Prepare it in final form: Check for grammar, punctuation, appearance

VI. **OUTLINE FOR A RECOMMENDATION REPORT**

   Is the report:
   A. Correct in information, grammar, and tone?
   B. Clear?
   C. Complete?

D. Concise?
E. Timely?
F. Worth its cost?

Will the report accomplish its purpose?

MANAGEMENT CONTROLS

I. CONTROL
What is control? What is controlled? Who controls?

The essence of control is action which adjusts operations to predetermined standards, and its basis is information in the hands of managers. Control is checking to determine whether plans are being observed and suitable progress toward stated objectives is being made, and action is taken, if necessary, to correct deviations.

We have a ready-made model for this concept of control in the automatic systems which are widely used for process control in the chemical land petroleum industries. A process control system works this way. Suppose, for example, it is desired to maintain a constant rate of flow of oil through a pipe at a predetermined or set-point value. A signal, whose strength represents the rate of flow, can be produced in a measuring device and transmitted to a control mechanism. The control mechanism, when it detects any deviation of the actual from the set-point signal, will reposition the value regulating flow rate.

II. BASIS FOR CONTROL

A process control mechanism thus acts to adjust operations to predetermined standards and does so on the basis of information it receives. In a parallel way, information reaching a manager gives him the opportunity for corrective action and is his basis for control. He cannot exercise control without such information, and he cannot do a complete job of managing without controlling.

III. POLICY

What is policy?

Policy is simply a statement of an organization's intention to act in certain ways when specified types of circumstances arise. It represents a general decision, predetermined and expressed as a principle or rule, establishing a normal pattern of conduct for dealing with given types of business events—usually recurrent. A statement is therefore useful in economizing the time of managers and in assisting them to discharge their responsibilities equitably and consistently.

Policy is not a means of control, but policy does generate the need for control.

Adherence to policies is not guaranteed nor can it be taken on faith. It has to be verified. Without verification, there is no basis for control. Policy and procedures, although closely related and interdependent to a certain extent, are not synonymous. A policy may be adopted, for example, to maintain a materials inventory not to exceed one million dollars.

A procedure for inventory control could interpret that policy and convert it into methods for keeping within that limit, with consideration, too, of possible but foreseeable expedient deviation.

IV. PROCEDURE

What is procedure?

A procedure specifically prescribes:
A. What work is to be performed by the various participants
B. Who are the respective participants
C. When and where the various steps in the different processes are to be performed
D. The sequence of operations that will insure uniform handling of recurring transactions
E. The paper that is involved, its origin, transition, and disposition

Necessary appurtenances to a procedure are:
A. Detailed organizational chart
B. Flow charts
C. Exhibits of forms, all presented in close proximity to the text of the procedure

V. BASIS OF CONTROL – INFORMATION IN THE HANDS OF MANAGERS

If the basis of control is information in the hands of managers, then reporting is elevated to a level of very considerable importance.

Types of reporting may include:
A. Special reports and routine reports
B. Written, oral, and graphic reports
C. Staff meetings
D. Conferences
E. Television screens
F. Non-receipt of information, as where management is by exception
G. Any other means whereby information is transmitted to a manager as a basis for control action

FRAMEWORK OF MANAGEMENT

I. ELEMENTS

A. Policy: It has to be verified, controlled.

B. Organization is part of the giving of an assignment. The organizational chart gives to each individual in his title, a first approximation of the nature of his assignment and orients him as being accountable to a certain individual. Organization is not in a true sense a means of control. Control is checking to ascertain whether the assignment is executed as intended and acting on the basis of that information.

C. Budgets perform three functions:
1. They present the objectives, plans, and programs of the organization in financial terms.

2. They report the progress of actual performance against these predetermined objectives, plans, and programs.
3. Like organizational charts, delegations of authority, procedures, and job descriptions, they define the assignments which have flowed from the Chief Executive. Budgets are a means of control in the respect that they report progress of actual performance against the program. They provide information which enables managers to take action directed toward bringing actual results into conformity with the program.

D. Internal Check provides in practice for the principle that the same person should not have responsibility for all phases of a transaction. This makes it clearly an aspect of organization rather than of control. Internal Check is static, or built-in.

E. Plans, Programs, Objectives
People must know what they are trying to do. Objectives fulfill this need. Without them, people may work industriously and yet, working aimlessly, accomplish little. Plans and Programs complement Objectives, since they propose how and according to what time schedule the objectives are to be reached.

F. Delegations of Authority
Among the ways we have for supplementing the titles and lines of authority of an organizational chart are delegations of authority. Delegations of authority clarify the extent of authority of individuals and in that way serve to define assignments. That they are not means of control is apparent from the very fact that wherever there has been a delegation of authority, the need for control increases. This could hardly be expected to happen if delegations of authority were themselves means of control.

II. MANAGER'S RESPONSIBILITY

Control becomes necessary whenever a manager delegates authority to a subordinate because he cannot delegate and then simply sit back and forget4 about it. A manager's accountability to his own superior has not diminished one whit as a result of delegating part of his authority to a subordinate. The manager must exercise control over actions taken under the authority so delegated. That means checking serves as a basis for possible corrective action.

Objectives, plans, programs, organizational charts, and other elements of the managerial system are not fruitfully regarded as either controls or means of control. They are pre-established standards or models of performance to which operations are adjusted by the exercise of management control. These standards or models of performance are dynamic in character for they are constantly altered, modified, or revised. Policies, organizational set-up, procedures, delegations, etc. are constantly altered but, like objectives and plans, they remain in force until they are either abandoned or revised. All of the elements (or standards or models of performance), objectives, plans, and programs, policies, organization, etc. can be regarded as a *framework of management*.

III. CONTROL TECHNIQUES

Examples of control techniques:
A. Compare against established standards
B. Compare with a similar operation
C. Compare with past operations
D. Compare with predictions of accomplishment

IV. WHERE FORECASTS FIT

Control is after-the-fact while forecasts are before. Forecasts and projections are important for setting objectives and formulating plans.

Information for aiming and planning does not have to be before-the-fact. It may be an after-the-fact analysis proving that a certain policy has been impolitic in its effect on the relation of the company or department with customer, employee, taxpayer, or stockholder; or that a certain plan is no longer practical, or that a certain procedure is unworkable.

The prescription here certainly would not be in control (in these cases, control would simply bring operations into conformity with obsolete standards) but the establishment of new standards, a new policy, a new plan, and a new procedure to be controlled too.

Information is, of course, the basis for all communication in addition to furnishing evidence to management of the need for reconstructing the framework of management.

PROBLEM SOLVING

The accepted concept in modern management for problem solving is the utilization of the following steps:

A. Identify the problem
B. Gather data
C. List possible solutions
D. Test possible solutions
E. Select the best solution
F. Put the solution into actual practice

Occasions might arise where you would have to apply the second step of gathering data before completing the first step.

You might also find that it will be necessary to work on several steps at the same time.

I. IDENTIFY THE PROBLEM

Your first step is to define as precisely as possible the problem to be solved. While this may sound easy, it is often the most difficult part of the process.

It has been said of problem solving that you are halfway to the solution when you can write out a clear statement of the problem itself.

Our job now is to get below the surface manifestations of the trouble and pinpoint the problem. This is usually accomplished by a logical analysis, by going from the general to the particular; from the obvious to the not-so-obvious cause.

Let us say that production is behind schedule. WHY? Absenteeism is high. Now, is absenteeism the basic problem to be tackled, or is it merely a symptom of low morale among the workforce? Under these circumstances, you may decide that production is not the problem; the problem is *employee morale*.

In trying to define the problem, remember there is seldom one simple reason why production is lagging, or reports are late, etc.

Analysis usually leads to the discovery that an apparent problem is really made up of several subproblems which must be attacked separately.

Another way is to limit the problem, and thereby ease the task of finding a solution, and concentrate on the elements which are within the scope of your control.

When you have gone this far, write out a tentative statement of the problem to be solved.

II. GATHER DATA

In the second step, you must set out to collect all the information that might have a bearing on the problem. Do not settle for an assumption when reasonable fact and figures are available.

If you merely go through the motions of problem-solving, you will probably shortcut the information-gathering step. Therefore, do not stack the evidence by confining your research to your own preconceived ideas.

As you collect facts, organize them in some form that helps you make sense of them and spot possible relationships between them. For example, plotting cost per unit figures on a graph can be more meaningful than a long column of figures.

Evaluate each item as you go along. Is the source material absolutely, reliable, probably reliable, or not to be trusted.

One of the best methods for gathering data is to go out and look the situation over carefully. Talk to the people on the job who are most affected by this problem.

Always keep in mind that a primary source is usually better than a secondary source of information.

III. LIST POSSIBLE SOLUTIONS

This is the creative thinking step of problem solving. This is a good time to bring into play whatever techniques of group dynamics the agency or bureau might have developed for a joint attack on problems.

Now the important thing for you to do is: Keep an open mind. Let your imagination roam freely over the facts you have collected. Jot down every possible solution that occurs to you. Resist the temptation to evaluate various proposals as you go along. List seemingly absurd ideas along with more plausible ones. The more possibilities you list during this step, the less risk you will run of settling for merely a workable, rather than the best, solution.

Keep studying the data as long as there seems to be any chance of deriving additional ideas, solutions, explanations, or patterns from it.

IV. TEST POSSIBLE SOLUTIONS

Now you begin to evaluate the possible solutions. Take pains to be objective. Up to this point, you have suspended judgment but you might be tempted to select a solution you secretly favored all along and proclaim it as the best of the lot.

The secret of objectivity in this phase is to test the possible solutions separately, measuring each against a common yardstick. To make this yardstick try to enumerate as many specific criteria as you can think of. Criteria are best phrased as questions which you ask of each possible solution. They can be drawn from these general categories:

- Suitability – Will this solution do the job?
  Will it solve the problem completely or partially?
  Is it a permanent or a stopgap solution?

- Feasibility - Will this plan work in actual practice?
  Can we afford this approach?
  How much will it cost?

- Acceptability - Will the boss go along with the changes required in the plan?
  Are we trying to drive a tack with a sledge hammer?

V. SELECT THE BEST SOLUTION

This is the area of executive decision.

Occasionally, one clearly superior solution will stand out at the conclusion of the testing process. But often it is not that simple. You may find that no one solution has come through all the tests with flying colors.

You may also find that a proposal, which flunked miserably on one of the essential tests, racked up a very high score on others.

The best solution frequently will turn out to be a combination.

Try to arrange a marriage that will bring together the strong points of one possible solution with the particular virtues of another. The more skill and imagination that you apply, the greater is the likelihood that you will come out with a solution that is not merely adequate and workable, but is the best possible under the circumstances.

VI. PUT THE SOLUTION INTO ACTUAL PRACTICE

As every executive knows, a plan which works perfectly on paper may develop all sorts of bugs when put into actual practice.

Problem-solving does not stop with selecting the solution which looks best in theory. The next step is to put the chosen solution into action and watch the results. The results may point towards modifications.

If the problem disappears when you put your solution into effect, you know you have the right solution.

If it does not disappear, even after you have adjusted your plan to cover unforeseen difficulties that turned up in practice, work your way back through the problem-solving solutions.

> Would one of them have worked better?
> Did you overlook some vital piece of data which would have given you a different slant on the whole situation? Did you apply all necessary criteria in testing solutions? If no light dawns after this much rechecking, it is a pretty good bet that you defined the problem incorrectly in the first place.

You came up with the wrong solution because you tackled the wrong problem.

Thus, step six may become step one of a new problem-solving cycle.

COMMUNICATION

I. WHAT IS COMMUNICATION?
We communicate through writing, speaking, action, or inaction. In speaking to people face-to-face, there is opportunity to judge reactions and to adjust the message. This makes the supervisory chain one of the most, and in many instances the most, important channels of communication.

In an organization, communication means keeping employees informed about the organization's objectives, policies, problems, and progress. Communication is the free interchange of information, ideas, and desirable attitudes between and among employees and between employees and management.

II. WHY IS COMMUNICATION NEEDED?

A. People have certain social needs
B. Good communication is essential in meeting those social needs
C. While people have similar basic needs, at the same time they differ from each other
D. Communication must be adapted to these individual differences

An employee cannot do his best work unless he knows why he is doing it. If he has the feeling that he is being kept in the dark about what is going on, his enthusiasm and productivity suffer.

Effective communication is needed in an organization so that employees will understand what the organization is trying to accomplish; and how the work of one unit contributes to or affects the work of other units in the organization and other organizations.

III. HOW IS COMMUNICATION ACHIEVED?

Communication flows downward, upward, sideways.

A. Communication may come from top management down to employees. This is downward communication.

 Some means of downward communication are:
 1. Training (orientation, job instruction, supervision, public relations, etc.)
 2. Conferences
 3. Staff meetings
 4. Policy statements
 5. Bulletins
 6. Newsletters
 7. Memoranda
 8. Circulation of important letters

 In downward communication, it is important that employees be informed in advance of changes that will affect them.

B. Communications should also be developed so that the ideas, suggestions, and knowledge of employees will flow upward to top management.

 Some means of upward communication are:
 1. Personal discussion conferences
 2. Committees
 3. Memoranda
 4. Employees suggestion program
 5. Questionnaires to be filled in giving comments and suggestions about proposed actions that will affect field operations.

 Upward communication requires that management be willing to listen, to accept, and to make changes when good ideas are present. Upward communication succeeds when there is no fear of punishment for speaking out or lack of interest at the top. Employees will share their knowledge and ideas with management when interest is shown and recognition is given.

C. The advantages of downward communication:
 1. It enables the passing down of orders, policies, and plans necessary to the continued operation of the station.
 2. By making information available, it diminishes the fears and suspicions which result from misinformation and misunderstanding.
 3. It fosters the pride people want to have in their work when they are told of good work.
 4. It improves the morale and stature of the individual to be *in the know*.

5. It helps employees to understand, accept, and cooperate with changes when they know about them in advance.

D. The advantages of upward communication:
1. It enables the passing upward of information, attitudes, and feelings.
2. It makes it easier to find out how ready people are to receive downward communication.
3. It reveals the degree to which the downward communication is understood and accepted.
4. It helps to satisfy the basic social needs.
5. It stimulates employees to participate in the operation of their organization.
6. It encourage employees to contribute ideas for improving the efficiency and economy of operations.
7. It helps to solve problem situations before they reach the explosion point.

IV. WHY DOES COMMUNICATION FAIL?

A. The technical difficulties of conveying information clearly
B. The emotional content of communication which prevents complete transmission
C. The fact that there is a difference between what management needs to say, what it wants to day, and what it does say
D. The fact that there is a difference between what employees would like to say, what they think is profitable or safe to say, and what they do say

V. HOW TO IMPROVE COMMUNICATION

As a supervisor, you are a key figure in communication. To improve as a communicator, you should:
A. Know: Knowing your subordinates will help you to recognize and work with individual differences.
B. Like: If you like those who work for you and those for whom you work, this will foster the kind of friendly, warm, work atmosphere that will facilitate communication.
C. Trust: Showing a sincere desire to communicate will help to develop the mutual trust and confidence which are essential to the free flow of communication.
D. Tell: Tell your subordinates and superiors *what's doing*. Tell your subordinates *why* as well as *how*.
E. Listen: By listening, you help others to talk and you create good listeners. Don't forget that listening implies action.
F. Stimulate: Communication has to be stimulated and encouraged. Be receptive to ideas and suggestions and motivate your people so that each member of the team identifies himself with the job at hand.
G. Consult: The most effective way of consulting is to let your people participate, insofar as possible, in developing determinations which affect them or their work.

VI. HOW TO DETERMINE WHETHER YOU ARE GETTING ACROSS

A. Check to see that communication is received and understood
B. Judge this understanding by actions rather than words
C. Adapt or vary communication, when necessary
D. Remember that good communication cannot cure all problems

VII. THE KEY ATTITUDE

Try to see things from the other person's point of view. By doing this, you help to develop the permissive atmosphere and the shared confidence and understanding which are essential to effective two-way communication.

Communication is a two-way process:
A. The basic purpose of any communication is to get action.
B. The only way to get action is through acceptance.
C. In order to get acceptance, communication must be humanly satisfying as well as technically efficient.

HOW ORDERS AND INSTRUCTIONS SHOULD BE GIVEN

I. CHARACTERISTICS OF GOOD ORDERS AND INSTRUCTIONS

   A. Clear
   Orders should be definite as to
   —What is to be done
   —Who is to do it
   —When it is to be done
   —Where it is to be done
   —How it is to be done

   B. Concise
   Avoid wordiness. Orders should be brief and to the point.

   C. Timely
   Instructions and orders should be sent out at the proper time and not too long in advance of expected performance.

   D. Possibility of Performance
   Orders should be feasible:
   1. Investigate before giving orders
   2. Consult those who are to carry out instructions before formulating and issuing them

   E. Properly Directed
   Give the orders to the people concerned. Do not send orders to people who are not concerned. People who continually receive instructions that are not applicable to them get in the habit of neglecting instructions generally.

   F. Reviewed Before Issuance
   Orders should be reviewed before issuance:
   1. Test them by putting yourself in the position of the recipient
   2. If they involve new procedures, have the persons who are to do the work review them for suggestions.

   G. Reviewed After Issuance
   Persons who receive orders should be allowed to raise questions and to point out unforeseen consequences of orders.

H. Coordinated
   Orders should be coordinated so that work runs smoothly.

I. Courteous
   Make a request rather than a demand. There is no need to continually call attention to the fact that you are the boss.

J. Recognizable as an Order
   Be sure that the order is recognizable as such.

K. Complete
   Be sure recipient has knowledge and experience sufficient to carry out order. Give illustrations and examples.

A DEPARTMENTAL PERSONNEL OFFICE IS RESPONSIBLE FOR THE FOLLOWING FUNCTIONS

1. Policy
2. Personnel Programs
3. Recruitment and Placement
4. Position Classification
5. Salary and Wage Administration
6. Employee performance Standards and Evaluation
7. Employee Relations
8. Disciplinary Actions and Separations
9. Health and Safety
10. Staff Training and Development
11. Personnel Records, Procedures, and Reports
12. Employee Services
13. Personnel Research

SUPERVISION

I. LEADERSHIP

All leadership is based essentially on authority. This comes from two sources: It is received from higher management or it is earned by the supervisor through his methods of supervision. Although effective leadership has always depended upon the leader's using his authority in such a way as to appeal successfully to the motives of the people supervised, the conditions for making this appeal are continually changing. The key to today's problem of leadership is flexibility and resourcefulness on the part of the leader in meeting changes in conditions as they occur.

Three basic approaches to leadership are generally recognized:

A. The Authoritarian Approach
   1. The methods and techniques used in this approach emphasize the / in leadership and depend primarily on the formal authority of the leader. This authority is sometimes exercised in a hardboiled manner and sometimes in a benevolent

manner, but in either case the dominating role of the leader is reflected in the thinking, planning, and decisions of the group.
2. Group results are to a large degree dependent on close supervision by the leader. Usually, the individuals in the group will not show a high degree of initiative or acceptance of responsibility and their capacity to grow and develop probably will not be fully utilized. The group may react with resentment or submission, depending upon the manner and skill of the leader in using his authority.
3. This approach develops as a natural outgrowth of the authority that goes with the leader's job and his feeling of sole responsibility for getting the job done. It is relatively easy to use and does not require must resourcefulness.
4. The use of this approach is effective in times of emergencies, in meeting close deadline as a final resort, in settling some issues, in disciplinary matters, and with dependent individuals and groups.

B. The Laissez-Faire or Let 'em Alone Approach
1. This approach generally is characterized by an avoidance of leadership responsibility by the leader. The activities of the group depend largely on the choice of its members rather than the leader.
2. Group results probably will be poor. Generally, there will be disagreements over petty things, bickering, and confusion. Except for a few aggressive people, individuals will not show much initiative and growth and development will be retarded. There may be a tendency for informal leaders to take over leadership of the group.
3. This approach frequently results from the leader's dislike of responsibility, from his lack of confidence, from failure of other methods to work, from disappointment or criticism. It is usually the easiest of the three to use and requires both understanding and resourcefulness on the part of the leader.
4. This approach is occasionally useful and effective, particularly in forcing dependent individuals or groups to rely on themselves, to give someone a chance to save face by clearing his own difficulties, or when action should be delayed temporarily for good cause.

C. The Democratic Approach
1. The methods and techniques used in this approach emphasize the *we* in leadership and build up the responsibility of the group to attain its objectives. Reliance is placed largely on the earned authority of the leader.
2. Group results are likely to be good because most of the job motives of the people will be satisfied. Cooperation and teamwork, initiative, acceptance of responsibility, and the individual's capacity for growth probably will show a high degree of development.
3. This approach grows out of a desire or necessity of the leader to find ways to appeal effectively to the motivation of his group. It is the best approach to build up inside the person a strong desire to cooperate and apply himself to the job. It is the most difficult to develop, and requires both understanding and resourcefulness on the part of the leader.
4. The value of this approach increases over a long period where sustained efficiency and development of people are important. It may not be fully effective in all situations, however, particularly when there is not sufficient time to use it properly or where quick decisions must be made.

All three approaches are used by most leaders and have a place in supervising people. The extent of their use varies with individual leaders, with some using one approach predominantly. The leader who uses these three approaches, and varies their use with time and circumstance, is probably the most effective. Leadership which is used predominantly with a democratic approach requires more resourcefulness on the part of the leader but offers the greatest possibilities in terms of teamwork and cooperation.

The one best way of developing democratic leadership is to provide a real sense of participation on the part of the group, since this satisfies most of the chief job motives. Although there are many ways of providing participation, consulting as frequently as possible with individuals and groups on things that affect them seems to offer the most in building cooperation and responsibility. Consultation takes different forms, but it is most constructive when people feel they are actually helping in finding the answers to the problems on the job.

There are some requirements of leaders in respect to human relations which should be considered in their selection and development. Generally, the leader should be interested in working with other people, emotionally stable, self-confident, and sensitive to the reactions of others. In addition, his viewpoint should be one of getting the job done through people who work cooperatively in response to his leadership. He should have a knowledge of individual and group behavior, but, most important of all, he should work to combine all of these requirements into a definite, practical skill in leadership.

II. NINE POINTS OF CONTRAST BETWEEN *BOSS* AND *LEADER*

  A. The boss drives his men; the leader coaches them.
  B. The boss depends on authority; the leader on good will.
  C. The boss inspires fear; the leader inspires enthusiasm.
  D. The boss says I; the leader says *We*.
  E. The boss says *Get here on time*; the leader gets there ahead of time.
  F. The boss fixes the blame for the breakdown; the leader fixes the breakdown.
  G. The boss knows how it is done; the leader shows how.
  H. The boss makes work a drudgery; the leader makes work a game.
  I. The boss says *Go*; the leader says *Let's go*.

EMPLOYEE MORALE

Employee morale is the way employees feel about each other, the organization or unit in which they work, and the work they perform.

I. SOME WAYS TO DEVELOP AND MAINTAIN GOOD EMPLYEE MORALE

  A. Give adequate credit and praise when due.
  B. Recognize importance of all jobs and equalize load with proper assignments, always giving consideration to personality differences and abilities.
  C. Welcome suggestions and do not have an *all-wise* attitude. Request employees' assistance in solving problems and use assistants when conducting group meetings on certain subjects.
  D. Properly assign responsibilities and give adequate authority for fulfillment of such assignments.

E. Keep employees informed about matters that affect them.
F. Criticize and reprimand employees privately.
G. Be accessible and willing to listen.
H. Be fair.
I. Be alert to detect training possibilities so that you will not miss an opportunity to help each employee do a better job, and if possible with less effort on his part.
J. Set a good example.
K. Apply the golden rule.

II. SOME INDICATIONS OF GOOD MORALE

A. Good quality of work
B. Good quantity
C. Good attitude of employees
D. Good discipline
E. Teamwork
F. Good attendance
G. Employee participation

MOTIVATION

DRIVES

A drive, stated simply, is a desire or force which causes a person to do or say certain things. These are some of the most usual drives and some of their identifying characteristics recognizable in people motivated by such drives:

A. Security (desire to provide for the future)
Always on time for work
Works for the same employer for many years
Never takes unnecessary chances
Seldom resists doing what he is told

B. Recognition (desire to be rewarded for accomplishment)
Likes to be asked for his opinion
Becomes very disturbed when he makes a mistake
Does things to attract attention
Likes to see his name in print

C. Position (desire to hold certain status in relation to others)
Boasts about important people he knows
Wants to be known as a key man
Likes titles
Demands respect
Belongs to clubs, for prestige

D. Accomplishment (desire to get things done)
   Complains when things are held up
   Likes to do things that have tangible results
   Never lies down on the job
   Is proud of turning out good work

E. Companionship (desire to associate with other people)
   Likes to work with others
   Tells stories and jokes
   Indulges in horseplay
   Finds excuses to talk to others on the job

F. Possession (desire to collect and hoard objects)
   Likes to collect things
   Puts his name on things belonging to him
   Insists on the same location

Supervisors may find that identifying the drives of employees is a helpful step toward motivating them to self-improvement and better job performance. For example: An employee's job performance is below average. His supervisor, having previously determined that the employee is motivated by a drive for security, suggests that taking training courses will help the employee to improve, advance, and earn more money. Since earning more money can be a step toward greater security, the employee's drive for security would motivate him to take the training suggested by the supervisor. In essence, this is the process of charting an employee's future course by using his motivating drives to positive advantage.

EMPLOYEE PARTICIPATION

I. WHAT IS PARTICIPATION

Employee participation is the employee's giving freely of his time, skill, and knowledge to an extent which cannot be obtained by demand.

II. WHY IS IT IMPORTANT?

The supervisor's responsibility is to get the job done through people. A good supervisor gets the job done through people who work willingly and well. The participation of employees is important because:

A. Employees develop a greater sense of responsibility when they share in working out operating plans and goals.
B. Participation provides greater opportunity and stimulation for employees to learn, and to develop their ability.
C. Participation sometimes provides better solutions to problems because such solutions may combine the experience and knowledge of interested employees who want the solutions to work.
D. An employee or group may offer a solution which the supervisor might hesitate to make for fear of demanding too much.

E. Since the group wants to make the solution work, they exert pressure in a constructive way on each other.
F. Participation usually results in reducing the need for close supervision.

II. HOW MAY SUPERVISORS OBTAIN IT?

Participation is encouraged when employees feel that they share some responsibility for the work and that their ideas are sincerely wanted and valued. Some ways of obtaining employee participation are:

A. Conduct orientation programs for new employees to inform them about the organization and their rights and responsibilities as employees.
B. Explain the aims and objectives of the agency. On a continuing basis, be sure that the employees know what these aims and objectives are.
C. Share job successes and responsibilities and give credit for success.
D. Consult with employees, both as individuals and in groups, about things that affect them.
E. Encourage suggestions for job improvements. Help employees to develop good suggestions. The suggestions can bring them recognition. The city's suggestion program offers additional encouragement through cash awards.

The supervisor who encourages employee participation is not surrendering his authority. He must still make decisions and initiate action, and he must continue to be ultimately responsible for the work of those he supervises. But, through employee participation, he is helping his group to develop greater ability and a sense of responsibility while getting the job done faster and better.

STEPS IN HANDLING A GRIEVANCE

1. Get the Facts
   a. Listen sympathetically
   b. Let him talk himself out
   c. Get his story straight
   d. Get his point of view
   e. Don't argue with him
   f. Give him plenty of time
   g. Conduct the interview privately
   h. Don't try to shift the blame or pass the buck

2. Consider the Facts
   a. Consider the employee's viewpoint
   b. How will the decision affect similar cases
   c. Consider each decision as a possible precedent
   d. Avoid snap judgments—don't jump to conclusions

3. Make or Get a Decision
   a. Frame an effective counter-proposal
   b. Make sure it is fair to all
   c. Have confidence in your judgment
   d. Be sure you can substantiate your decision

4. Notify the Employee of Your Decision
   Be sure he is told; try to convince him that the decision is fair and just.

5. Take Action When Needed and If Within Your Authority
   Otherwise, tell employee that the matter will be called to the attention of the proper person or that nothing can be done, and why it cannot.

6. Follow through to see that the desired result is achieved.

7. Record key facts concerning the complaint and the action taken.

8. Leave the way open to him to appeal your decision to a higher authority.

9. Report all grievances to your superior, whether they are appealed or not.

DISCIPLINE

Discipline is training that develops self-control, orderly conduct, and efficiency.

To discipline does not necessarily mean to punish.

To discipline does mean to train, to regulate, and to govern conduct.

I. THE DISCIPLINARY INTERVIEW

Most employees sincerely want to do what is expected of them. In other words, they are self-disciplined. Some employees, however, fail to observe established rules and standards, and disciplinary action by the supervisor is required.

The primary purpose of disciplinary action is to improve conduct without creating dissatisfaction, bitterness, or resentment in the process.

Constructive disciplinary action is more concerned with causes and explanations of breaches of conduct than with punishment. The disciplinary interview is held to get at the causes of apparent misbehavior and to motivate better performance in the future.

It is important that the interview be kept on an impersonal a basis as possible. If the supervisor lets the interview descend to the plane of an argument, it loses its effectiveness.

II. PLANNING THE INTERVIEW

Get all pertinent facts concerning the situation so that you can talk in specific terms to the employee.

Review the employee's record, appraisal ratings, etc.

Consider what you know about the temperament of the employee. Consider your attitude toward the employee. Remember that the primary requisite of disciplinary action is fairness.

Don't enter upon the interview when angry.

Schedule the interview for a place which is private and out of hearing of others.

III. CONDUCTING THE INTERVIEW

   A. Make an effort to establish accord.
   B. Question the employee about the apparent breach of discipline. Be sure that the question is not so worded as to be itself an accusation.
   C. Give the employee a chance to tell his side of the story. Give him ample opportunity to talk.
   D. Use understanding—listening except where it is necessary to ask a question or to point out some details of which the employee may not be aware. If the employee misrepresents facts, make a plain, accurate statement of the facts, but don't argue and don't engage in personal controversy.
   E. Listen and try to understand the reasons for the employee's (mis)conduct. First of all, don't assume that there has been a breach of discipline. Evaluate the employee's reasons for his conduct in the light of his opinions and feelings concerning the consistency and reasonableness of the standards which he was expected to follow. Has the supervisor done his part in explaining the reasons for the rule? Was the employee's behavior unintentional or deliberate? Does he think he had real reasons for his actions? What new facts is he telling? Do the facts justify his actions? What causes, other than those mentioned, could have stimulated the behavior?
   F. After listening to the employee's version of the situation, and if censure of his actions is warranted, the supervisor should proceed with whatever criticism is justified. Emphasis should be placed on future improvement rather than exclusively on the employee's failure to measure up to expected standards of job conduct.
   G. Fit the criticism to the individual. With one employee, a word of correction may be all that is required.
   H. Attempt to distinguish between unintentional error and deliberate misbehavior. An error due to ignorance requires training and not censure.
   I. Administer criticism in a controlled, even tone of voice, never in anger. Make it clear that you are acting as an agent of the department. In general, criticism should refer to the job or the employee's actions and not to the person. Criticism of the employee's work is not an attack on the individual.
   J. Be sure the interview does not destroy the employee's self-confidence. Mention his good qualities and assure him that you feel confident that he can improve his performance.
   K. Wherever possible, before the employee leaves the interview, satisfy him that the incident is closed, that nothing more will be said on the subject unless the offense is repeated.

www.ingramcontent.com/pod-product-compliance
Lightning Source LLC
Chambersburg PA
CBHW081812300426
44116CB00014B/2333